FOOD, FREEDOM, COMMUNITY

HOW SMALL LOCAL ACTIONS CAN SOLVE
COMPLEX GLOBAL PROBLEMS

ISA PEARL RITCHIE

TE RĀ AROHA PRESS

CONTENTS

Supermarket Culture

I stare at the packets
Bright colours
Meaningless labels: lite, original, new and improved, natural
And zone out
Hoping for enlightenment out of this surreal fluorescent hyper-reality
Nothing looks like food anymore
I take a picture of 'free range' next to 'normal' chicken breast at $10 less
a Kilo
We can pay 75% more to feel better about our consumption
If we can afford it
And are enough – or have enough guilt – to need to alleviate it…
I find a new pasta-like substance:
Low carb, made from a Japanese vegetable
And wonder if I still care enough today to try not to get type 2 diabetes
later on…
Supermarket
Culture
A parody
A spectacle of awful proportions and pre-packaged single-serve portions
Only humour can save me
Everything is so clean
But feels so dirty
I laugh out loud and talk to myself
Not caring about the breach of social rules
Strange looks only add to the amusement
I used to take this so seriously
Before I cracked like a free-range egg into an organic omelette
Before it became so ridiculously complex
To the point where I can only engage as comedy or bizarre meditation
Before I started thinking – compulsively – about poverty and privilege and
powerlessness
I enjoy this aisle most of all

The packet sauces for your butter chicken or other ethnic cuisine
Full of stabilisers, spices, flavour enhancers
Which only imitate the joy of real flavour, real connection
I know too much
And now I don't see these packets as viable
Just a combination of things I could make a better hash of with cumin and an onion at home
I appreciate how utterly unlikely all this is
I buy fairtrade chocolate – because it's necessary
And dream of a better world – where real food is normal

- Isa Pearl Ritchie, 2015

1 LOCAL SOLUTIONS AND THE POWER OF AUTHENTIC STORIES

Every time it rained, the harbour turned brown. The muck would stay there for months. Every time it rained farm animals would be caught up and swept into the harbour and rot. People became accustomed to that. You couldn't even collect shellfish. So Freddie put a flier up which said, "Does anybody care that every time it rains the harbour turns brown?" Fiona saw the note and gave him a ring. He said there was a survey which said that Whaingaroa Harbour was the worst for recreational fishing. It took eighteen hours to catch a single fish. He said "I remember when we could go out and a family could catch a feed. I want to have that back again." For Fred the motivation was wanting to catch a fish, for Fiona it was wanting to sit on her deck and see sparkling water instead of brown.

Freddie's flier didn't just attract the attention of recreational fishers or people who liked a nice view of the harbour, it also brought together local ecologists and activists, living in the Whaingaroa community. There were probably already a high proportion of such people in the area, drawn by the local history of activism lead by the legendary Tuaiwa "Eva" Rickard whose brave and powerful activism and community organising saw the early return of a significant section of land to the local indigenous people.

After Freddie put the flyer up, people came together and formed Whaingaroa Harbour Care in 1995. They got organised and began working to fence off and plant riparian lines to repair the freshwater systems that ran into the harbour. They planted well over a million trees. It took less than twenty years for the harbour to transform from one of the most polluted in the country, to one of the healthiest.

The harbour is now much better for recreational fishing, and that isn't the only outcome. People coming together to create Whaingaroa Harbour Care also lead to nuberous other community groups and powerful food activism, some of which is covered in this book.

Connection, alienation and paradox

These days whakapapa [ancestry][1] has been dumbed down to this simple notion of who your parents and great grandparents are... but I reckon whakapapa is actually a fuller concept about the journey of all things through time and space. All things have whakapapa. A rock has whakapapa, snow has whakapapa, stars...

-The Bro

What kinds of alternatives are possible in a food and agriculture system dominated by global corporations, where time and space are disconnected? (Hendrickson and Hefferman 2002, 347).

In 2002 activist anthropologist, David Graeber, commented that he found it hard to think of another time in history when such a wide gulf of disconnection between intellectuals and activists had ever previously existed (Graeber 2002). However, in the short stretch of time since the turn of the 20th century there has been a surge of intellectual activists. These include many of the key researchers and theorists presented in this book, among them Capra and Luisi (2014), Korten (2010), Shiva (2012) and the 'organic intellectuals' of the food sovereignty movement as framed by Rose (2013). In recent years awareness has been building around myriad social, cultural, environmental and ethical problems with the global corporate food system noted by scholars such as Germov and Williams (2008), Mason and Singer (2006) and Curry (2011), and many others. Alongside this growing awareness, there is a noticeable emergence of a common vocabulary with the proliferation of words such as 'sustainability', 'eco-friendly', 'free-range', and 'organic', attributed to a rising political and social awareness.

Alongside this surge of activist research, contemporary grass-roots initiatives have emerged[2] focussed on producing or redistributing food locally. These include new community gardening and land sharing initiatives, co-ops, food hubs and other means of distributing local food; as well as food foraging and public food production. Some scholars, including Holt-Gimenez and Patel (2009) consider these initiatives as part of a broader social movement towards food sovereignty. These are the subjects to which my attention has been drawn as researcher.

Globalising corporate capitalism can be perceived as a form of colonisation, achieved through overt and covert violence, disconnection and domination. The definition and connotations of 'capitalism' are especially relevant here. Although the term 'capitalism' was invented by socialists as a critique of an exploitative model of power relations, it seems to have appropriated its own term and transformed the meaning into something positive. This creates confusion, especially for those still using the word as a critique, when talking to people who are used to 'capitalism' meaning something synonymous with freedom and the ability to buy and sell, to which the only alternative is a communist dictatorship[3].

The research that this book is based on takes a complex systems view, an ecological approach to understanding connectedness and complex situations (Capra and Luisi, 2014). This perspective rejects mechanistic ways of understanding the world that have become common under the dominant Western scientific approach as it is unable to grasp complexity enough to address the numerous multi-faceted crises humanity is facing.

Human beings are always embedded in wider eco-systems and are part of these systems from an ecological perspective. This view sees humans as part of, rather than oppositional to, nature. This kind of perspective is compatible with many indigenous perspectives, including Māori conceptions of environmental ethics (Gunn 2007). This eco-centric perspective is also articulated in Aldo Leopold's pioneering Land Ethic:

The land ethic simply enlarges the boundaries of the community to include soils, waters, plants, and animals, or collectively: the land... In short, a land ethic changes the role of Homo Sapiens from conqueror of the land-community to plain member and citizen of it (Leopold 1949, 239).

This ecosystem framework resonates well with my experiences of Māori Cosmology, of the valuing of the anthropomorphic Ranginui [sky father] and Papatuanuku [earth mother]. These key deities are parents to many of the other gods in the pantheon who protect and care for domains such as Tāne Mahuta, god of forests and Tangaroa, god of the ocean. Through this perspective intrinsic value is also placed in anthropomorphised mountains, and in the taniwha [fabulous water monsters] that protect each bend in a river. Leopold's land ethic also relates well to the complex systems approach articulated by Capra and Luisi (2014), and these, in turn resonate with what Rose (2013), in his research on food sovereignty in Australia, calls: an ontology of connectedness.

The term 'ontology' invokes questions about the nature of 'the world', how the universe works and what forces can be said to exist within it. Both Rose (2013) and Graeber (2009) present ontological dichotomies. Graeber (2009) positions the anarchist activists which are the focus of his ethnographic study as operating from an ontology of imagination and creativity as in contrast to the dominant system's ontology of violence. He argues that the state and market are interdependent, and that the coercive force of the state is everywhere. Most of all, this force adheres in anything large, heavy, and economically valuable that cannot easily be hidden away. Graeber claims that while the state and the market operate on ontologies of violence, the activists he has worked with operate on an entirely different ontology: one of imagination. The former is continually engaged in destruction and maintaining lopsided power dynamics while the latter is continuously in the process of creation in order to challenge those power dynamics (2009, 511, 512). These represent basic underlying understandings upon which 'the activists' and those adhering to the dominant perspectives sometimes called 'the system' operate on which differ fundamentally.

The concept of alienation is also relevant in this theoretical framework:

Just as alienation forms part of the capitalist rationality in an ontological sense, it is connectedness which lies at the core of the food sovereignty rationality, which is aimed at healing the ecological and social rifts. In its practical manifestations to date, I regard food sovereignty as constituted by three foundational 'pillars', namely: redistributive agrarian reform, agro-ecological methods of production, and (re)localised and democratised food systems. Each in its own way contributes to the healing of the ecological and social rifts; and integrated as a whole they express the ontology of connectedness (Rose 2013, 11-12).

Ontologies of connectedness are a recurring theme in this book as it supports the concept of food sovereignty which envisions and works towards replacing the capitalist food system, with its ontology of alienation and disconnection, with a more connected and democratised mode.

In place of the anonymous 'cash-nexus' which constitutes the sole bond between primary producer and end-consumer in the capitalist food system, food sovereignty is premised on the recovery of social connectivity via more intimate and direct personal relationships between producers (farmers) and the end consumers achieved through localised food systems. In such direct and personal exchanges, it can also be argued that something is being altered in the minds of the participants as regards their understanding of food itself. A monetary exchange is still taking place, but the value of food – its sensuous, cultural nature, and its true ecological and social cost – is being recovered, and more properly reflected in the price. The primary consideration is no longer simply about profit; in the process food becomes de-commodified; and this represents a deep and effective engagement with a central element of the common sense of the globalising capitalist food system (Rose 2013, 28).

Another contemporary theorist whose work is relevant to both the ecosystem framework and 'ontology of connectedness' is the Indian ecologist Vandana Shiva (2012). Shiva emphasises the importance of local knowledge systems which are disappearing and being colonised by dominant Western knowledge and the globalising system. She argues that although Western knowledge has been constructed as universal, it is actually just a globalised version of a local parochial system based in particular cultures, gender and class (2012, 9). Therefore, the common dichotomy between the universal and the local is misplaced when applied to Western and indigenous traditions because what is perceived as 'universal' was actually a local system "which has spread world-wide through intellectual colonisation" (Shiva 2012, 10).

Shiva argues that just as intensive corporate farming practices create unsustainable biological monocultures which erode both biodiversity and cultural diversity, the dominant scientific paradigm "breeds a monoculture of the mind" (2012, 12). It makes local alternative knowledge systems disappear by destroying the possible conditions required for alternatives to exist. It does this through its 'superior' exclusivity and through a violent process of reductionism which destroys diverse local meanings. Shiva states that in local knowledge systems there is no artificially imposed separation between 'resources': "the forest and the field are in ecological continuum". Local agriculture is modelled on forest ecology and both supply food (2012, 14). In contrast the supposedly 'scientific' system segregates forestry from agriculture. Forestry is reduced to resources like timber and is no longer connected to food. "Knowledge giving systems which have emerged from the food giving capacities of the forest are therefore eclipsed and finally destroyed, both through neglect and aggression" (2012, 14). Shiva uses the examples of 'scientific management' based on narrow commercial interests and enforced through legislation in India to illustrate her arguments on the destruction of diverse knowledge systems (2012, 18).

For the purposes of this research, 'contradiction' is apparent when two ideas appear to in conflict, in a kind of opposition where it is difficult to see how they could possibly co-exist. On further exploration, a contradiction is often revealed to be a paradox: a dialectic relationship between two or more competing yet coexisting influences creating tension. Seo and Creed (2002) suggest the conscious and reflective negotiation of paradox presents opportunity for raising awareness, resolving tensions or stimulating further action. Such a paradox can be experienced internally by those who seek to protest the globalising cabitalist system while being part of it.

From a United States perspective, Hendrickson and Hefferman (2002) comment on this kind of corporate colonisation, relating it in particular to food movements:

This gradual transformation, or colonization, of the lifeworld by the same systems logic that governs economic and political transactions is the significant transformation of Western society in the late 20th century. Therefore, the critical issue we in Western society are facing is resisting the commodification of our personal, private relationships by the same logic that rules our political and economic lives – and perhaps nowhere is this more evident than in the social movements surrounding food (Hendrickson and Hefferman 2002, 348).

Despite common arguments claiming there are some strengths in a globalised food system, there are also great costs in the loss of specialised localised knowledge, diminishing biodiversity and exacerbation of wider social and environmental exploitation. In this context, alternative food movements offer potential solutions:

The true measure of these alternatives might well be the inspiration they give to others to envision an alternative way of being in the food system. Moreover, these alternative projects may turn out to be effective models to be used if the global system ultimately proves unsustainable. The most important aspect of these movements might well be their ability to protect the lifeworld from encroachment by the dominant logic of the systems world, or to reorder time and space. Without these spaces for the creation and implementation of these alternative visions, we condemn those farmers, workers and consumers who are actually striving to make their way in the food system to the despair of no hope (Hendrickson and Hefferman 2002, 365-366).

The concept of, and the campaign for, food sovereignty can be described as a broader frame for such a movement. The term 'food sovereignty' was initially coined by Vía Campesina, an international peasant movement representing more than 180 organisations advocating for migrant workers, landless peasants and small farm owners (Rose 2013). Disillusioned with the term 'food security' and its capacity to be co-opted by corporations, this movement deliberately coined the notion of 'food sovereignty' as a concept that is about people and communities having control over their food supply (Wittman et al 2010). According to the International Planning Committee for food sovereignty, the ideals of the movement can be summarised as follows:

Food sovereignty is the right of peoples to healthy and culturally appropriate food produced through ecologically sound and sustainable methods, and their right to define their own food and agriculture systems. It puts the aspirations and needs of those who produce, distribute and consume food at the heart of food systems and policies rather than the demands of markets and corporations. It defends the interests and inclusion of the next generation. It offers a strategy to resist and dismantle the current corporate trade and food regime, and directions for food, farming, pastoral and fisheries systems determined by local producers and users. Food sovereignty prioritises local and national economies and markets and empowers peasant and family farmer-driven agriculture, artisanal – fishing, pastoralist-led grazing, and food production, distribution and consumption based on environmental, social and economic sustainability. Food sovereignty promotes transparent trade that guarantees just incomes to all peoples as well as the rights of consumers to control their food and nutrition. It ensures that the rights to use and manage lands, territories, waters, seeds, livestock and biodiversity are in the hands of those of us who produce food. Food sovereignty implies new social relations free of oppression and inequality between men and women, peoples, racial groups, social and economic classes and generations (International Planning Committee for Food Sovereignty 2007, 1).

The principles of food sovereignty include focussing on enabling people to produce their own food, valuing community food providers, encouraging local sustainable food systems, giving control over land and resources to communities (rather than corporate interests), building knowledge and skills within communities, and valuing diverse eco-systems (International Planning Committee for Food Sovereignty 2007, 1). Food sovereignty is presented in much of the surrounding academic literature as a potentially radical and powerful critique of the neoliberal discourses that are reflected in the contemporary practices of the corporate capitalist food industry. It also provides alternative models for agriculture that are intended to be more environmentally and socially just (Wittman et al 2010, 3).

The grass-roots origins of 'food sovereignty' as well as the diverse and inclusive nature of the groups who have constructed this concept, is arguably one of its greatest strengths. This lends to the campaign and concept the ability to connect diverse groups, from a variety of different countries and socioeconomic situations, which are able to unite under the common purpose of attempting to prioritize the interests of people and communities over corporations.

My story

As someone who was raised in a kaupapa Māori[4] environment, the word 'whakapapa' has been important to me. As a child I was taught to map my whakapapa on coloured paper, to introduce my family to my kōhanga reo [early childhood centre]. Connectedness is an important thread in this book, which goes beyond conventional conceptions of ancestry, however, my ancestry is as good a place to start as any.

My heritage is Scottish, Scandinavian, Cornish, and Lithuanian-American-Jewish. I was born, the oldest daughter of the oldest daughter of the oldest daughter of a woman who was given $1,000 dollars when she completed her undergraduate study in the late 1920s. While her older sister, in a similar position, had chosen to buy a fur coat, my great grandmother, Pearl Malsin, chose to travel from the United States to England to study at the London School of Economics. There she met my great-grandfather, Ernest Beaglehole, a New Zealand-born cultural psychologist working toward a PhD on the psychological basis of property, and together they later documented ethnologies of Pacific peoples, among others. This book charts the process I went through, as a fourth generation ethnographer, academic and feminist, undertaking a fourth generation PhD[5]. Despite my unusually academic heritage, this work has not been easy for me. While I now feel a deep connectedness and deep appreciation for life, a sense of belonging has not come easily, but has been worked for out of experiences of alienation and isolation.

For me, kai [food] has always been connected to empowerment or disempowerment. I was born into the 1980s, the first child of a solo mother. At the time, the welfare-state established post-Depression was quickly being dismantled under a virulent strain of the neoliberal project. My mother cried into the phone to the social welfare department when they cut her Domestic Purposes Benefit by $50 without warning. That was our food money. As her income grew, so did our family, until there were six children. We were never wealthy, but we didn't starve. I often didn't have school shoes or new clothes, but we were a lot better off than some of the kids at Te Ara Rima school, a decile 1[6] kura kaupapa [total immersion Māori school]. Here, my step-sister Piata and I were among the lucky ones who usually had lunch to bring to school, even if it was occasionally stolen by other kids. I have warm memories of the term when the father of some school pupils was employed to come in and cook hot meals for the kids: pale green leek and potato soup, mince and gravy on mashed potatoes. He had cooked in the army, and there were extra plates, even for the kids who could not afford the $5 a week.

Growing up, we did not have a vegetable garden. I was raised on processed bread and margarine; skim milk and meat that came in polystyrene packets; canned tomatoes and uniform vegetables that I often refused to eat. Food came from the supermarket. Once a fortnight when Mum got paid, all the kids would push the trolley around the Pak 'n Save supermarket asking for treats. By the end of the fortnight there wasn't much left, especially for that most precarious meal: school lunches, so easily ruined by stray odours or liquids, vulnerable as it sits for hours in a plastic box, in a school bag, in a cloak bay, going stale.

As the oldest children in an ever-growing family, Piata and I were taught to take on domestic responsibilities. We were expected to make our own lunches from the time we first started school. Tired in the morning, I often did not get organised in time and spent many days feeling hungry. Later, at the middle-class school I attended, I learned that if I pretended to have ordered my lunch from school, the teachers would feel sorry for me and eventually microwave a pie for me from the staff-room freezer. I learned to bake and cook dinner for the family at around the age of eight. Mum always had a baby, and I remember going into her room, where she lay with a newborn and asking instructions for cooking, which usually started with "First chop an onion…"

In my early twenties, as a fairly young mother with a sociology degree and strong critical analysis, food took on a different kind of significance in my life. Concerned about the industrial food system and potentially harmful additives, I sought more control over my baby's food. I felt I had to claw some power back from corporations. I was seeking more connection to food and health. I wanted to focus on micro-level solutions to the concerns that were now prominent in my consciousness. These concerns became the focus of my Masters' research, where I explored nourishing food movements. My Doctoral research followed on from this interest in food, health and wellbeing. It was sparked from excitement about the proliferation of food democratisation initiatives and prospects of greater food freedom I was becoming aware of.

I came to this research with a deep commitment to social justice, and a deep concern for human impacts on the ecosystems of this planet. My focus on food has been influenced by experiences of food insecurity in my childhood; observations of abject poverty in my immediate surrounds; by ongoing negotiations in my life around food as healthy, ethical and affordable; by an acute awareness of the ruthless social and environmental exploitation involved in the corporate food industry; by a deliberately cultivated attitude of optimism; and by a strong compulsion to search for and promote more sustainable models of food production.

Stories and solutions

Just as fabricated stories are an instrument of social control, so authentic stories are an instrument of liberation (Korten 2010, 252).

'Focusing on solutions' assumes that there are possibilities of resolving complex problems – which, in this context means that there are alternative systems that are more sustainable, with more capacity for facilitating environmental, cultural, economic, and social justice, with more space for generating human freedom while reducing inequality. It is a standpoint that seems to require some bravery – and it is a stance that seems necessary. It is also a position that many of the researchers cited in this book also employ. A similar perspective of deliberate optimism is expressed by Naomi Klein:

What if we realised that real disaster response means fighting inequality and building a just economy, that everyone working for a healthy food system is already a climate warrior? So too are people fighting for public transit in Brazil, housing and immigrant rights in the United States, when there are movements battling austerity in Europe, extraction in Australia, pollution in China and India, environmental crime in Africa, and the bad trade deals that lock in all of these ills everywhere. I believe the movement we need is already in the streets, in the courts, in the classrooms, even in the halls of power. We just need to find each other. One way or another, everything is going to change, and for a brief time the nature of that change is still up to us. - Klein (2015, NP[7]).

There is a sense of urgency building among the voices of scientists, activists, citizens and social researchers; awareness that we are heading towards multi-faceted crises that could ultimately mean the demise of our species; crises comprising global warming, social exploitation, increasing socioeconomic disparities, environmental destruction, the peak of our energy capacity within our current global system dependent on fossil fuels, the peak of an economic system, dependent on exponential growth, and the devastation of the planet's ecosystems, upon which our species depends.

Narratives of imminent crisis are nothing new. Indeed, their strong historical prevalence may indicate deep embeddedness in the make-up of 'humanity'. There are many 'Armageddon' stories, the world has been coming to an end for a very long time – be it by volcano, pre-nuclear war, nuclear war, meteor, sun surge, or 'the hand of God'. The contemporary story of 'climate change', can be seen as a modern manifestation of such a narrative, but the repetition of the story of significant threat does not mean it is not serious, just as threats of nuclear war must still be taken seriously. The difference this time, is that it is a secular, scientific argument, perhaps reflecting a growing secular, scientific dominant 'religion'. We can see the evidence on many levels. We can see the vulnerability of the systems on which we currently depend. We can measure change that is becoming increas-ingly uncomfortable as polar ice-caps melt and weather patterns become more erratic and extreme. In this globalised world, recorded and broadcast though various media, we can learn about problems happening in far-flung places, and see wider patterns than ever before. We know people are being exploited and environments are being devastated to serve profit motives. The welfare of the many is being crushed in the hands of the few.

In the face of these multiple intersecting stories of exploitation, humanity needs now more than ever to develop coherent counter-narratives — stories of solutions. We need to tell genuine stories that inspire hope, that resonate with people, and that connect people and inspire compassion and empathy, because this seems to be the most obvious way to counter alienation, depression, and exploitation. I intend to tell, re-tell, and explore some such stories in the course of this book, through the gathered narratives of research participants in the community of Whaingaroa[8] and wider New Zealand.

For further information on my research process and methodology, including using the permaculture design system for my research method, see the **Research theory and Methodology** section, near the end of this book.

2 FOOD SOVEREIGNTY AND AOTEAROA

Explaining food sovereignty

The global production and distribution of food is highly political. Food shortages have been manufactured by the power-plays of governments and large corporations (Fairbairn, 2010). The concept of food sovereignty came from the international peasant movement Via Campesina, who represent more than 180 different groups of small farmers and migrant workers around the world in 1996. Via Campesina were disillusioned with the United Nations' concept of 'food security' a concept which is focussed on households having access to adequate food. This concept is favours food policies that maximise food production and access opportunities, without questioning how, where and by whom food is produced. 'Food security' co-opted by big corporations. Companies like Monsanto were putting pressure on the United Nations to support their Genetically Engineered crops in the name of food security, often at the expense of indigenous people and small-scale farmers. Because 'food security' offered no real possibilities for transforming the existing system which is both socially and environmentally exploitative. Therefore, Via Campesina called for a new term, one that could not be co-opted by big corporations because its focus is strongly connected with communities having empowerment over their food system. (Wittman, Desmarais and Wiebe, 2010)

According to the International Planning Committee for Food Sovereignty can be summarised as follows:

"Food sovereignty is the right of peoples to healthy and culturally appropriate food produced through ecologically sound and sustainable methods, and their right to define their own food and agriculture systems. It puts those who produce, distribute and consume food at the heart of food systems and policies rather than the demands of markets and corporations. It defends the interests and inclusion of the next generation. It offers a strategy to resist and dismantle the current corporate trade and food regime, and directions for food, farming, pastoral and fisheries systems determined by local producers. Food sovereignty prioritises local and national economies and markets and empowers peasant and family farmer-driven agriculture, artisanal fishing, pastoralist-led grazing, and food production, distribution and consumption based on environmental, social and economic sustainability." - Declaration of Nyéléni, 2007

According to a vast and growing body of research, food sovereignty is a potentially radical and powerful critique corporate food industry. It also focuses on alternative models for agriculture that are intended to be more environmentally and socially just. The grass-roots origins of 'food sovereignty' as well as its inclusive nature one of its greatest strengths. With its strong focus on caring for people and the environment, and its obvious similarity with permaculture, agroecology and indigenous values, it has the ability to connect diverse groups of people variety of different backgrounds. It has also been used as a platform to influence government policy in a range of different countries including Ecuador, Venezuela, Mali, Bolivia, Nepal, Senegal and some parts of the United States. Food sovereignty is intentionally linked directly to democracy and justice by putting the control of land, water, seeds and natural resources in the hands of the people who produce food. A core purpose of the food sovereignty campaign is to redistribute land and the power over food production to enable marginalised communities to produce their own food.

The six pillars of food sovereignty

Food sovereignty...

Focuses on food for people: *The right to food which is healthy and culturally appropriate is the basic legal demand underpinning food sovereignty. Guaranteeing it requires policies which support diversified food production in each region and country. Food is not simply another commodity to be traded or speculated on for profit.*

Values food providers: *Many smallholder farmers suffer violence, marginalisation and racism from corporate landowners and governments. People are often pushed off their land by mining concerns or agribusiness. Agricultural workers can face severe exploitation and even bonded labour. Although women produce most of the food in the global south, their role and knowledge are often ignored, and their rights to resources and as workers are violated. Food sovereignty asserts food providers' right to live and work in dignity.*

Localises food systems: *Food must be seen primarily as sustenance for the community and only secondarily as something to be traded. Under food sovereignty, local and regional provision takes precedence over supplying distant markets, and export-orientated agriculture is rejected. The 'free trade' policies which prevent developing countries from protecting their own agriculture, for example through subsidies and tariffs, are also inimical to food sovereignty.*

Puts control locally: *Food sovereignty places control over territory, land, grazing, water, seeds, livestock and fish populations on local food providers and respects their rights. They can use and share them in socially and environmentally sustainable ways which conserve diversity. Privatisation of such resources, for example through intellectual property rights regimes or commercial contracts, is explicitly rejected.*

Builds knowledge and skills: *Technologies, such as genetic engineering, that undermine food providers' ability to develop and pass on knowledge and* *skills needed for localised food systems are rejected. Instead, food sovereignty calls for appropriate research systems to support the development of agricultural knowledge and skills.*

Works with nature: *Food sovereignty requires production and distribution systems that protect natural resources and reduce greenhouse gas emissions, avoiding energy-intensive industrial methods that damage the environment and the health of those that inhabit it.*

Nyéléni 2007 - Forum for Food Sovereignty

Vía Campesina no longer juxtaposes food sovereignty and food security, choosing instead to frame the former as the route to the latter. Advocates explain that the oppositional framing was useful to begin with, to differentiate food sovereignty and define it (Rose 2013).

Vía Campesina critique the way neoliberal governments and corporations have used the concept of food security to promote increased agricultural trade liberalisation. Fairbairn (2010) argues that this has resulted in a concentration of food production in the hands of fewer, and larger, agri-business corporations, and the 'dumping' of excess food strategically through international trade at prices below the production cost, devastating local agriculture which cannot compete. Some international aid agencies subscribe to the view that food insecurity is the result of a lack of supply, and promote the idea that more food must therefore be mass-produced, despite the vast food waste that exists in the global system. In contrast, food sovereignty is intentionally linked directly to democracy and justice by putting the control of land, water, seeds and natural resources in the hands of the people who produce food (Wittman et al 2010; Patel 2009; Masioli and Nicholson 2010; Rosset et al 2006).

Little was published in relation to food sovereignty until around 2008. However, since then an abundance of academic articles and books have emerged. The bulk of this literature takes on an aspirational tone. Treating 'food sovereignty' almost as an entity with desires and demands.

Wittman, Desmarais and Wiebe (2010) assert that food sovereignty has emerged in recent years as a radical and powerful critique of neoliberalism as enacted by the global corporate food industry. They also claim that it has "the potential to foster dramatic and widespread change in agricultural, political and social systems related to food by posing a radical challenge to the agro-industry model of food production" (Wittman et al 2010, 4). This transformation involves an integrated, democratised and localised food system.

Criticism of neoliberal theory and practice is central to the concept of food sovereignty. The words 'neoliberal' and 'neoliberalism' are used frequently and rather simplistically as 'catch all' terms to encompass the problems with contemporary corporate capitalism and governance (Wittman et al 2010; Handy and Fehr 2010). Neoliberalism is also specifically linked, in theory and practice, to political shifts favouring the rights of corporations over communities. The concept of food sovereignty is deliberately constructed in direct contrast to neoliberalism in that it promotes the decentralisation of corporate power structures and advocates on behalf of marginalised communities especially, providing alternative models for agriculture that are more environmentally and socially just (Borras and Franco 2010; Patel 2009).

Food sovereignty is presented in much of the literature as an ethically persuasive and achievable objective, yet as a movement it is not immune to critique. Borras and Franco (2010) highlight some key challenges to achieving food sovereignty. They focus primarily on difficulties with access to and distribution or redistribution of land under changing political systems which are heavily influenced by corporate interests. Borras and Franco (2010) claim that the first step in achieving food sovereignty involves reforming land-based social relations so that the rural poor can access and have control over land resources and, therefore, the ability to produce food. They argue that because large powerful corporations have recently had renewed interest in rural land for producing agrofuels it is likely to be a difficult struggle to achieve food sovereignty for the rural poor (Borras and Franco 2010, 116).

Other challenges have come from Philipp Aerni (2011) who claims that food sovereignty makes what he calls 'wrong baseline' assumptions. He makes the point that subsistence farming is not necessarily a chosen or preferred lifestyle for all peasants. He also argues that the challenges faced in the Global South are not easily comparable with those in the Global North. Furthermore, Aerni asserts that although food sovereignty literature is vocal about the problems with neoliberal ideology, it is silent about how some communist regimes have contributed to famines. Along similar lines, Bernstein (2009) makes the point that Vía Campesina, in its critique of individualism and modernism and its reassertion of rural peasant identity, too easily generalises a unified peasant identity. Other potential conflicts, as mentioned by Wittman (2009) have arisen in the food sovereignty literature regarding the role of the state in the implementation of food sovereignty, which sometimes calls for greater state power.

Rose (2013) notes the lack of alliances with trade unions and worker groups as a weakness of Vía Campesina's campaign. Despite these criticisms, Rose maintains that the movement has many strengths and good potential to influence and transform aspects of the current globalising capitalist food system. One of the core strengths is the inclusiveness of the campaign, which embraces the aspiration of diversity in a deliberate ideological way. As a critical and reflexive movement there is also room to address these limitations, and Rose (2013), maintains optimism about this potential.

Food sovereignty has become an important framework in Europe where it is increasingly difficult for rural populations to maintain dignified livelihoods (Holt-Gimenez and Patel 2009, 159; Masioli and Nicholson 2010). This challenge has been responded to by farmer unions, consumer groups, environmental and fairtrade organisations, as well as economic solidarity networks and others, creating a range of alternative policies and practices for sustainable production (Holt-

Gimenez and Patel 2009, 84). Vaarst and González-García (2012) relate the concept of food sovereignty to food systems in Europe, focussing particularly on Denmark and France, and emphasising what they call social food networks and consumer-farmer networks.

Grass-roots initiatives that are openly linked to Vía Campesina also have emerged in the Global North such as the National Family Farm Coalition (NFFC), one of two United States based members of Vía Campesina. The NFFC is a not-for-profit organisation that was founded in 1986, a few years before Vía Campesina. It promotes grassroots movements towards food sovereignty and represents family farms and rural groups in the USA where members face economic recession and corporate pressures. It works alongside a network of domestic and international organisations with similar goals, towards empowering farmers and "securing a sustainable, economically just, healthy, safe and secure food and farm system" (National Family Farm Coalition 2012, 1).

Holt-Gimenez and Patel (2009) assert that various marginalised populations in the US have taken the lead in food justice struggles in their country: "A broad-based, home-grown food movement led by youth, underserved communities, community groups and family farm and labour organisations, is steadily taking back control over the food system" (Holt-Gimenez and Patel 2009, 159). They argue that these kinds of groups are reaching out to form global networks to further sustainability and food sovereignty, and that international similarities are widespread. They describe that this "outpouring of practical initiatives" collectively reflects a necessary condition for the transformation of the current system to one of food sovereignty. Similar outpourings of practical initiatives can be found located in Whaingaroa and wider New Zealand.

Community gardens are also of high relevance to the research presented in this book. In his USA-based ethnography, 'The Social Impact of Community Gardens in the Greater Cleveland Area', Flachs (2010) notes that the contemporary community gardening movement is motivated by wider environmental and social as well as personal and financial concerns, but also that community gardens have existed throughout history. Flachs reflects on the great complexity and diversity presented by community gardens and of their potential to foster personal and communal growth through participation and shared experiences (7). Flachs also argues that the personal and functional motivations of community gardens, including greater food security and financial benefits, are interconnected with wider social and environmental concerns. He refutes the claims made by other researchers that gardeners from higher socio-economic sectors of society are more focused on environmental justice concerns while lower socio-economic gardeners focus on personal motivations, finding that personal food and financial motivations were common across demographics and that gardeners with lower socio-economic means were also politically and environmentally conscious. Furthermore, Flachs claims that the communities themselves did not recognise the dichotomy of class motivations presented in other community gardening literature.

Freeganism, the practice of living off food that would otherwise be wasted, has been linked to the food sovereignty movement both in the refusal to contribute to the corporate food system and in the associated outspoken activism (Le Grand 2010; Partridge 2011; Galli and Cliff 2012; Scanlan 2009). Partridge seeks to critically engage with Freegans and Freeganism in London in order to locate them in relation to the wider discourses of sustainable consumption. He explores the paradox inherent in protesting against a system one is benefiting from and discusses how some Freegans negotiate this paradox. Partridge (2011) claims that Freeganism is not just about opting out of consumerism, but is also about deliberate self-marginalisation: "'existing in the cracks' and subverting the materialities created by commodified spaces and reinscribing them with alternative values" (38). Partridge (2011) argues that by subsisting on surplus food, Freegans take an active role in their negotiation of ways of living within a commodified society and, in doing so, their consumption constitutes an act of resistance rather than compliance with cultural expectations (39). I encountered similar reactions and resistance to commodified society in New Zealand.

Despite food sovereignty being a relatively modern concept, it can also be seen in the context to the history of food and industrialisation. In support of food sovereignty Handy and Fehr (2010) weave a powerful critique of neoliberalism from its philosophical roots in the writings of Adam Smith. In doing so they document the progression of industrialisation through the eighteenth and nineteenth centuries' forced migration of British peasants from the 'commons', where they had the ability to grow and produce their own food, to the cities. This shift, they argue, was encouraged and entwined with the widespread uptake of Adam Smith's pro-market and pro-capitalist ideas. Handy and Fehr (2010) depict these beginnings of neoliberal ideology as involving superstitious religious-type worship, fetishism, and the naturalisation of 'the market', all elements that continue in contemporary neoliberalism. They conclude that modern agriculture was based on exclusions and land enclosures fundamental to the development of capitalism, and that myths about the market and industrial agriculture have been constructed and reinforced to make injustices easier to tolerate. They also affirm the important role of the framework of food sovereignty in challenging this system (Handy and Fehr 2011).

Although the eighteenth and nineteenth centuries are seemingly distant, the process of actively driving peasants from the land in the name of development is a common contemporary occurrence, both for marginalised populations in the Global North and Global South. This process of deliberate dislocation of peoples from their land, resources and livelihood in the name of progress can be linked to the historical experiences of Māori in New Zealand, particularly in relation to land confiscations, colonisation and forced urbanisation (Walker 2004).

Supporters of neoliberalism claim that the only way to solve the problems of inequality (which are arguably exacerbated by neoliberal practices like market deregulation) is by further market deregulation presenting a rosy view of 'progress' as visiting and improving 'under-developed' places, ignoring the necessary further exploitation of these countries in sustaining the more advanced 'developed' countries (Handy and Fehr 2010). This occurs, they argue, despite evidence that even in developed countries neoliberal ideology, in practice, has been shown to lead to increased social inequalities. This can be seen in New Zealand where, as Kelsey (1995) and Larner (2000) have argued, since the 1980s neoliberal policies have had detrimental effects on health, education, work and social support systems. The New Zealand example of neoliberal ideology in practice has been upheld by powerful institutions as a model for the rest of the world (Kelsey 1995; Larner 2000).

Kiwifood

There are an infinite number of possible stories to tell about food across every human community and culture. New Zealanders, with our diverse landscapes and cultures could tell many stories ranging from those of whitebait fritters we have loved and 'eeling with the cuzzies', to swanky café culture, and food reality television. We can also tell stories about food poverty (McNeil 2011), about children going hungry at school and the increasing lack of affordability of 'healthy' food. Alongside such heart-breaking narratives we can inspire hope with stories about the Enviroschools program that facilitates connection and understanding between children and the wider environment[1]. Occasionally in this country which has always been my home, I have recognised great change: 'this is not the New Zealand I grew up in'. There are many different worlds here – some invisible, some private, all political and interconnected by a few degrees of separation among people in this small, colonised, isolated, island nation.

Any discussion of contemporary food systems, or indeed anything contemporary in New Zealand is set against a backdrop of British imperialism and historic colonisation. As Came (2012) describes, colonial policy in New Zealand required land to be removed from Māori, the indigenous people, for the pursuit of individual occupation or profit for colonial settlers. In this process the communal use of land by Māori people was marginalised through colonisation and through the individualising and alienating processes of the organisation of capitalism (Came 2012; Walker 2004).

McCormack (2011) highlights how continued widespread commitment to neoliberal principles in so many aspects of economic and social policy has opened up opportunities for iwi [tribe/s] self-determination and also the development of the 'Māori-self' or Māori trading entity. This development is said to be in keeping with the overall neoliberal goal of reducing state welfare and strengthening individual property rights to encourage self-interested competition under the seductive guise of individual 'freedom'. However, McCormack (2012) also notes that the concept of private ownership reduces the broad, holistic, spiritual and intergenerational concepts and traditions of communal ownership. The valuing of private property for the sake of commodity production divides humanity into competing groups. It enables those with advantages to 'win' and encourages dominance through winning. The dominance of market based organisations and of productivity measured by Gross Domestic Product marginalises interconnected, interdependent, sustenance based, reciprocal ways of being human. Casey-Cox (2014) links this to the colonisation of our life-world, a concept that speaks to the personal internalisation of dominant narratives of power and privilege.

Food, privilege and poverty in New Zealand

Freedom is a privilege. I'm really not saying that it should be, but unfortunately it often is. The freedom to easily participate in society is something many people can't afford and too often these are the people who crowd our prison system. Food freedom is a middle-class luxury too much of the time. Farmers markets are mostly populated by well-dressed (if sometimes eccen-

tric) white folk. Whaingaroa is somewhat of a bubble, where class and privilege seem to break down a bit more than usual. Lots of people here are on low incomes but have a high quality of life because they can grow their own food, share, and participate in community activities. I know foragers and people who want to plant as many public fruit trees as possible. It's easy to help out in someone's garden and then share lunch with them or take home some of the harvest. These are the invisible (and non-taxable) things that can overcome issues of monetary privilege. It's certainly not the default world, but maybe it's a step in the direction of positive food freedom.

- My fieldwork reflections from August 2013.

The purpose of this section is to hold space for further discussion in order to recognise the growing social inequalities in New Zealand which reflect a global pattern of increasing inequity as documented by Graeber (2011). In any research focussing on social relationships to food, the lack of access to safe, sufficient, and culturally appropriate food is worthy of discussion. McNeil's (2011) doctoral research on experiences of food scarcity in Hamilton, New Zealand (less than an hour's drive from Whaingaroa) is a relevant example, highlighting these often invisible, struggles in New Zealand.

It struck me, during my fieldwork and through wider conversations around poverty, that privilege is often invisible to the privileged, and that narratives around poverty in New Zealand too easily take on neoliberal discourses around 'laziness' and 'personal choice'. Over the past five years homelessness and begging has become increasingly visible in my home town and other cities around New Zealand. Simultaneously, campaigns for feeding kids in schools and ending child poverty have grown more audible out of necessity. These campaigns and their reach demonstrate, to my mind, that there is a public ethos of caring – that we do care about injustice, especially when innocent children are at risk. It is, however, much harder to raise public concern around poverty for adults, because of the dominant neoliberal narratives around personal choice and meritocracy. The paradox here is that the populist neoliberal narratives of freedom and choice seem to result in the very opposite when put into political practice. This paradox is becoming clearer with the increasingly widespread awareness of child poverty, homelessness, and growing inequality in New Zealand in recent years. The following ethnographic reflection from my fieldwork demonstrates some of the mixed attitudes to poverty:

Feeding People: problems with how we think about poverty

There's a woman in our small town who feeds people. She makes soup and jam and drops it off on the door steps of people who need it. It's the old people who know, and they tell her: so and so is struggling this week, they could do with some help. She often comes home to find a bag of apples on her door step or other seasonal produce. She also finds the containers returned to her door-step, cleaned. She says it's like Christmas, she's so excited to find those cleaned containers. She doesn't know how they know to return them. They just do. She feeds people because her family has always done it. Where she comes from the haves feed the have-nots. That's just what's done. They don't seem to have that culture so much in New Zealand, she says.

The other day a woman came up to her on the street. "Are you feeding people?" the woman asked. "Now why would you think a thing like that?" The woman who feeds people replied. "You're feeding people. I know you are," the response came in a snarl. "You shouldn't feed people. You should stop. You know why? Because if you feed them the drug addict parents don't need to spend their money on their kid's food. They can go right ahead and spend their money on drugs. You shouldn't let them. They should have to spend their money on feeding their kids."

"Come here," said the woman who feeds people. She gestured with her finger. "Come closer." She didn't want to yell, she kept her composure, as she always does. The other woman leaned in. "I don't care what you think. I don't care what you say about those parents, you know, I don't care about any of that. The only thing I care about is that those kids get fed, so you tell me not to feed people, I don't give a damn." Then she went right on with her day.

There's a problem with how we think about poverty in this country. There's a big problem. People like to think that there isn't real poverty in New Zealand but there is. There are hungry children living in cold, damp, drafty housing. There are kids going to school with no lunch because after the bills are paid there's nothing left over – if the bills can be paid at all. The bills have all gone up: rent, power and especially food. While the minimum wage and benefits have only moved sluggishly, everything else has sky-rocketed. We do have a problem with poverty in New Zealand and it's only getting worse. The Salvation Army is on the news imploring people to vote for the political parties that are going to do something about it. They have too many people waiting in line outside their food banks.

We'd like to think there's no real poverty – not like in other countries. We'd like to think that anyone who is struggling to get by is just not trying hard enough – not working hard enough. We'd like to believe that with a bit of hard work and Kiwi ingenuity, anyone can get to the top. We'd like to think that poor people are just not budgeting properly, that they're making bad choices, that they're degenerates, wasting their money on cigarettes and alcohol, that they're drug addicts, and maybe sometimes they are, because when you have very few choices and a crushing tonne of social pressure those "bad choices" seem like they might make the present just a little bit more bearable. I can't believe the lack of empathy that people show people who are less privileged than themselves, all that ugly, hateful, beneficiary bashing all the simplistic judgments and advice: they should just... Just what? Has it not occurred to us that if the problem was that simple to solve we would have solved it by now? If it was such a simple choice, people wouldn't choose poverty, would they?

- My fieldwork reflections, March 25, 2014.

Through this ethnographic process a juxtaposition of food privilege has arisen, between struggles of scarcity and inequality, and the growing demand for 'ethical food', often associated with the upper and middle-class. Privileged middle-class food ethics fetishism is not new and has been the subject of wide critique as have the academics writing about localism and slow food (Slocum 2007; Guthman 2003;

2008; Laudan 2001; Donati 2005). A potential problem with 'ethical food' and the rise of value-based labels such as 'free-range', 'organic', 'local', 'fairtrade' and so on, is that these are generally more expensive and therefore less accessible to a growing number of the population who are living in poverty. While there is much to celebrate in the invigorated cottage industries and in raising awareness around ecological, social and animal welfare, this 'ethical consumption' has potential to become a force of hegemonic injustice in itself – if only the relatively wealthy can afford to be ethical. This uncomfortable possibility can be made more palatable though with the addition of a more optimistic aside. There is potential for 'ethical food' to raise awareness, to lower prices through 'the market', and to diffuse this tension through a greater common purpose. Food scarcity and various kinds of 'ethical food' justice issues can illuminate the cracks in this system of growing inequality.

Food sovereignty in Aotearoa

A food evolution is taking place in New Zealand. Right now, right here, new ways of producing, preparing and sharing food are slowly being established. Some of the new ways are not too different from some of the good old ways, which have been displaced over the past century by the industrial food system… It's time to move on to something better (Dann 2012, 9).

In her book *Food@home*, organics writer and academic, Christine Dann (2012) describes many grass roots initiatives and activities in New Zealand that are also evident in the food sovereignty movement, although she does not explicitly use the 'food sovereignty' term. These include community gardening, Māra Māori [traditional Māori gardening], food foraging, seed-saving and sustainable small-holders. Dann (2012) refers in her preface to the food transformations occurring in New Zealand communities. This statement, and many of the initiatives covered in Dann's (2012) book, can be seen as inter-linked with the concept and campaign for food sovereignty in their intentions as well as their motivations, and can be considered part of a general global movement towards food sovereignty, as described by Holt-Gimenez and Patel (2009, 2).

'Food sovereignty', though not a usual part of the dominant discourse in New Zealand, was mentioned in the Food Bill (which became the Food Act 2014), the proposed replacement of the parliamentary Food Act (1981). This generated much interest during the time of my core fieldwork. For example, a lobby group, The Food Bill Issues List, challenged the Food Bill claiming that the proposed legislation would 'make fundamental changes to New Zealand's food supply and food sovereignty' (Foodbill.org 2012, 1). Issues were raised around the potential threat to food sovereignty posed by the legislation through restricting practices such as 'wwoofing'[2], seed saving and gifting food, including garden produce. This lobby group asserted that the proposed legislation was designed to appeal to international trade agreements, to the detriment of the public good. This was picked up by national media and while the Bill was topical, before it was passed in mid-2013, the term 'food sovereignty' was regularly mentioned on news bulletins on the public broadcast station, Radio New Zealand National (2014). However, in this discourse the use of the term was applied in a different sense, as the Food Bill was described as a potential threat to New Zealand's national food sovereignty. In positioning the Bill as a threat, there is an assumption that 'food sovereignty' is something New Zealand, as a nation, already possessed, rather than something to move towards at the community level. This use of 'food sovereignty' differs from its general use in the literature which ascribes aspirational qualities to the term.

Despite a large and growing body of international food sovereignty literature, when I first began this research I could not find any New Zealand based publications focussed explicitly on the subject aside from a brief mention in relation to food regimes by Roche (2012). Since then it has been the focus of several articles. Hutchings, Tipene, Carney, Greensill, Skelton and Baker (2013) discuss food sovereignty in relation to 'Hua Parakore', the certification system provided by the Māori organics association, Te Waka Kai Ora. They argue that Te

Waka Kai Ora are contributing to the wider food sovereignty movement and draw connections between Hua Parakore and the Western-based organics systems in New Zealand, as well as the international Slow Food movement. Hutchings et al (2013) frame this group as an expression of indigenous food sovereignty, which is making a key contribution to indigenous organic food producers in New Zealand, as well as representing Māori food sovereignty at an international level, and responding to the 'global triple crisis' of climate change, peak oil, and food insecurity:

Hua Parakore is a development opportunity in the form of an indigenous food sovereignty initiative that seeks to address and respond to this triple crisis from a kaupapa Māori [Māori philosophical] framework and assert rangatiratanga [self-determination] with regard to food production. Critical within this Hua Parakore framed response to the triple crisis is the reassertion within Māori tribal collectives to save and protect traditional seed from commodification and to return to the land to grow food to feed families (Hutchings et al 2013, 133).

This article states that strengthening relationships between the Māori and non-Māori organics sectors has broadened the paradigm of organics in New Zealand and that although the philosophies are based on different epistemologies, they are both holistic paradigms for food production which include a focus on ecosystems, soil, biodiversity, and animal welfare, as well as strong resistance to genetic modification, nanotechnology, and chemical herbicides and pesticides. The resistance to genetic modification among Te Waka Kai Ora members includes concerns over risks to human health, traditional farming and biodiversity, as well as intellectual and cultural property right issues (Hutchings et al 2013). This resistance is integral to the organisation:

The development of Hua Parakore is not only about supporting Māori well-being though the commercial, community and home-growing of Hua Parakore food and products, but it is also a means by which to demonstrate resistance to biopiracy[3], GM[4] and neo-liberal free trade policies which continue to act as a vehicle to displace and colonise indigenous peoples globally (Hutchings et al 2013, 132).

In another article focussed on the concept of food sovereignty in New Zealand, Rosin (2014), approaches the topic from a human geography perspective, as an example of potentially transformative utopian politics. He points out that the country's export-focussed agriculture, rooted in colonial history, means that an excess of food is produced, rendering food security of little concern at a national level. He also states that food sovereignty does not fit well within the dominant food production paradigm, despite the reality of food scarcity for some economically vulnerable populations, and that these situations in New Zealand are mistakenly treated as discrete and localized problems. Rosin (2014) argues for the important role of utopian scholarship in re-imagining a food system that is just, fair, secure and abundant, and which supports the production of safe, nutritious and culturally valued food.

Other research focussed on community gardening and similar activities in New Zealand can also be considered relevant to food sovereignty, including Anna Casey-Cox's (2014) research on local community gardening. Casey-Cox makes note of connectedness, values and wider relating to the environment in her work:

I notice that the action of gardening together can open a space for communication. I have noticed that often when people till the soil together, a conversation stirs. Stories and reflections are shared and often relationships develop. I notice how a conversation in the garden often starts organically, gently and spontaneously as people busy themselves in the soil, looking at Earth, listening to each other. As a researcher in the garden, but not only, I have found it hard to prioritise or instigate conversations pertaining to the 'noticing' of values and dominant order when conversations about life and how each of us are in the day seem more important to us. Community gardens as a space to talk about life and the things that matter to us, is something I consider to be an important finding of this research. (Casey-Cox 2014, 57)

In making these connections to land and place in New Zealand, Casey-Cox acknowledges the complex history of colonisation, and emphasises the importance of having discussions around it:

Community gardening is an activity that involves land, shared land, public land, land that holds stories. In Aotearoa New Zealand, these stories invariably connect to colonisation. However, the connections between land, history and oppression, the wider context of our action together are not what everyone wants to talk about. Yet, I question – how can it be ethical for these issues not to concern us? If community gardening is an action that people consider to be contributing to a 'better world' then part of this action needs to consider how humanity came to be facing today's economic, social and environmental problems. (Casey-Cox 2014, 64)

Food democracy initiatives

New Zealand has a thriving permaculture community and many alternative economic initiatives including active online Freecycle groups, through which goods can be given away or requested. The image below, from the Hamilton Freecycle email newsletter, demonstrates how a variety of items can be shared, including food:

Figure 6: Offers and requests from the Hamilton Freecycle group, 2013.

Alongside Freecycle[5], other new initiatives have been set up to facilitate the re-distribution of food that would otherwise be wasted, especially from retail stores including supermarkets and bakeries. These include food rescue organisations like Kaibosh[6] which collects food from shops and takes it to food banks and community organisations. Free stores have also been set up in Wellington, Auckland and Palmerston North, often supported by other organisations including churches, and in one case, a petrol station. These free stores, stocked with freshly rescued food, are intended to provide a less stigmatised distribution point than traditional food banks, and more free choice. Other food redistribution in New Zealand includes informal foraging or dumpster-diving, the excess of which is generally shared among friends, as well as groups like Food Not Bombs[7], a chapter of which has been active outside the Dunedin Farmers' Market. Food Not Bombs is a long-standing global network, which takes donated or foraged food then prepares and shares meals in public with anyone who wants, as described by Giles (2013). He makes the strong connection between excessive food waste and neoliberal ideologies:

The material wealth I have found, cloistered away in Seattle's factory, wholesale, and retail dumpsters (or on its way there) is hardly out of the ordinary. Or, if you like, it's business as usual. The market has not been the efficient arbiter of resources some free-market ideologues imagine. Rather, it makes waste in absurd quantities… Waste is a quiet, ongoing crisis at the heart of capital, which, no less than want, stalks the noisier, episodic economic calamities we are more accustomed to hearing about (Giles 2013, 39).

As I was conducting food research during the time that the 'Food Bill' controversy was in mainstream, as well as more peripheral online media, people have often asked me about the Food Bill. As part of my fieldwork I talked to people involved in a variety of different food democratisation and food activism activities that can be linked to the framework of food sovereignty, as explained by Patel (2009). The following sections in this chapter present long-form narratives sourced from interviews with people involved in some of these activities. They introduce many themes that relate to the following chapters focussing on the food providers of Whaingaroa, tensions, values, practices and alternative economics. These themes will be drawn through into the final discussion and explored further in Chapter Nine.

3 WHAINGAROA

The narratives presented in the previous chapter can be seen as representing two separate but interconnected sites: of Wilderland and of urban New Zealand.

The purpose of the present chapter is to introduce and describe Whaingaroa, the third, and main site of my fieldwork. Whaingaroa is located on the west coast of the central North Island of New Zealand.

Nestled beneath Mt Karioi (Te Ara 2011), the township in many ways resembles a typical New Zealand sea-side holiday settlement with pastel coloured weatherboard houses and tongue-and-groove baches [holiday homes] interspersed with more modern concrete and glass constructions. These houses are clustered between the hills, and the quaint town-centre.

Figure 7: The bridge from the township across to Te Kopua, 2014.

Whaingaroa is described in tourist brochures as "A charming coastal town only 30–45 minutes from [the significant city of] Hamilton... [with] a large harbour perfect for fishing and boating, as well as several beaches spread along the coastline"[1], and "An unspoilt holiday destination. Whether you're looking for world class surf, stunning scenery, beautiful beaches, inspiring arts or simply a good old cup of coffee, laidback Raglan offers the perfect escape from the hustle and bustle of everyday life"[2]. It is known as an international surfing destination, with a famous left-hand surf-break (Corner 2008), a kiwi holiday spot, and is home to many commuters who work in Hamilton (Te Ara 2011). As of the 2013 census, the township had a permanent population of 2,736 (Statistics NZ 2013).

Figure 8: Karioi and Whaingaroa, 2012.

Demographic statistics of this population show that it is slightly older than that of the wider Waikato Region signifying its popularity as a place of retirement. Over the summer the population of the township has been recorded as approximately 10,500, around three times the usual number of inhabitants (Corner 2008). This summer influx helps to support local businesses which are known to struggle during the winter months.

Ethnic groups in Raglan and Waikato District		
2013 Census		
Ethnic group[1]	Raglan (percent)	Waikato District (percent)
European	81.1	79.1
Māori	27.3	24.3
Pacific peoples	2.8	3.5
Asian	2.4	3.8
Middle Eastern, Latin American, African	0.7	0.4
Other ethnicity	1.3	1.8
1. Includes all people who stated each ethnic group, whether as their only ethnic group or as one of several. Where a person reported more than one ethnic group, they have been counted in each applicable group. As a result percentages do not add up to 100.		
(Statistics New Zealand, 2016)		

Figure 9: Ethnic groups in Whaingaroa from 2013 census (Statistics New Zealand 2006).

The table in Figure 9 shows the recorded percentages of people categorised in ethnic groups in Whaingaroa in the 2013 census. This presents a higher Māori population and lower Asian population than the wider region or the nation as a whole. Due to its desirability as a tourist and in particular, surfing destination, Whaingaroa is inhabited by a noticeable number of travellers or semi-permanent international people. These 'internationals' are often European, North American or South American. They have a visible influence on the cultural landscape of the township and surrounding area, lending a more cosmopolitan atmosphere to what would otherwise be an isolated small coastal town.

Figure 10: Bow Street, 2014.

On arrival, the first signs of the township are several new subdivisions encroaching on the surrounding farmland. Just beyond these is the top of the main street, Bow Street, remarkable for its tall phoenix [non-indigenous] palms set in a row down the grassy median strip, which descends down-hill, past war memorials, towards a view of the harbour inlet and indigenous pohutukawa trees.

Local produce and bread are present on the menu at some of the cafés but this is not immediately obvious at an initial view. On closer inspection, there is a very small bread shop, open only three to four mornings a week, selling locally made sourdough bread and, in view from the bottom of the street, the Herbal Dispensary stocks vegetables grown nearby by Kaiwhenua Organics.

Locally roasted coffee, at Raglan Roast, can be found in the alley behind the main street as well as at the wharf which is a short walk from town. This coffee is also sold in Te Uku, the township just before Whaingaroa, and across the one-way bridge, in the pizzaria and gelato shop which was once the Raglan West dairy.

History and activism

Like other early settlements in New Zealand, Whaingaroa has a colonial past replete with the still visible legacies of missionaries and flax trading, and an indigenous history that goes back much further. The Tainui waka [canoe], the vessel bringing a vanguard of people from Hawaiki [the legendary place of origin of Māori people] is said to have landed here before making its way to its final resting place in Kawhia.

This area, by some accounts, was originally named Whangaroa "Long Harbour", however, in a typically colonial gesture, to distinguish it from the more northern harbour of the same name, early missionaries inserted an "i" (Vennell and Williams 1976). Other local accounts argue that the name "Whaingaroa" is correct, meaning "long pursuit", referring to the lengthy journey of the Tainui waka.

The geographic isolation of the area was a prominent factor regarding access in earlier history, and today still appears to be a factor in the size of the town. Early [non-indigenous] settlers grew wheat and ran sheep on the cleared land. An old settler who lived in Whaingaroa in the 1890s reminisced in the local newspaper, the *Chronicle* in 1956:

As one who had not seen Whaingaroa for fifty years, I was greatly surprised at the progress and the lovely grasslands which have replaced the scrub and bush. Every person I met appeared prosperous and content, and so from a financial point of view as well. From the sentimental point of view it was sad to find the miro groves that sheltered the pigeons and wild pigs gone for ever.

Also, where are those streams that were alive with mountain trout and eels? The bush was chopped by some of the finest axe men... Like dominoes falling, a chain reaction would sweep through the bush as a hillside of trees crashed to the earth (Vernon 1981, 87).

In more recent history, Whaingaroa featured prominently in the beginnings of the Māori rights movement in the 1970s. The land known as Te Kopua was taken by government from local Tangata Whenua [people of the land] for use as an aerodrome during World War II, and was not returned after the war as agreed. Instead, it was retained by the local council, leased to the local golf club, and converted into a golf course.

Eva Rickard, the legendary local activist, is known for leading the long struggle to win back the land. She was arrested in 1978 during a sit-in protest, but eventually won back the land (Ministry for Culture and Heritage 2015). Some of Eva's impact on the area is described by research participants Liz and Rick:

Liz: Eva did it first.

Rick: Yeah, Whaea Eva Rickard and the land down at the Kōkiri centre. The land was taken during the war as an emergency air strip. Then the day-to-day control, i.e. the lawn mowing, was done by the council, then they decided to get a bit of money out of it so they started establishing a golf-course, which was all put up with by the Tangata Whenua, but when they started bulldozing her grandmother's grave, Eva was arrested for trespassing on her tribal land and it went to court. They got the land back and everyone said: 'Oh no, the 'Māoris' have got their land back – what will happen?' The first thing they did was they gifted most of the land back to the community: the camp grounds, we still have an air strip. Down at the Kōkiri Centre they set up amazing things. She realised the kids coming out of school had no skills for employment so they set up all these workshops for them.

I remember, as a child, eating slices of watermelon at the festival Eva held on the land every year to commemorate its return. More recently, members of the community, including local Tangata Whenua, have been involved in ongoing activism against proposed seabed mining by corporate interests.

My family's involvement in Whaingaroa started in 1967, on January 7th when, on a day trip from Hamilton, my grandparents, Jane and James, learned of the auction of a section at Whale Bay. My mother (aged 7) took her two younger brothers to the Duck-Inn dairy to buy ice blocks leaving her parents free to bid successfully on the section later to hold the Skyline garage known as 'The Shack' which my grandparents used as a family bach [holiday home] and allowed surfers to use as well.

In more recent history it has become the namesake of the café on the main street of town called The Shack, originated by a surfer and frequenter of the original Shack. My grandparents lived in the area full-time from 1990.

My aunt moved to Whaingaroa later in the 90s and started a family and my mother took up residence near-by in the early 2000's. Although I have spent significant time in the area over the course of my life, it was only in 2011 that I moved here, pulled by the need to be closer to the ocean, my family, and excited at the prospect of being involved in what has become an unusually creative small-town community.

Figure 11: Famous surf breaks near the original 'Shack', 2013.

Many things in Whaingaroa have changed since my childhood: the Duck-Inn dairy was transformed into a café and then a Cambodian restaurant, before becoming yet another café; 'Petchells' the local supermarket was sold by the Petchell family and became '4-Square' before changing chains and becoming a Supervalue, with a sign on the outside 'Owned and operated by locals', despite no longer selling local produce; another 4-Square has since opened up near the main street of town; the former post office became a Post Shop, and now stands as an empty shop as the franchise has been bought by, and now occupies, a small corner of the Supervalue; the fruit and vegetable shop that was once on the main street moved to a side street, then vanished completely.

Since then, two different greengrocers have opened on Bow Street, only to close after a year or less. The past fifteen years in particular have seen the development of more cafés, gift shops and local art galleries, as well as more live music and creative workshops, adding to a complex and diverse small-town culture. These changes have been driven, in part, by tourism and local residents attempting to make a living.

Whaingaroa is often described as a transient place. Because of its traveller-friendly culture, its celebration of creativity, its picturesque qualities and its desirability as a surf destination it often becomes the temporary home of travellers, for months or years, before visas run out or other commitments call people back. There are noticeable numbers of British, German, French, Italian and other European residents, both short and long term.

This transience seems to create a culture of general friendliness to newcomers while simultaneously close friends, and longstanding locals tend to form more closed groups. Many people experience Whaingaroa as a very friendly place. In a small town it does not take long to get to know familiar faces. It is usual for new acquaintances to hug or kiss on the cheek, although, it is a common experience for this friendly-acquaintance level to continue without deepening into closer friendships.

Jenny makes sourdough bread and sells it in a tiny shop on the main street. She explains that the transient international visitors enjoy her bread:

A lot of American tourists are really excited by it. A lot of Europeans who are really missing the bread back home are surprised to see the little shop – they think it's really funny and almost every day – I think so far there's only been about one or two days that someone hasn't taken a photo.

She describes the growing local food initiatives as follows:

In Whaingaroa we've got some interesting things happening. It seems like we're on the cusp of being a foodie place. We could make ourselves into a foodie place if we had more of a farmers' market thing happening on Saturdays. It's a beautiful climate. I can grow citrus here all year round. There's the fish at the wharf.

Being geographically situated within a small town means relatively close physical proximity between residents, and while the township has particular distinctive characteristics which can be seen as community identity, Whaingaroa is nevertheless imagined and experienced subjectively by each participant.

A particular brand of local pride is evident in the way people talk about the town, and is displayed, to some extent in the bumper stickers adorning local vehicles bearing the town's name, the emblem of the coffee roastery, or the anti-mining group which was started locally, KASM [Kiwi's Against Seabed Mining[3]]. The community, however, can take a while to include people to a level deeper than casual acquaintance. Justin and Alex who have owned a local café and lived rurally for several years, have found it a slow process getting to know the local community:

It can be a hard group to break into, I think we are slowly getting in there but I think that's kinda normal. It takes time for people to become friends and get involved. We are not the kind of people that are jumping out there and getting involved. We just sort of let it happen; that's just us.

People often fall in love with the small, diverse township, with the casual lifestyle and the spectacular views, and do not want to leave. The geographic isolation of the township lends a cul-de-sac quality to the town, in that Whaingaroa is seen to be 'at the end of the road', not being on the way to anywhere else in particular.

Because of the absence of through-traffic there are few corporate franchises and no corporate fast-food outlets. This relative geographic isolation, combined with accessibility from two large neighbouring cities (Auckland and Hamilton), as well as beaches and scenic views, appear to be attributes shared by other New Zealand locations such as Waiheke Island, the Coromandel Peninsula, and Golden Bay at the top of the South Island, which are also known for their 'alternative' creative counter-cultures.

The population can be described as consisting of a wide variety of overlapping subcultures. There is the older generation of retirees who congregate at the Light Exercise Group, the Horticultural Society, the Museum Society and The Raglan Club, a social centre featuring cheap meals and alcohol.

Some have lived here for most of their lives, others have deliberately retired to the sea-side. Because the small town has a limited supply and range of employment opportunities there are many residents who commute to Hamilton as well as people who have set up their own businesses, some of whom can work from home.

Overlapping with these working groups is the large number of young families, whose incomes and education levels vary widely. Compared with wider New Zealand, there is a larger-than-usual population of people who might be grouped under the marketing term *Lohas* [lifestyles of health and sustainability], as described by Rose (2013). This term was created to describe a growing number of health-conscious people with ethical concerns regarding social and environmental exploitation. This subsection of the community are sometimes colloquially referred to as 'hippies' and dubbed by one local the 'curtain-pants-wearing' people.

Although the marketing term *Lohas* refers to a middle-class group with disposable income, many people in Whaingaroa with lifestyles focussed on health and sustainability are living on relatively low incomes, often without suffering from deprivation. This will be explored further in Chapter Eight.

The following figures show Whaingaroa and wider New Zealand, according to the *NZDep2013 Index of Deprivation* (Singh 2014). The areas that are darkest green are deemed most deprived.

The areas that are darkest brown are deemed least deprived. Deprivation here is measured by a number of factors including income, employment, qualifications, home ownership, as well as access to support, to adequate living space, to transport and to communication technology.

Figure 12: Deprivation mapped from most deprived (dark green) to least deprived (dark brown) (Singh 2014).

The *Index of Deprivation* images show Whaingaroa as dark green 8 or 9 on the deprivation index scale (10 is most deprived). The town's dark green can be seen as less deprived than the lighter green and light yellow of the rural area surrounding it:

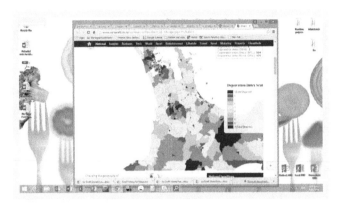

Figure 13: Whaingaroa (circled) compared to deprivation in wider area (Singh 2014).

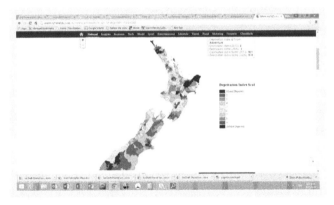

Figure 14: Wider New Zealand's mapped deprivation (Singh 2014).

Set against this wider deprivation context, the dark green areas such as Whaingaroa, can be seen to reflect areas with higher populations of Māori residents. In the online access point to this interactive deprivation map health policy researcher, Professor Crampton, based on his reflection that most Māori and Pacific people still live in socially deprived areas, states: "I am struck and still taken aback by how ethnic patterns [of socio-economic deprivation] have remained stable" (Singh 2014, 1). This socioeconomic deprivation pattern is linked to New Zealand's history of colonisation as described by Walker (2004).

This deprivation is an underlying theme and tension – a thread that runs through this book. Most people do not seem to experience Whaingaroa as a place of deprivation, rather, their experience is of an eco-friendly, surf-savvy, creative community. It is likely that some of the low incomes contributing to the dark green belong to people with a lot of multi-faceted sources of wealth as described in more detail in Chapter Eight. However, for others in the same community, the sense of deprivation is very real. These themes will be explored several times in the following chapters.

A typical social gathering in Whaingaroa will be comprised of a particular cross-section of the heterogeneous population. An art exhibition opening at the Old School Arts Centre will host a sample of all ages who happen to be interested in the arts. Sunday Sessions at the Yot Club, where local DJs entertain in the courtyard in the summer, will appear to be populated by trendy casually dressed people, some of whom are members of the community, while others are international travellers or visiting out-of-towners. A talk at Xtreme Zero Waste, the local recycling centre, will be attended by the more politically and environmentally motivated: members of the community who are active in environmental education, recycling and 'upcycling', which is like recycling but involves making the old objects 'better', as implied by the 'up'.

Figure 15: My 'upcycled' jandals made from re-purposed
conveyer belts and upholstery fabric by local shoe-maker
Ben Galloway, 2014.

To further illustrate the 'upcyling' culture of the town, recent upgrades of the local library situated in the main street created an opportunity for some handy local artists, as shown in this piece from the local newspaper, the Raglan Chronicle:

Quirky furnishings real Raglan style

Raglan's identity as an artistic, nature-conscious community has been stamped on the revamped Raglan Library space, thanks to the hard work of the local place-makers group... using material that had been recycled or donated by the community. There were ottomans made from old wooden pellets, with squabs and beanbags covered in kiteboard sails... and wooden book stools made by Xtreme Waste. (Raglan Chronicle 2014, 2)

This 'upcycling' culture is further highlighted by events such as the annual wearable art awards which largely consist of costumes constructed from recycled materials and the annual 'Save Maui Dolphins' recycled raft race, organised by the Whaingaroa Environment Centre, described later in this chapter.

In the summer, when the population quadruples in size due to holi-day-season, local people express relief in seeing a familiar face and even more relief when the autumn sets in and the pace quietens. The holiday season is widely regarded as 'a bit of a pain' by many locals. This time of the year is filled with parking problems and crowded spaces, but is also regarded as good for business. Many local busi-nesses make the bulk of their money over the summer, and struggle to stay afloat during the quieter months, especially with the high rents which have been driven up by property investment and other factors. Although Whaingaroa is less popular as a holiday destination in colder seasons, the surf is still good, so even in winter there is a steady stream of international tourists, if to a lesser degree than in the warmer months.

There is a richness to the small township that goes well beyond the financial dimension. People who have relatively low incomes are able to attain a quality of life that is more dependent on relationships, community activities, and creative pursuits than just on financial means. Whaingaroa has a reputation for being progressive with its art, recycling, environmental and local food initiatives, but this is largely a recent development. Twenty years ago, aside from being a surfing destination, it was much like any other small seaside town. There are numerous complex factors that have led to these develop-ments. Geographically, Whaingaroa is on the wilder west coast of the North Island, and is therefore less desirable for wealthy holiday-home owners who tend to prefer the east coast's white sandy beaches rather than the black iron sand and rocky shoreline of this coast. The Regional Council influenced Whaingaroa's landscape with its purchase of prime beach front land in the early 1990's, which was being proposed for development, turning it into Wainui Reserve, thus saving the land from being used for luxury beach-houses. The early development of trendy cafés has had an effect on Whaingaroa too, by creating a café-culture which has been supported by the active pres-ence of the local coffee roastery.

The heterogeneous nature of the township is not without its tensions. When I began to write an ethnographic description of the local township, I decided to show my first attempt to a few locals for feedback. One respondent queried the lack of socio-political issues in my writing, especially regarding tensions between Tangata Whenua who have an ancestral connection to the land here yet have little compared to wealthy people who can freely come in and purchase property. The land prices in Whaingaroa have increased remarkably in the past two decades, along with its desirability as a holiday destination, and commutability from nearby Hamilton. These reflections reaffirm the widely recognised tensions between 'haves' and 'have-nots'. For the most part, these tensions remain largely invisible, as does the local 'drug problem', which I have been told has been exacerbated by the current prevalence of amphetamine addiction. More audible, are the frequent complaints about the high price of shop rentals in town. This has been topical for over a decade and is largely blamed on several monopolies in commercial property ownership. The group nicknamed the 'tight-five' is known to own many of the shops in Whaingaroa, as are several other individuals. The rents in town are said to be comparable to the prices of those on K-Road in Auckland, a busy metropolitan street which has a lot more foot-traffic than a small town that is particularly quiet in winter.

There are also visible tensions between the members of the town who want things to remain as they are and those who are seeking various kinds of change. The sub-sets of the population resisting different kinds of changes tend to vary based on the values held by different individuals and groups within the population. At a recent town meeting called to discuss proposed changes to the centre of town, more conservative members of the population out-numbered those who were excited about the proposed developments which included creating a more lively, pedestrian-friendly 'town square' styled area. Opposition has also been met by developers proposing new subdivisions near the township. Some locals who are opposed to housing developments for environmental or personal reasons are supportive of creating a more social and interactive space in the centre of town while others who oppose new subdivisions are also resistant to the idea of changing the centre of town as it may decrease parking, already a rare resource, thus inhibiting access for elderly and less physically able residents.

A 'green bubble': gentrification and playing monopoly in Whaingaroa

I guess Whaingaroa is quite a bubble in a way... I see it as almost a child's playground, you know it's a place where you can do stuff. So since being here I haven't really paid a lot of attention to national politics, yeah I've just been focusing on the people and what we can do here, and hope that we can show the rest of New Zealand... such a good place because the community is so supportive. There's always a lot of support to do whatever you do. So since I've been here I've just been focusing on the community – Robz.

The concept of a 'green bubble' came up at a particular point in conversations during my fieldwork. These conversations were sparked by an online discussion, described below, in which some participants realised that the 'green' values relating to ethical consumptions were a kind of privileged choice not accessible to many people who were struggling financially. 'Green' values, relating to environmental and social justice are particularly evident in Whaingaroa. The township is widely known to have a particularly high Green Party voter-ship in compared to the total Green party vote of the recent general elections[4]. There is a great deal of ambiguity around privilege and ethics in Whaingaroa. There are many local examples, including key participants in my research, who achieve a quality of life that they are happy with despite having relatively low financial incomes as Robz describes here:

I feel very rich and I'm way below the poverty line. We live a life that people dream of, spending our summers just cruising around, you know in the mountains, in the bush, and then come back to Whaingaroa, beautiful Whaingaroa.

This 'rich lives, small wallets' phenomena will be explored further in Chapter Eight. It is mentioned here as a factor in the socioeconomic complexity of the small town. Another relevant factor is the commercial real-estate situation in the centre of town, where a few groups of investors own most of the shops. This has created a situation where rent prices are considered by many locals to be unreasonably high, despite the seasonality of business, and many retail and hospitality businesses have been forced to close. I asked my Grandmother, Jane, as a long-standing resident of Whaingaroa, about the real-estate situation.

There's two lots, I think. There's the 'tight five' and they own those two blocks, they built those two new buildings behind, and Raglan West store is owned by them, they bought it probably 10 years ago. Then there's Pat, he's the other lot, he pops up in real estate, he seems to be attached to the real-estate agency. He owns some of the shops on the other side of the road. I think they must sort-of leverage off one another. I don't quite know how you do it but there are people who do it – and don't go broke. There's a sort of difference between the "haves" and the "have nots" and it is difficult for people to own property, particularly now that it's gone up. I think property's not particularly cheap now in Whaingaroa.

The following example illustrates factionalism and diverse perspectives within the township. Interestingly, this conversation may not have had the means to occur without the particular technological platform of the Raglan Noticeboard, a Facebook group, set up for locals to exchange goods and information.

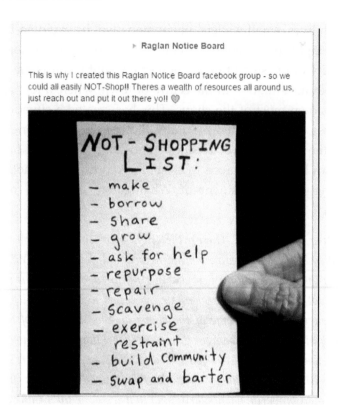

Figure 16: Raglan online noticeboard's 'not shopping list'
created by Melissa McMahon, 2013.

The Raglan Noticeboard only allows people who live or have lived locally to join the group. At the time of writing the group has over three thousand members, indicating that a large percentage of the local population can be included in discussions. The term 'green bubble' was not mentioned in the discussion below, but came up in the conversation through which I learned of a discussion in which friends of modest financial means reflected on the realisations of their own privileged eco-friendly mentality: 'I totally agreed with the post, then all these people were commenting about struggling in Whaingaroa and wanting to buy their kids toys and I thought "maybe I *am* living in a green bubble." The initial post, mentioned here was made in September 2014 by an eco-conscious member of the Whaingaroa community:

Feeling disappointed. Not particularly impressed to hear that there is a 'two-dollar' store opening on Bow St. Seriously, does Raglan really want one? Especially considering most of that cheap plastic finds it's [sic] way into landfills because it can't be recycled. I wonder what message it will send to people visiting from out of town?

This immediately sparked a lot of supporting messages, followed by many expressing conflicting viewpoints. It was pointed out by several commentators that other similar businesses, selling cheap mass-produced goods, had not lasted long in Whaingaroa. Some echoed the sentiment that it was a bad look for eco-tourism and harmful to the environment. Some questioned the safety standards and empha-sised the exploitation of factory workers in China, where it was assumed that most of the goods are produced. There were calls from some to use 'consumer power' and boycott the shop.

Others complained of the negativity of these posts and argued that the affordability of the shop was a positive thing. It was pointed out, by several business owners, that running a retail business in Whain-garoa is very difficult due to high rents and that having so many empty shops is not a good look for the town either. Many of the conflicting replies focussed on identifying the realities of living on limited incomes, as opposed to the 'green bubble' that the initial conversation seemed to represent.

Whats this "we" business? Just koz we are lucky enuff and shud be gr8full enuff to be here in Whaingaroa !! You people sound like ya live in a bubble !! Grow up !! I hope the new owners do well with sum positive insights from real conscious people like me who are on a budget with kids trying to make it in this bald headedness system… Its called freedom of choice people !! Not all of us can afford a $30 toy [sic].

Many replies expressed the freedom-of-choice sentiment: "If you don't like it, don't shop there". Someone even questioned whether the people complaining of the 'two-dollar' shop even lived in Whain-garoa, demonstrating the very different perspectives co-existing in the same small town. The 'green bubble' people did not particularly address the affordability issue for those who are struggling, other than to suggest buying second-hand toys from the Xtreme Waste shop, Kahu's Nest. They stressed the 'big picture' and ethical implications of 'plastic crap', while those on the other side of the discussion pointed to a complex and contradictory socio-economic 'big picture'.

One contributor expressed the opinion that the loudest voice on what should and should not be in Whaingaroa should come from the local hapū [Māori subtribe]: "After all, the rest of us are all manuhiri [guests]." She did not feel that local Māori had been shown the respect they deserve with regard to many of the decisions that have been made lately. One tangata whenua [local Māori] respondent agreed that it is very difficult running a business in Whaingaroa "and it's sad to see shops closed". While she personally does not buy from 'two-dollar' shops, many of the town's youth population felt they could not afford to buy from local shops, and suggested that this might offer an alternative to people travelling 'the twisted journey to the Tron [Hamilton]' for cheap goods: 'Put the pitchforks and burning torches down and give them a break.' This respondent supported awareness and education around environmental factors and people being conscious of their choices, but felt that the criticism as voiced in the original post was harsh and unhelpful.

Although it was suggested by some that the building owners or the council should take responsibility over which shops were being allowed to set up in Whaingaroa, others were concerned about the implications of councils making decisions of this nature: "Imagine the political corruption then!". One commenter suggested that those complaining about the shop should pay the difference in price, and he would buy the good quality products. Another accused the 'green bubble' of being anti-progress: "[I] think you're not keen for growth, full stop." Many complained about 'moaning'. Others disputed this:

There is a big difference between voicing one's opinion in response to an issue raised and 'moaning' (as someone has suggested it is being done on this thread). Some of us chose to move here recently because of Whaingaroa's *awesome vibe and clean eco-friendly community. The very first thing noticed was the total lack of crap-shops...a welcoming sight compared to majority of other NZ towns. Sustainability starts with every business decision made, and it is ultimately the business owner's choice. I feel for the new owners risking their finances in this venture, but I simply cannot wish them bon'chance based on their product choice and everything that a '$2 shop' stands for (which is nothing really, apart from promoting very cheap, very unsustainable and some plainly dangerous products). Growth is not achieved by unsustainable practices...simple as that [sic].*

Following this, many more replies complained of moaning and suggesting that anti-'two-dollar' shop people 'get a life'. The apparent hypocrisy and self-righteousness of the 'green bubble' was pointed out, repeatedly:

all u whinging humans STOP using PLASTIC altogether...see how that feels...2014..everything is PLASTIZISED so to speak. u'll continue to drive cars & use ya computer & watch tv &&&&&&&& on & on!!!!!!!! [sic].

Is the computer or phone you're posting this from made of wood from a sustainable source, harvested by well paid workers? I think not. Wot a hypocrite u are [sic].

The 'green bubble' people did not explicitly express awareness of their apparent privilege in this discussion. They tended to argue instead that speaking up and promoting eco-consciousness is important. Despite this lack of acknowledgement, from face-to-face conversations, it was evident that the challenge of privilege had sparked some awareness of the socio-economic realities of those outside the 'bubble'. It was also pointed out by one respondent in the online conversation that there were broader interconnected political and social issues:

This isn't simply a matter of a cheap shop in town, we should be looking at living wages – enough for our bills to be paid, our rent/mortgages, and food, we should be looking at GST[5] on food, a fairer taxation system and keeping our national assets, when communities have more they can then make different choices, particularly when it comes to purchasing [sic].

Some respondents integrated several different perspectives, arguing that "we are lucky to be moving towards sustainability" in Whaingaroa, and also acknowledging the reality that people are driving cars and use computers: "Lets not beat our selves and others up over it... You don't have to shop there.... But I will, and I wont feel guilty for it [sic]." It was also pointed out that many local shops already sell similar "cheap plastic crap", and that these products are often manufactured in the same factories that produce more expensive branded items.

Several people came to the defence of those accused of 'green bubble' hypocrisy, claiming that while it's hard to be completely 'green', the person who made the initial post "does a pretty darn good job of being as environmentally conscious in the way she lives her life in the areas that are attainable." It was argued that there is a difference between being hypocritical, contradicting one's own values, and being a 'conscious consumer' actively aware of contradictions while trying to live as sustainably as possible. Another respondent lamented the 'small welfare-town attitude so predominant in NZ', and encouraged the community to 'lift your game' and 'be the change you want to see.' This last comment seemed to be the closest to actually acknowledging class privilege, though it was also contradictorily positioned as an attack.

Humour entered into the discussion, with one critic of the original post commenting "very sensitive [topic] must be a full moan... whoopsey daisy I mean Full Moon [sic]." This can be easily read as a light-hearted teasing of the stereotypical hippy/curtain-pants-wearing obsession with the full moon, although it could also be read as more malicious[6]. Around this point, the conversation reached one hundred comments and someone jokingly suggested a two dollar giveaway, another playfully expressed a hope it would be made with used toothpicks. This seemed to cause a momentary break in tension before a new respondent contributed that they 'would be more concerned about the crap that pollutes our Moana [ocean], dumb sewage system – does that mean you all won't be using your toilets?' This comment referred to the overloaded sewage system that faces particular difficulties in summer with the annual population explosion. It can also be read as an attempt to identify hypocrisy, as is the following comment:

kia ora everyone very touchy topic the environment... but it's sad that some people still think they know whats good for you... where were all you enviro eco plastic haters 35yrs ago when our grand parents were fighting for the WHENUA and the MOANA the ones you should be mad at are the land lords creaming it they decide what bizzo stays and goes plus the only rubbish i see spilling out of the bins are coffee cups,lids,sushi packaging [sic].

Throughout the conversation there were many other references to history. The landlords and 'ridiculous' high rental prices were also implicated, as major barriers to local commerce, as were the non-resident holiday-makers.

Most of the commercial real estate in Whaingaroa has been owned for quite some time by a handful of people. Having said that the rents are struck in line with valuations. Valuations are based on rents. It's a vicious circle but Whaingaroa's massive growth around the 90s would have had a major impact on these figures now. Problem is the population growth has not been as rapid with many owning holiday baches. When they rock into paradise it's not to boost the local economy but to mow their lawns, clean their gutters and get a Sunday rest [sic].

This online conversation could be seen as an example of the democratisation potential of the internet and the importance of conversations in raising awareness. Overall, the attitude to Whaingaroa as expressed in the conversation was of love, pride and being lucky to live there: "There are so many unique reasons why we live here, sometimes you can't have it all ways, but I wouldn't move for all the plastic in china! [sic]"

People who have chosen eco-friendly austerity over more lavish consumer lifestyles may find it difficult to see their privilege because they have less than what they could have. Just as choice is the primary difference between a deliberate hunger strike and unwanted starvation due to factors outside one's control, the freedom to be able to choose is the major difference between lifestyles of 'empowered eco-simplicity' or of externally inflicted poverty. People who lack the privilege and choice of a deliberately eco-friendly lifestyle understandably resent the judgement of those who appear to be more privileged.

Ironically, as Korten (2010) notes, people surviving on lower incomes are likely to have a lower carbon footprint than wealthier eco-consumers, simply because they cannot spend as much. From his perspective, all economic activity supporting the current destructive corporate capitalist system can be seen as contributing to further destruction. 'Green consumption' might be a more eco-friendly alternative but less consumption will have even less environmental impact (Korten 2010, 60–61). This is not necessarily the case in Whaingaroa, and it may be that those living within the 'green bubble' are consuming less, considering their low incomes, and are also contributing more to the local economy. Further research would be required to determine this, although I would speculate that carbon footprints would vary quite widely between 'green bubblers', yet may well be roughly in proportion to their income.

For those being confronted with their own privilege, the experience can feel like a violent attack which leads to shame and anger. This may be because it comes from people who are continuously exposed to the violent pressures of inequality and discrimination and the shame and anger often associated with these things. When presented with an opportunity to point out their realities, people suffering from deprivation do not often adopt middle-class manners, or feel inclined to be gentle. Unfortunately, such attacks promote defensiveness, leading to arguments where each is trying to push their agenda on the other, rather than seeking to understand where the different perspectives are coming from. Even when approached in a gentler way, privilege is awkward or uncomfortable. One participant compared it to underwear: something that is not appropriate to wave around in public, but is usually invisible. This unease often seems to have the effect of generating silence rather conversation. Privilege is seen as something to be ashamed about, rather than as potential to exercise the agency it affords to contribute towards balancing out the inequalities, the awareness of which trigger the shame. At best, the 'green bubble' and 'ethical consumerism', with its espoused aspiration towards social and environmental justice, are a form of this action, at worst, they are a potential source of shame, guilt, resentment and anger for those who are unable to pay the higher prices, and therefore, cannot afford to be 'ethical'. Ackerman-Leist (2012) touches on this tension and asserts that the onus is on the privileged:

People who are food insecure are generally far too busy trying to convert their own personal energy into food dollars to spend much time researching and thinking about the national food and energy dilemma. The onus is upon those who are concerned enough to care and are able to do something about it" (Ackerman-Leist 2012, 30)

He notes that economic constraints create greater dependency on cheap commodities produced by large corporations within the industrialised food system as well as the jobs that drive this system. It is partly for this reason that 'ethical consumption' can be seen as part of an ethical responsibility of those who have the agency to exercise it. People who do not have this kind of agency, such as those in the Raglan Noticeboard online conversation who supported the 'two-dollar' shop, cannot logically be held responsible for acting in accordance with those particular values.

"Food choice" for them is not about "local," "organic," or "animal-welfare approved" but whether they can feed the kids even just one meal a day… and how. It is here that the push for local food systems hits a paradox in the shape of something like an enormous wall. How can more just, inclusive local food systems be built upon a fair and equitable representation of all community

members when some of the most oppressed members are so embedded in and reliant upon a much bigger and more powerful food system? In fact, we may well be jeopardising their jobs or even their personal well-being by advocating for change (Ackerman-Leist 2012, 139).

This ethical contradiction is central to the notion of 'ethical consumption' in a wider system of vast social inequalities. Tensions here can be linked to the paradox discussed in the theory section of Chapter One. Ackerman-Leist (2012) also discusses this contradiction, arguing that it is often an opportunity for creativity. He describes the increasing ecological constraints facing food systems as tensions that will 'inevitably force us to span the contradictions with commonsense bridges' (140). Ackerman-Leist also link food initiatives, such as those described in the following section, to this concept of bridging the gaps of contradiction with creative and practical solutions. Many of the underlying strands of tensions between lived experience and idealism also carry though into these groups.

Relevant groups

This section introduces are a number of groups and initiatives relevant to food sovereignty in and around the small township of Whaingaroa. Kaiwhenua Organics, a charitable educational trust run by Kaiwaka and Lynn, provides courses on Māori organic growing, and is involved in the national Māori organic organisation Te Waka Kai Ora. Much of their educational work is focussed on helping Marae [Māori community centres] to set up gardens. Kaiwhenua also produces organic fruit and vegetables that are served in Whaingaroa cafes and have been available for purchase at some local shops.

Known in the Whaingaroa community as "Liz and Rick's", Taunga Kereru [the name indicates the arrival of the kereru, the native wood pigeon] is a small permaculture farm, approximately 4 km outside of the Whaingaroa township, comprising both gardens and orchards. They host wwoofers and offer a limited number of year-long apprenticeships. At Liz and Rick's people may participate in gardening on 'community day', Tuesdays, and sometimes other days of the week. In doing this they assist in the maintenance of the property and some also grow their own produce on the land in an informal land-sharing operation. Liz and Rick's stall at the monthly creative market is a regular feature, including their vegetables and locally-famous pesto, which also for sale locally.

Figure 17: Elderflowers gathered from Liz and Rick's on community day, to be made into syrup, 2014.

Solscape is an eco-retreat located ten minutes south-west of the Whaingaroa township. Solscape also hosts wwoofers who help in the running and maintenance of the establishment in exchange for lodgings. It also hosts permaculture and sustainability courses. Solscape is closely connected with environmental activism within the Whaingaroa community, including KASM [Kiwi's Against Seabed Mining] which aims to stop the mining of the iron from local black sand by large corporations.

There are three community gardening initiatives in Whaingaroa. One is a modest community garden behind a church which is organised by members of the congregation but is open to the public. Another community garden is present on the grounds of the local police station. Wayne, who started the community police garden, is not a police officer. He got the idea for the garden from a similar garden which was started in Hamilton with the intention of making healthy connections between the community and the police. The third community gardening site is a 'food forest', so named because it incorporates permaculture principles to balance fruit trees with food producing shrubs and vegetables, imitating a forest arrangement. This has been planted on public land on the west side of the town, in a series of six circular gardens. During my fieldwork I spent some time in the community police station garden, and visited the food forest regularly.

Whaingaroa Organic Kai (WOK) is an organic food co-op, run by Jon, which was initially run out of a double garage at his residential address. Because it was run like a club, rather than a shop, Jon was able to keep his overheads low and then pass cost savings on to members through lower-priced organic food. Jon stocks as much local produce as possible, including fruit and vegetables grown by Liz and Rick. He tries to find 'more local' exotic items such as chocolate from the Pacific Islands.

Te Mauri Tau is an organisation based in Whaingaroa that has been involved in developing the Māori curriculum of Enviroschools, a national program that early childhood services and schools may adopt for teaching children about sustainability and connection with the environment. They also run facilitation training for Enviroschools coordinators, as well as courses in nonviolent parenting and educa-tion for which they are developing a Māori based system. Te Mauri Tau are focussed on wellbeing and Māori tikanga [protocol]. They have produced several cookbooks focussed on seasonal, local and nutritious food. Madi, who is involved in Te Mauri Tau, describes how the organisation developed:

It started with a group of parents who wanted to home school their kids. Then it evolved into education for everyone, so running workshops on a needs basis. At that point there was not a base, so they were run out of the

Kōkiri [the Māori community centre]. Eventually this place could be purchased with the help of some inheritance, so then those workshops became more localised. Sometime after that Mauri Tau became involved with Enviroschools, so a lot of the activity became Enviroschools focused.

It may seem ironic that a group of home-schoolers became involved with developing the Māori Enviroschools curriculum. At the time, they were asked by the friend who approached them: 'What would you want school to look like for you to put them back in?' and that became the focus for their work.

Xtreme Waste Recycling Centre, the community-based refuse and recycling centre, also provides education to schools in the region. Rick and Liz have been heavily involved in its formation and day-to-day running, along with other members of the community. This small business intentionally employs as many people as it can to create jobs and keep money circulating within the community.

Figure 18: Xtreme Waste, retrieved from website, 2013.

Xtreme Waste's aim is to reduce landfill waste and they have already achieved a diversion rate of around eighty percent. One of their recent projects is a trial of organic waste recycling for food scraps. They have also been involved in eco-activism, including sending unrecyclable packaging back to the company that produced it, sometimes resulting in changes in the company's practices towards more recyclable materials. These activities are described in more detail in Chapters Seven and Eight.

Figure 19: Gardening resources for sale at WEC, 2014.

The Whaingaroa Environment Centre (WEC) is involved in various community-based initiatives. It hosts a seed bank where gardeners who save their seeds may deposit excess, and members of the public may draw from the seed stock for their own gardens. Seed banking systems aim to help proliferate successful food seeds and keep heirloom (50 years old or older) varieties of fruits and vegetables from becoming extinct. At this point the Whaingaroa seed bank only has a few local contributors and buys in bulk organic seed from a catalogue, making it cheaper for locals. The intention is to transition to being supplied predominantly by locals, although the environment centre has many other projects to juggle at present. These include: providing education to schools and the public; hosting the annual 'Sustainable September' talks and workshops; and organising the annual Maui's Dolphin Day, the biggest event on the Whaingaroa Calendar, which features a community recycled raft race. WEC also facilitates a 'curtain bank' which lends good-quality curtains to families on low incomes to help with home insulation. The Whaingaroa Time Bank is also run out of WEC. Time Banking is a global community-building initiative where time functions as a currency, everyone's time is worth the same, and transactions are recorded using software on the internet.

All the people and organisations outlined above can be seen as interconnected, with complex and diverse community economies functioning alongside, and interacting with, the dominant economic system (Gibson-Graham 2006).

Figure 20: Curbside garden outside WEC, 2014.

The beginnings of many sustainability-focussed community initiatives in Whaingaroa can be traced back to the late nineties after the harbour had become polluted from surrounding farmland. As Fiona from Harbourcare describes:

Every time it rained, the harbour turned brown, and then you walked in the mud. It would stay there for weeks and months. Every time it rained stock [farm animals] would be caught up and swept into the harbour and it would rot. People became accustomed to that. You couldn't even collect shellfish. So Freddie put a flier up which said "Does anybody care that every time it rains the harbour turns brown?" I saw that and gave him a ring. He said there was a Ministry of Agriculture and Fisheries survey done which said that Whaingaroa Harbour was the worst for recreational fishing. It took eighteen hours to catch a single fish. He said "I remember when we could go out and a family could catch a feed. I want to have that back again." For Fred the motivation was very much about wanting to catch a fish, for me it was about wanting to sit on my deck and see sparkling water instead of brown.

The story that started with a man who could not catch a fish led to the establishment of Whaingaroa Harbourcare which has fenced off many farm water-ways and planted 1.2 million indigenous plants to catch the nutrient run-off from farmland. This has helped to restore health to the harbour which is now much better for recreational fishing. Harbourcare also directly led to the creation of the Whaingaroa Environment Centre which was part of the plan set out in the Whaingaroa Environment Catchment Plan. These initiatives were also interconnected with the beginnings of Xtreme Waste Recycling Centre.

Figure 21: Plants from Whaingaroa Harbourcare nursery, 2014.

These beginnings coincide with the first permaculture course taught in the area in 1999. The philosophies of permaculture, with their ecological approach to lifestyle and food production, are a key influence in the community. I have been told that over forty people living in Whaingaroa have completed a Permaculture Design Certificate (PDC).

When Liz, Rick and their family came back from several years spent living in the Cook Islands, Te Mauri Tau had been running home schooling from their house and had a strong interest in learning more about the land. Together they spent a whole winter running community evening classes and weekend workshops on topics including beekeeping and organic gardening which led to organising a permaculture design course for twenty interested locals. This course was really the beginnings of Xtreme waste as well. The key participants in the following chapter are interconnected within the groups described above. Their stories reflect similar values and tensions to those described in the vignettes of Chapter Two. These values and tensions are explored in further detail in Chapters Five and Six.

4 LOCAL FOOD PRODUCERS IN WHAINGAROA

In the process of my fieldwork, through various conversations with locals in Whaingaroa, a number of key local food providers were identified. I made contact with these food providers and asked if they would like to participate in my doctoral research. I explained the context of the research and that I was interested in learning about their perspectives, values and experiences. The following sections of this chapter introduce the Whaingaroa research participants, many of whom have been involved in the relevant groups described in chapter three.

Liz and Rick

Within the Whaingaroa community Liz and Rick are widely regarded as the best people to talk to about local food. They are permacultural-ists and local food producers, with a regular stall at the monthly Creative Market. As mentioned earlier, Liz and Rick are locally famous for their pesto and garlic, as well as their involvement in setting up and running Xtreme Waste. Fortunately I had known them as acquaintances for a few years, through friends and family. Much of my fieldwork was carried out at the weekly 'community day' on their small farm, Taunga Kereru. I was interested in how they first became interested in food and gardening:

Liz: It's been a long time for me, as I grew up with a big food garden, and was kind of coerced into gardening together. Usually it worked as long as it was playful – we had lots of playing in the garden and house. We kind of went into the garden and did a bit of work in short bursts. And then after leaving home I always had a garden, except for when I was in the city, wherever possible. The taste of fresh food – I've always known that it seems so nutritious if you've grown it yourself. It's become a bigger issue in my adult life as things have changed, access to good food has changed, it's much harder to go to a market and buy fresh, locally grown produce. Especially in the last 20 years with the rise of supermarkets. So the reasons for gardening have changed over time.

Rick: For me, we moved around a lot as a family, we always used to have a little garden but not producing a huge amount. But baking was always part of us. My Mum never bought biscuits or cakes or snack foods, so there was a lot of home baking. In my early teens we moved to Fiji, so all around I was surrounded by people gardening, even my friends would come to school with their cane knife and their sack and it would be part of the daily routine to do a bit of weeding on the way home, and to pick a bit of kumara or tapioca or taro for dinner. They were production gardens, but often curbside, so it would be a convenient little plot or piece of grass on the way home, and people would respect that and never interfere with each other's gardens. Also, spending school holidays in the village there would be an everyday wild harvest of fish or firewood, fresh water prawns or foods from the forest. My Dad was always quite keen on duck shooting, so right from an early age, and trout fishing and catching pig and deer was all part of it, so we more enjoyed those foods than we would supermarket foods.

Liz grew up, on the English-Welsh border, with a lot of wild food harvesting too:

There was quite an abundance of food around there, lots of edible things in the hedge rows, nuts and fruits, we ate lots of rabbit, pheasants and other wild things. We enjoyed them and the interesting flavours of the wild food.

Liz first heard about permaculture when she was travelling in the 1980s. She stayed on a sheep farm in South Australia where they were experiencing a severe drought. Liz and the friend she was travelling with noticed the lack of trees in the landscape and realised the climate that had been created by the farmers was a desert. At that time permaculture was quite a new system developed in relation to land management in Australia. The farmer offered his farm to permaculture pioneer, Bill Mollison, as a pilot farm. Liz did not stay around long enough to see the results but she had the opportunity to read about permaculture and thought 'well that sounds really smart'.

Both Liz and Rick have backgrounds working as ecologists for the Department of Conservation. Liz had studied environmental science, ecology and natural systems. Permaculture, with its ecological approach to farming, made sense to her. This was especially in relation to water management, particularly after her experiences travelling the world and seeing people wasting a lot of water. Permaculture seemed to her to be a really sensible well-grounded philosophy. After reading about it, Liz had the chance to do a course in Wales over one weekend to deepen her understanding. She did not really get to be a practitioner until she had a piece of land to practice on. When she got together with Rick, they realised they both had the same philosophies and enjoyed gardening together. Liz and Rick started thinking about New Zealand ecology in relation to permaculture. Using their ecological background and knowledge of birds, seeds and wetlands they set about to see if they could build a system. They decided to buy some land in Whaingaroa in 1991, as the next step to becoming practitioners. They were inspired by a man nearby who had set up some interesting orchards, "as an example of someone we can look at and say 'yes, we can do that' – that's a glimpse of what can be achieved".

Like Liz, Rick too became interested in permaculture in the mid-1980s:

I was working for the wildlife service, specialized in endangered species, so designing reserve systems and realising the need to be holistic in the management. Everyone was focused on predator control but I've seen examples, especially in the Pacific, where bio-abundance is actually an alternative to predator control. If there is heaps of food and no competition then animals can coexist. I was given an opportunity in '85–'87 with another guy who was interested in permaculture to write a management plan for a reserve in the King Country. So we tried to integrate some permaculture ideas, particularly designing a system of young and modified forest with plantings of exotic trees, with things like plum and apple, and the wildlife service in those days thought that was outrageous, planting exotics in the nature reserve! I had a little bit of a frustration that many of the projects which I worked on at that time were really focused on recovery of the individual, the ambulance at the bottom of the cliff. Frustrated with that, I moved out to Whatawhata [a small town between Whaingaroa and Hamilton] and started gardening more seriously there.

Liz and Rick eat as much as they can from the produce at their farm and focus on growing the foods that their family enjoy, especially beetroot. On a weekly basis, they let Jon, at WOK, know what surplus they have so that he can use it for the 'veggie boxes' that he sells. Liz and Rick also add value by transforming and preserving their surplus, especially through making pesto, preserves and sauces. In the past, they have sold produce through green-grocers in the township, which are no longer running. They participate in the Whaingaroa Creative Market.

We've been part of the Creative Market since the beginning, which must be around eight years. Initially when that market was set up people were thinking of a farmers' market, but there wasn't really any food producers around here. So we suggested we could be there and Kaiwhenua Organics, the other big garden. But they said they were too busy just servicing the cafes and the supermarket, and we only have one day off a week. That's how it became the Creative Market – to include the arts.

As well as providing practical education on permaculture gardening, Liz and Rick's farm has proved to be a 'gateway', introducing new people, who arrive as wwoofers, to the community, as Liz describes:

"So many of them come through the gates and are introduced into the community, find an interest or an opportunity and stay and they all have something to do with local food." After buying their land and some initial planting Liz and Rick spent a few years in the Cook Islands. Their return to the Whaingaroa in the late 1990s coincided with the establishment of Harbour Care, which they became involved in, applying their skills as ecologists. Around that time, Te Mauri Tau was being established and the first Whaingaroa Permaculture Design Course was held. Rick comments: "That was really the start of Xtreme waste as well."

Kaiwaka

Kaiwaka is a well-known local character. He and his wife Lynn have been running Kaiwhenua Organics since the late 1990s on his traditional family land which sits on the slopes of Karioi Mountain and overlooks a spectacular ocean vista. As stated earlier, Kaiwhenua Organics is a charitable trust providing education on organic gardening. They grow fruit and vegetables, and are well known for their salad bags which include some edible flowers and herbs. I interviewed Kaiwaka in the old farm house at Kaiwhenua Organics during his lunch break. I brought some local bread which we ate with butter and a cup of tea. Kaiwaka expressed a strong connection to the land: "Well, without the land we can't grow our kai, grow our families, sustain our families." His personal history is one of reconnecting with the land:

We came here in 1999. I was released from incarceration in 1997. Whilst I was in there I did a certificate in small business. So I got out and came home and came up here and looked around. First me and my son were going to get into carving, buy a shop in town, close the doors, work really hard and open just before Christmas. And then when I got home I saw his younger brother, holding a baby and I thought what can we all do? So I came back up here, just sitting on the balcony. When I came up here all this was here lying here waiting for someone to love it. I said to myself, let's see if this is any good. Let's see if you learn something. The rest is history; it's been 13 years now.

Their first crop was kamokamo [squash] and potatoes and it did not take long before they were selling produce in different ways:

We didn't have to buy potatoes for 18 months. We had a concrete basement, where we put all our potatoes. Well straight away it told us it worked because we didn't have to buy this or that. We were saving money. And then we started with the honesty box, which worked really well for two years, then people started to take advantage of it. And back then, Vinnies [restaurant] was there, so [the owner of Vinnie's] was coming up to Kaiwhenua a lot. And he used to say, 'I'll have all of that, I'll have all of that'. 'Yeah, ok bro.' Just from that it became 'oh you can supply me with rocket and k.g.'s of salad mix'. And Wayne Petchell was eating at Vinnies, and he said he tried the salad and liked it, and would we like to sell it in the shop. We started off with ten bags, and then it went to sixty bags and we had plenty of workers and the whole place was covered in gardens. There's no difference, except there's less money now. Everything is the same but there's less money.

For a while, the government subsidised the wages of employees who were previously on unemployment benefits, a mutually beneficial arrangement for Kaiwhenua and for the workers. This, combined with charitable trust grants, supported the process of establishing the business. Reduction in these subsidies has made employing workers more difficult, resulting in a decline in the productivity of the gardens.

Kaiwaka and Lynne have received national media attention for their work at Kaiwhenua Organics. Kaiwaka's story of putting his horticultural skills, originally gained from growing cannabis, to use in organic vegetable gardening has been shared as a success story. This has been encouraging. Kaiwhenua is also involved in Te Waka Kai Ora, the Māori organics organisation, as he explains:

How I met them was, when Lynn and I first wanted to start the garden, we didn't know anything about gardens! That weekend the Ministry of Social

Development had a couple of guys that were going around to groups and helping them get set up. They were funding guys. We went up North for the weekend... we stayed at their house in Auckland... we jumped in these vans and we went to the Waipu forest and had a look at what Māori were doing up North. The majority had backyard markets and were selling produce at markets. They all had their own little home gardens. They were growing anything they could, picking and boxing it. They had a shop which was a registered trust. So all those people who were doing things on their own, they'd take it to the shop and sell it there. We met all those people Friday to Sunday. It was about 18 months after we came home we invited them down. They were blown away because we had surpassed them, packaging our kai and selling it downtown. They gave us this tohu [a certificate]. When they came on the land and looked around and signed the tohu – about sixty signatures. That gave us the mana to say that we were Te Waka Kai Ora producers. We fed them and spent the day up here and they congratulated us, and presented us with our organic certificate. And we never looked back. Well – until [the subsidies] changed.

Another big set-back came more recently when the local supermarket stopped taking Kaiwhenua produce because they didn't have a particular certification:

For the thirteen years we were serving them, they just chopped us off, and said we can't take your salad anymore. And he said all we need is a food certificate! And I said no, we're not going to do that, we are not going to pay $1800 a time just to be in there!

Kaiwhenua still supply The Shack [café] and The Herbal Dispensary. They are making plans to sell their other produce from a large shed on the property, to "cut out the middleman." Kaiwhenua also provides education on organic gardening to Marae [Māori community centres] and are looking to transitioning to focus more on those services. I asked whether he thinks his lifestyle of growing vegetables has made Kaiwaka more healthy "Yeah," he replied, "people say to me 'gee you look healthy!' Probably 'cause I can walk along and eat straight from the earth."

Mike

During my initial fieldwork in Whaingaroa Mike was mentioned to me several times as a good person to talk to about food sovereignty and local food production. I had already met him, when buying organic milk from the farm. He struck me as knowledgeable, down to earth, and practical. Over the years I have sporadically made the effort to drive out to the farm again. Mike is well-known in the community and also supplies many of the other participants. The farm that he and his wife Mady run sits among the lush rolling pastured hills of the valley. Their farm is particularly notable for the trees, deliberately planted along fence lines and native plants on the banks of fenced-off water-ways. In New Zealand, farming livestock contributes significantly to water-way pollution. Practices such as fencing off and planting along riparian lines assist the land in retaining nutrients, and help to protect the water from nutrient pollution and animal related pathogens like E.Coli. They also enhance the picturesque qualities of the farm.

The main enterprise on the farm is dairying, with 125 dairy cows providing the bulk of the farm's work and income. Only about five percent of the milk is sold to people from the farm gate. Most of the milk is picked up by Fonterra, the New Zealand-based multi-national dairy co-operative. The farm also runs sheep and beef cattle for meat. Mike and Mady grow most of their own seasonal fruit and vegetables, including potatoes. They have been looking into further diversification, such as planting feijoa hedges to increase the financial sustainability of their operation.

When Mike took over his family farm it was run using conventional, rather than organic, agricultural practices. The lack of sustainability in these practices was part of the reason organic farming methods were pursued:

We were becoming disillusioned with conventional agriculture. It was creating imbalances with urea to grow more grass, but that grass lacked the nutrients it needed, so then you bought a whole lot of magnesium in to keep the cows on their feet because they were short of magnesium – so you've spent money to grow this grass and a whole lot of extra money to try to get things back into balance. Then the products you're using are acidic, so you buy more lime to try to reduce the acidity. Then cows wouldn't cycle well in their reproduction, so you'd get the vet out to fill them with drugs to get them to cycle. And while you had a good gross income, the net income was less than a living wage, and we thought 'There actually has to be a better way', and started looking around at what might be a better way to farm... So we did a bit of a review of the farming options and ended up going down the organic track.

At the time when Mike and his family decided to transition to an organic mode, twelve to fourteen years ago, there was not an accessible market for organic milk in New Zealand, but they felt that "With the way the world was going, there would be a demand for it – and we were right." By the time they had completed a three-year changeover to become certified as organic, "Fonterra had been created at that point and they were interested. Now, twelve years later, we're actually reviewing it again and saying "Okay, we've learnt a lot about organic farming and the principles. Do we stay certified? Because we can still follow the driving principles without being certified, and it will probably make our life a lot easier [not to remain certified], because the paper trails and the loops you've got to go through are just pretty demanding."

At the time of this interview, Mike expressed some concern over the stability of Fonterra's commitment to their organic programme: "There's a lot of indecision with Fonterra about whether they want to stick with it or not. They go hot and cold with it. They keep changing the leadership and to be honest, we don't really know what they want". Also around the time of out interview, two late summer droughts in a row had put pressure on the farm. Although Mike considered the organic methods and planting systems he was using to be more resilient than those of his conventional neighbours, the strict FDA (the United States Food and Drug Authority) organic certification standards applied by Fonterra posed a challenge to the financial and environmental sustainability of the farm – buying in organic feed is expensive and must come from further afield. USFDA[1] standards are also ill-fitted to the New Zealand farming context in that they do not allow some nutrients to be sprayed onto the pasture, but do allow it to be added to feed: "In New Zealand, the pasture is the feed".

The milk sold unpasteurised from the farm gate provides added value for the farm. As sales have grown, Mike and Mady have had to adapt and create new systems to make managing this aspect of their operation more efficient. Mady is currently upskilling so that she can use new software to manage payments.

On a local level, for us it's growing. We've gone from supplying milk to five or six locals, to a few people in Hamilton and a few in Whaingaroa, to around about 150 families now. We used to spend a lot of time in the evenings bottling and had people ringing up all the time. While it was working, it wasn't working well. So we put in a purpose-built vat, and we put in each morning what we feel we will need each day – to a pattern – and then people can bring their own containers and fill that themselves.- and that's been working well. But even that's started to out-grow the systems we've had in place, so we're just putting in new systems.

"We're very lucky", Mike comments. "A fair bit of hard work goes into it, not just luck." He notes that the land is not the easiest farming land for dairying, "…but it's a good area to live in"

Cally

I met Cally through the local writers' group, and found out later through my grandmother that she was an avid bee-keeper and a leader of the local bee-keeping group. Cally lives with her husband a short drive from the township on their rural property in view of Karioi mountain. Aside from the bees, they grow vegetables and fruit, and raise chickens. Cally grew up with vegetable gardens and attributes this to the value she places on fresh produce:

My parents always had veggie gardens. We weren't very well off so I grew up knowing what home-grown vegetables, fresh vegetables and things tasted like and fruit and that's actually really important, you know, food needs to taste good.

Cally and her husband both grew up on farms. After living on the edge of a sprawling town for twenty years they decided in the year 2000 to move back to the peace and quiet of rural life. Moving to the country sparked Cally's interest in bee-keeping:

When we came here everything was farmed and there were two feral hives down in the bush and in 2000 they just all disappeared: varoa. Yeah the varoa [bee parasite] hit the Waikato and our bees just all disappeared. There were no bees on anything other than bumble bees. So I was quite worried about that. I never really thought about bee-keeping until I went to an organic gardeners' meeting in Hamilton and they had a talk about bee-keeping and it turned out it was an old friend that I'd lost touch with and she's the same age as me and I thought: 'well, if she can do it I can do it'. So she was actually teaching a night class at Fraser [a Hamilton high school] and I went along and got into it and then after I'd had my bees for a wee while I did a course [through Lincoln University].

Over the years, Cally has noticed the bees being affected by varoa mites. This has made beekeeping a lot more work and affects not only the pollination of fruits and vegetables, but the whole ecosystem as many plant species rely on insect pollination. This has elevated the importance of back-yard beekeeping. This is Cally's major motivation in keeping bees:

I really enjoy bees although it's frustrating there never seems to be any certainty. Every question you ask there's a dozen answers. It's all a bit of a mystery and it's a lot harder to bee keep now that we've got varoa. But I have bees on my veggie garden and bees on my fruit trees now so it's worth it for that. We did have years when things just didn't seem to get pollinated, we didn't do well at all, and after seeing a video of people in China up ladders with paint brushes pollinating their trees I thought: I'm really not into doing that. So basically [getting into bee keeping] was about pollination but I do like having honey too.

Cally joined the Hamilton bee club before she started keeping bees and started the Whaingaroa beekeeping club with a friend. There are around sixty people on the local beekeeping club mailing list and between six and fourteen members attend any one meeting:

We just meet and we start and go round in a circle and say how our hives are doing and questions come up out of that and they get answered or not answered as the case may be, and we might if that doesn't take too long have a talk about what we should be doing in the next month before the next meeting... what we should be doing in the hive. So it's very informal but you get a lot of help and suggestions on what you should be doing for your own specific situations... and it's good 'cause you meet people and if you need a hand you know there's somebody you can ring up.

Cally got interested in organic gardening in the 1970s when she was still flatting and started to care about her health. She started going to the Hamilton meetings of the Soil and Health Association to learn a bit more. She describes herself as 'organic by default' rather than actively organic, because she always had a vegetable garden and did not like using chemicals. She became interested in permaculture in the late 1980s but didn't do a Permaculture Design Course until after her kids, who were home-schooled, had left home. Although she has led a relatively alternative life, Cally feels quite ordinary until she socialises with 'normal' people:

I feel like I've been a real boring ordinary stay at home mum... and then I start talking to people on my occasional excursions into normal society and realise I've become quite radical over the years, it's sorta snuck up on me without me noticing. So yeah, I guess my lifestyle is quite different from most people's but I don't think of it like that because I don't mix with people like that much. Maybe I should do and then they might start thinking too.

Jon

I had met Jon a few times, through mutual friends, before beginning my fieldwork, but had not made the connection between him and the organic co-op that I'd heard about called WOK (Whaingaroa Organic Kai). When I began to inquire about WOK and made the connection Jon was happy for me to join the co-op, which in some ways is run like a small business, although he was pushing his upper-limit in terms of members. I called around to the address Jon gave me to discover what appeared to be a normal residential dwelling. Jon let me into the outside room which appeared on the inside to resemble a small organic shop with cans and packets of food as well as bulk-bins containing grains, dried fruits, nuts and seeds. I noticed quite a few imported organic foods like almonds and dried bananas. There were a few local jams and chutneys and Jon told me that he tries to stock foods as locally as possible, especially the fresh produce in the Tuesday 'veggie boxes'. He likes to support local growers, including Liz and Rick, and believes that imported foods, though enjoyable, are ultimately unsustainable because of the food-miles involved in transporting them around the world.

Because WOK was run like a club where only members are allowed to shop, many of the regulations and expenses of running a public shop can be avoided and the cost of organic food can be kept down. I was interested to learn how Jon and his partner Roz had come up with the idea:

My partner and I were living in Wellington and we had the opportunity to travel without having to pay rent while we were away. We thought we'd go north for better weather and so we ended up wwoofing in different places and it occurred to us that we were looking for a different place to live. We like to grow food and be outside a lot so climate's very important to us and we like to drink rain water rather than chlorinated water so rainfall is important to us. We travelled the Coromandel and in Northland and here and we decided that the west coast ticked more of our boxes. We've got family in Hamilton and in Auckland. Whaingaroa just seemed like the right place for us when we arrived – lots of pairs of open arms – and so we just went with that.

Along with a new place to live, Jon was also seeking a new livelihood. He and Roz began to brainstorm plans for living in Whaingaroa, considering there seemed to be few employment opportunities. Inspiration came from the tension between their desire for organic food and its lack of affordability:

We like to eat organic food but we despair at the price of it. We realised that a large proportion of the population of this country is priced out of organic food so we thought 'how can we make this more affordable?' We thought about running a shop but we realised there are enough organic food shops selling high-priced food and we realised there's no call really to do that again so we thought if we could do something similar but with massively reduced overheads then that would make the prices much cheaper, and if we could do it in such a way that there was a lot of local co-operation that people could meet each other and have time to talk and we could save packaging and all these kind of things, then that would really be a good thing. So we thought 'well, what about if we do it from home?' – some kind of food-safe area at home, and we did some research and it turns out that it's perfectly within the law to do that as long as the public can't just walk in from off the street.

Around that time Jon and Roz were wwoofing with some local people who resonated with the idea and handed them a phone book full of interesting local characters. Jon called people in the phone book and received very good feedback from them. Jon's idea was to bulk order organic food and offer it to members in a way that made the food cheaper than it would be at retail prices and that also paid him a wage. There were a few organic co-ops running in Whaingaroa at the time with several people in each but some were not going well because they needed to be organised. Jon printed out a flier and handed it around. Fifteen people joined the first day and within ten weeks Jon had forty-five members and had to close the doors to new members because the numbers were more than he could handle.

At the time of the interview, in 2013, WOK had been going for over five years and had reached its upper limit in terms of members which included about forty regulars, twenty people who came in "reasonably often" and another twenty who came in once in a while, "so I'd say in any three month period I'd see about 80 different people". Since the interview John has moved premises and expanded WOK. This meant that he could accommodate more members.

Jon has been involved in several other initiatives in Whaingaroa including the early stages of the local food forest and the seed bank at the Environment Centre. Both projects have been handed on to other people. Other than running WOK, Jon raises seedlings from home and the gardens on Liz and Rick's farm. He also picks fruit from spray-free orchards around Hamilton:

We pick it to eat and to sell and I believe that my friend has some kind of lease arrangement on some of the orchards and others are more casual arrangements, but it's really about picking fruit that would otherwise all rot and getting it to people and making a bit of money at the same time.

Jenny

I first noticed Jenny and her Ruapuke Sourdough bread at the Whaingaroa Creative Market several years ago. Shortly after that her 'Tiny Tiny Bread Shop' appeared on the main street of town. After chatting with her about her bread it became clear that she was a suitable research participant. I interviewed her while sitting in the sun on the public bench outside the shop. Like Cally, Jenny grew up with vegetable gardens and this has played a big role in her relationship to food:

When I was young I lived with some old relations who were living the old-fashioned way. At the time I didn't think much about it but looking back I can see how much I learnt about harvesting and eating seasonally. It certainly wasn't trendy then. Everything was cooked in a pot on the back of a coal range – slow cooking – everything was seasonal. When peaches were in season we ate and bottled peaches and made peach jam and when they weren't we didn't, so I had that experience when I was young and it was really interesting. It gave me a feeling of how food was a couple of generations before me.

Jenny tries to grow as many vegetables as she can in her vegetable garden at home. She estimates that she produces around forty percent of all the vegetables she eats as well as some of her fruit and meat. She says she does not often buy meat and feels it is more ethical "if you've grown a beast on your farm and you've looked after it and you've killed it humanely". She especially avoids buying cling-wrapped polystyrene meat at the supermarket, as "it's not real. You have to respect it." Jenny's emphasis on 'real food' extends to her soughdough bread. She describes how she got into bread-making:

A couple of years ago I had an epiphany. I was on the dole and I hated it and I thought: what can I do at home, that I can work from home and make a living that gave me a sense of pride and a sense that I was actually doing something rather than just existing? I've always been interested in bread and so I thought I could make bread, how hard can it be? I discussed it with my sister who said "that's a crap idea because you hate maths and you don't like baking" So I thought: 'fair comment'. Then I told my best friend I was going to make bread and she said "do you know how to make bread?" so I thought: 'fair comment', so I just started making bread every day. I got up and I made bread and I made bread and I made bread. Then I talked to WINZ [Work and Income New Zealand, responsible for administering benefits and social services] and I had to submit a business plan and I spoke to two friends in Wellington who were successful single business women and they liked the plan so much they decided they wanted to put some money in and it came together quite quickly and now I bake bread.

Many months of research went into setting up her business because she started off with "no idea" of what was involved. Despite never having made sourdough before and her dislike of baking in general, the venture seems to work well for Jenny: "I like the process of sour-dough – the fact that it's all one process and it keeps on going and going." The process of starting her business has involved a lot of learning. Jenny says she's not fanatical about food and didn't actually know what yeast was or what was in commercial yeast and didn't know how to find out so she decided to stick with the sourdough. She bought her first starter from the Trademe website, from a baker who also has a home bakery and supplies bread to Commonsense Organics, a large organic shop in Wellington. Since then he has become something of a mentor: "every time I have a disaster I ring him up and he's been very supportive".

Jenny started out slowly in establishing her business. She wanted to avoid being in competition with anyone else so she talked to local businesses before she began selling bread to make sure they knew what she was wanting to do "and didn't have a problem with it." She started off just supplying neighbours and friends and sending it out on the rural delivery postal service. When she was taking her grand-children to school she also sold it from her parked car. Sales were progressing slowly at first...

Then, I don't know how but, the Chronicle [local newspaper] found out, and there was a little article in the Chronicle and I was approached by Orca [a Whaingaroa restaurant] who wanted to buy local bread so they, very, very early in my career, put in a big order and were very supportive. So once I had that order I was away. Only a couple of months ago people were wanting to buy it and they [customers at Orca] were robbing it from the kitchen so they said: 'could I supply more?'

Jenny sees the Creative Market as "just sort of an aside" as it is only once a month and a very long day for a modest remuneration. The fish shop at the wharf have recently begun to stock her bread as well. Jenny set up her tiny shop in an unused passage way belonging to the shop rented by the local Trade Aid, a not-for-profit fairtrade shop:

I'd always been aware that there was a passageway there. I love renovating and I saw this little gap and I thought – wow, there could be a shop there – so I wrote a proposal and it went to the Trade Aid head office and they said yes. It's in-line with their values and what they want to do.

Jenny still insists she does not like baking, but bread is different. She is critical of commercial processed bread.

There's a whole bread scene and bread people and bread websites and it's just much more satisfying to turn out 30 or 40 loaves that are quite similar. A lot of commercial bread, with all due respect to the big companies, is crap, and I just wanted to make something good – healthy good. I enjoy making the bread. I never think "oh dammit, I have to go bake", although sometimes there are other things I want to do instead.

Wayne

I met Wayne after discussions with people at the Whaingaroa Environment Centre. We spent some time gardening together at the eco-retreat, Solscape, where he is the main gardener, and at the community garden at the local police station which he set up. Still in his mid-twenties, Wayne was among the youngest participants in my doctoral research. Like most participants, he grew up with gardening as a big part of his early life, and despite some hesitation, he has come back to it:

My parents were market gardeners on quite a large scale, over 400 acres. So I have had that background experience. When they moved out to Whaingaroa [in 1998] they changed to organics, when I was maybe eight. So I was sort of born into it and then from a very young age I was working in the garden whether I liked it or not. It just had to be done, but it was very enjoyable being on the farm and it was quite a nice way to be brought up. I never thought I'd end up growing vegetables (laughs). When I left home I went farming and I had seen how hard my parents worked to make a living by growing food for a living and it can be very difficult and long hours so I thought that's not really a path that I want to go down but as I've gone through various jobs... I've realised that this is a skill-set I have and I'm fairly good at it and I can make a living out of it and it's very good to be able to live in Whaingaroa and have a lifestyle when I can still go to the beach relatively when I want – choose my own hours – and it's something I've enjoyed. So as far as growing produce goes, nothing has really changed except my perception of it.

Before working at Solscape, Wayne had been earning income through private gardening jobs in the area. He was offered the job as the main gardener at Solscape when the position became available and someone mentioned his name to Phil, the owner. When he first started at Solscape, in the busy season, there was a paid position to take charge of the gardens and then at winter time it was not viable to keep someone employed so the arrangements were adjusted in a way that suited both parties:

I'm basically leasing the land off Phil and paying him a percentage of the profits that I make. It seems to be working well so far. Really over the summer will be the key time to see how viable it really is. Vegetable gardens can be planted for seasonal produce so I think it's quite viable to have a year-round income source and it's quite a good climate up here so you can grow a lot of different stuff all year round whereas even in lower parts of Whaingaroa where there's more frost it restricts the crops you can grow. It's my own little business, essentially. Phil is also contributing some funds to things like straw and mulch, but as far as seeds go I'm purchasing all the seeds – [and I] try and save as much [seed] as possible.

From the gardens Wayne runs at Solscape he sells some things through Jon of WOK. He has also sold produce at the Whaingaroa West shop, the organic shop in Hamilton and at the monthly Whaingaroa Creative Market, although there is an issue of food waste as the vegetables must be picked with no definite number of buyers. Wayne also supplies for courses at Solscape and when the café is open, during the busy summer season, a lot of the produce from the gardens will go there. Wayne tailors his growing practices so that he can produce an ongoing supply of vegetables:

I do a lot of planting, so I'm not doing huge crops of just one thing and then harvesting that. It's always a revolving cycle, so in the seed house there are always plants going in and coming out, a continuous cycle. This time of year, planting summer crops, the majority of my days are spent watering. By now most of the summer stuff should be planted so it's just maintenance really and watering. I stagger my planting so there's an ongoing supply, when the harvest is quite short, because it goes to seed quite quickly at this time of year. Because I've got so many varieties I have to keep planting to keep a continuous supply going. You've always got some plants coming into season and some going out of season. So you've still got to maintain seasonality.

Wayne says he would like to see beehives put in place at Solscape and also more fruit trees. He never expected that he would grow vegetables for a living but he finds that it fits his lifestyle very well, to the point that it doesn't really feel like work:

There's two kinds of people: those who work and those who don't want to work and I don't really feel like I'm working. When I'm working I enjoy what I'm doing. I'm not thinking "oh this is my job".

The Bro

I met The Bro through several groups and acquaintances. His role as a key character in local food was partly due to his history of involvement in Te Mauri Tau, his apprenticeship at Liz and Rick's and his more recent catering business in which he sources as many local ingredients as possible. The Bro says that he moved to Whaingaroa because of food and describes a childhood of economic challenges, food foraging and alternative economy:

The way that we grew up, it was the 1980s, in rural New Zealand, so it was like neoliberal restructuring of the whole political economy, and so they ripped out the farm subsidies, and suddenly farmers had no money and all of the freezing works and shit closed down.... No one had no money, our family we didn't have any money 'cause we kinda, like the business that my parents were in, well my mum was a freezing worker and the business that my dad was in, it relied on business from farmers, but the farmers got no money so we used to get paid in food, like, I grew up drinking raw, unpasteurized milk, because that was currency. Dad would do some rewiring on the tractor lights or whatever for a farmer and he'd pay him in milk and meat, or whatever he had. So we were really poor and we couldn't really afford to buy meat that often, so we had a garden at home and we used to do a lot of foraging as well, like we had in the family, well mostly my dad really, had like a map of all the food sources in the local area, you know like fruit trees on the side of the road, and places where you could go and get watercress... So it's funny, we grew up doing all of these things that hipsters do these days for fun.

This childhood of foraging has had lasting affects in The Bro's life, although he is critical of people foraging to be fashionable.

The Bro lost touch with foraging and growing food when he moved to Auckland for university. Living in a city was very different to growing up in a small rural town. He got involved in the Tino Rangatiratanga [Māori sovereignty] movement and other activism, and he noticed that he was always the guy that baked cookies and bought fruit to the protests. After a protest against the Iraq War he noticed some other protesters going to McDonalds, despite the war being driven by corporate interests. The Bro had a realisation:

McDonald's feeds the troops... Fucking McDonald's and Halliburton. So it's interesting to me that people have that level of political analysis but they weren't applying it to what they were putting into their bodies. I was like 'Fuck!' And I had this realisation that probably as one person the single most powerful thing that you can do to create change is to take control of eating, the things that you eat and knowing where they come from, as one person I reckon that's the single most important thing you can do to effect change is food, I reckon.

The Bro decided to get involved in growing food again, but although he had childhood memories of gardening he did not really know how to do it. He happened to come to Whaingaroa for the 'Nice and Native' gathering for young indigenous people from all over the world which included a tour of places like Kaiwhenua Organics.

I remember sitting there on that grassy lawn up above the ocean and listening to Kaiwaka talk about food and his journey from growing dope to growing organic lettuce on a garden that his ancestors have been gardening for a millenia. That was a real 'wake-up' moment. I partially wanted to move here because I knew there were people like that here, like Rick and Liz, and Mike and all the rest of it.

The Bro wanted to reconnect with food, to learn practical growing skills and be more grounded in his activism. He lived in a flat near the township for four or five years with other keen gardeners and learnt bio-intensive gardening. He got back into foraging and went to community gardening days at Liz and Rick's farm. Later he spent a year and a half living there as an apprentice. Since then he has moved away from the area and travelled before coming back to establish a catering business where he puts his food values into practice.

Justin

I chose to interview Justin because he and his wife, Alex, own and run the popular café, The Shack, which openly aims to supply as many local, organic, and free-range ingredients as possible.

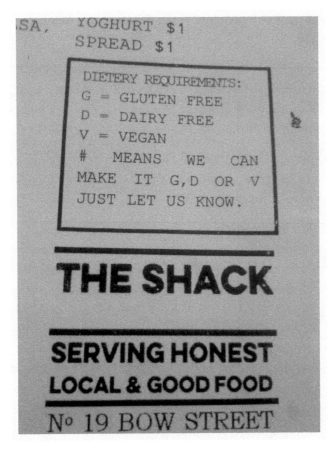

Figure 22: Local food is mentioned on the menu at The Shack, 2014.

At the time of the interview they had been running the business for almost two years. I asked Justin if there was a local food focus before he took it over:

Not so much, my brother was running the kitchen, and he was using little bits, you know Kaiwhenua and that sort of thing, but he was heavily guided by the current owners so they sort of dictated what had to be done, minimal.

Justin had been in the hospitality industry for twenty-five years, working "all over the world, most of it in Auckland and Waikato." His time has been split between working in the kitchen and front of house as a general manager. Like Wayne, his involvement in the industry has a family connection:

Well my family has always done it, we grew up in this [hospitality] business so we kinda had no choice. My brother does it. My sister does it. My mum and dad did it. My uncle and aunt, my grandfather so it's just one of those family curses... [said humorously]

Justin deliberately introduced the local food focus to the menu in line with his and his wife's personal values, gained through their experience of local food traditions in Europe:

It's one of those things, like I said, Alex and I have always, we've been doing a lot of it at home, and we spent a lot of time in Spain in a really small rural community, where we just sort of lived on this little farm and we worked at a restaurant on the farm and everything was local. Like a little town called Belafia which wasn't far from us. If we wanted a pig, we'd go to the pig farmer. If we wanted some corn we'd go to the corn grower. If we wanted some flour, we go to the mill. It was all walking distance and it just made sense that everything you needed was right there and there was only like 50 families in this little community. It worked really well and so we came home and it's really hard to do that where we live 'cause we live out in the sticks and there's nothing. There's no shops for 20 kilometres either way. You try and trade off people, your neighbours, but that doesn't work in New Zealand. We're not really set up for that. They're all producing sheep out my way and pine trees. It doesn't really work. So yeah, we just took that idea back [from Spain]. They have a free [range] farming over there and their pigs are just going through the bush and doing the truffle thing. This community we were part of didn't have that caged sort of environment. It just seems more natural.

Justin and Alex came back to New Zealand and decided to try to carry on "doing our bit for what we think is right." Over time their food values have permeated other members of the family, including Justin's father-in-law who he describes as an "old-school farmer". Justin reflects that a few generations ago it was normal to have a vegetable garden in New Zealand and everyone knew how to make a soup from leftover chicken but that this seems to have been lost. Having grown up in kitchens, he feels he is lucky to have cooking skills passed down to him. These skills seem to him such a basic necessity. At home Justin and Alex have a big garden and although they bring in what they can to supply the café, they are not able to produce much at a commercial level:

We bring in a lot of stuff, a lot of herbs and stuff in from home, whatever we can, again it's really hard, yes we've got a big garden but it's not big enough, it's not a commercial size. We tried growing asparagus last year, well this is our fourth year, and we got six spears of asparagus, which really isn't going to help anybody.

Justin deliberately stocks as much local produce, and as many free-range and organic ingredients as possible, within the confines of running a profitable business.

Madi

When I contacted Te Mauri Tau asking if I could talk to someone about local food they recommended Madi, as she is in charge of the gardens there. I had met Madi several times at events organised by Mauri Tau, and when I went to interview her, she was busy hulling amaranth, a very small South American grain, that she had been growing as an experiment to see how well it did in the climate. Madi first moved to Whaingaroa after she finished high school. She had tried university for half a year and decided it was not for her. She wanted to get out of the city, so she did a 'room swap' with her cousin who was living at Mauri Tau and wanted to experience city life. Unlike many local food providers with rural childhoods, Madi was born and raised in the city but had a feeling that her 'heart lay beyond the realms of urban life.' I asked Madi if she had always been interested in food:

I was always interested in justice, and it wasn't until I moved here that it really became food focused. I stepped in the door on the first day and Katarina said Ok, you're making 45kg of muesli and 5kg of hummus [to cater for a workshop]. I'd never done any kitchen work before. I worked alongside her for five years in the kitchen, and during that time became more involved in food outside of the kitchen as well.

Madi's years managing the kitchen were spent cooking for up to twenty-five people, feeding the people who live on-site and catering for the workshops held at Te Mauri Tau on topics including facilitation training, nonviolent parenting and Enviroschools. Her main passion now is working in the garden and orchards and re-generating the boundary of the Te Mauri Tau land with native plants.

Madi began learning about gardening from a bio-intensive gardener friend and is still particularly interested in that method with its strong focus on quick regeneration of the soil. It was Madi who first invented the idea of having internships at Liz and Rick's. She spent a year as the first long-term permaculture intern there. At the time of the interview, she had been back at Te Mauri Tau for eight months, after a long sailing voyage with her partner. Her focus was on re-establishing the gardens, and once they are established she talked about having a community day, where the public can come and garden, like at Liz and Ricks but perhaps in te reo [the Māori language]. She expressed amazement at the amount of attention her 'tiny garden' at Te Mauri Tau attracts from visitors, and thinks the garden has a good potential to engage with people. Over the past eight years, Madi says, she has developed a good relationship with the land at Te Mauri Tau, and is now focussing on setting up good systems.

I'm finding my feet myself and what I would really like would be a model to work from. At the moment, coming back and touching down with the structures that are in place... finding them really inefficient: having three separate gardens. And are they for just the whanau [family] here or bigger education? I guess I'm in a phase of developing a coherent system.

Robz

I first met Robz several years ago, before he moved to Whaingaroa, when he was in town visiting some friends. At the time he was splitting his time between his very social nomadic lifestyle, travelling and sleeping in a van with his infant son, Matai, and a more isolated lifestyle in a house bus on some rent-to-own land in the far North. Since then he has sold the van and continues his nomadic lifestyle by bicycle every summer, with Matai in a special seat at the front, making his way as far south as Dunedin, in the South Island. His lifestyle, both 'on the road' and in Whaingaroa, is focussed on living as 'money-free' as possible. He achieves this through wild foraging as much as possible. He also often uses his skills in building and installing solar-power and is frequently given food in return, although he would prefer to think of this less in terms of some kind of barter or exchange and more in-terms of gifts, freely given.

A big believer in free food, Robz has devoted a lot of his time and energy and the money he does have, to planting as many public fruit trees as possible, as well as building and running his 'nature classroom', designed for teaching children about edible plants and foraging. For this purpose Robz built a roundhouse, mostly out of recycled materials including a tarp which was once part of an old bill-board. The 'nature classroom' sits among Robz' other constructions including the outdoor kitchen and living space, also largely made of foraged materials, amidst young pine trees on the corner of land owned by friends who do not mind him and Matai living there.

Before moving to Whaingaroa Robz had planned to live off the land in the far North, but he had only got as far as planting his first garden when a change in personal circumstances left him a solo parent in a very isolated situation. This prompted his move. At first Robz and Matai lived in their van, then they lived in a rented batch for a few months, while looking for some land to build a life on:

We were looking for a place, a piece of land to rent or lease, and I put it in the Chronicle a few times and put flyers in letterboxes and places and that, but didn't really get any response and I think I'd only met Lenny once and he brought Andreas to a solar power workshop I was running and Andreas mentioned "Oh I heard you're looking for a place to live" and I said "Oh, I've got a caravan" and we kind of loosely checked it out and it was very unofficial but when we returned from our cycling trip we asked "Are you open to it?" We came out here and pointed at this little area which was covered in branches... yep made it home.

Robz started to learn about wild foods about a year prior to the interview. He got inspired while staying with friends in Otaki, helping them to build a solar hot water system. After that he bought books on foraging and began to eat wild foods he found on his long cycling trips. Many of the edible plants Robz eats are often considered weeds, including plantain, wild carrot roots and dandelion leaves. To supplement his and Matai's food supply and provide more free food to other people, Robz was motivated to plant public fruit trees:

One day I had an idea to plant a community orchard, I think it was when I was looking for some land, I was looking for land for us to live on and I had this idea of – if someone's got a spare paddock or something, we can just plant it in fruit trees and live in it at the same time and look after the orchard. I think that was when the seed was planted, and it just grew from there. I like the idea of there being lots of free food around the community to share. It would definitely be beneficial to us but lots of other people as well. So yeah it kinda stuck and it became kinda important to do, that's kinda been my main priority since we've been back from our trip.

Together with some friends Robz estimates he had planted around 200 to 250 trees last year and is hoping to do the same again this year. It can take years for fruit trees to fruit so Robz is just "whacking them in," but he did get into a bit of trouble for doing so, from his friend at the Environment Centre who wanted them to be more structured in their approach. The Environment Centre is interested in getting funding to plant fruit trees in the gardens of low-income rental properties, an idea that Robz is not too enthusiastic about because he has seen such fruit go to waste. He prefers the idea of fruit being available for anyone to harvest. Along these lines, Robz has taken the lead in organising the local food forest started by Jon and other volunteers.

The following chapters focus on the themes which emerged from interviews. Chapter Five explores the various tensions experienced by the participants in Whaingaroa in their shared resistance to perceived problems with global corporate capitalism, local and national government, and in navigating the paradoxes apparent in their daily lives. Chapter Six examines the values and ontological basis that interacts with these tensions. Chapter Seven observes the common theme that interactions between these values and tensions often lead participants to practices around deliberately focussing on small-scale local solutions. Chapter Eight concentrates particularly on solutions involving alternative economic models. These themes are combined with key reflections from Chapters One and Two, including those presented by the urban and Wilderland based interview participants, into Chapter Nine, the discussion chapter.

5 CULTIVATING RESISTANCE

On a sunny November Saturday in 2014, My daughter, Tesla, and I sat at the large communal picnic table outside Raglan Roast eating locally made Dizzy Blocks [ice-blocks] and drinking coffee. Some friends came to join us.

"Are you going to the protest?"

"The one about the TPPA?"

"Yeah, we thought we'd check it out."

Twenty minutes later we made our way to the end of Bow St to hear Robz playing protest songs amid stacks of placards painted by volunteers. A small crowd gathered around as we mingled. Tesla played on the bank with other children as several people, including local tangata whenua, gave speeches against the Trans Pacific Partnership Agreement [TPPA] – a proposed free-trade agreement with the United States and other Pacific-rim countries. For a protest, the atmosphere was noticeably relaxed, cheerful and inclusive.

Figure 23: Locals holding protest signs, 2014.

One of the speeches was given by Eva Rickard's daughter, Angeline Greensill:

In the 60s three local women chained themselves to those trees to save them so we can enjoy them today. So that was one victory for people taking action – a few women.

The second big action was a march down the street for the Raglan golf course land in 1978 and in 1983 a political settlement was made – no money – but the land was handed back. In 1981 we had a big march in Hamilton, a lot of people came from here to the rugby field. That was the turning point of apartheid being destroyed in South Africa, and Nelson Mandela actually made a comment about the light shining through on the day that that happened...

We've had all these trade agreements that government, not only National, but Labour. They started selling our assets in the 1980s and the TTPA is the final nail in that coffin. The Pacific itself is the next territory to be colonised and it's going to be colonisation by corporation...

The TTPA is really a breach of the Treaty of Waitangi[1] because the Treaty gave the government the right to govern... If we stand up united we can fight this… If they're not willing to govern in the interests of our people, then we need to stand up, agitate and change them.

If you look at the internet you see the citizens are fighting back, because they're sick of surveillance. They're sick of not being able to have a say. They actually want their freedom – to be people living in their own land – deciding what they're going to eat – knowing that this is their place to stand on.

The speeches were followed by several songs written specifically about the TTPA. The final speaker urged the crowd to grab placards and prepare to march down the main street – so we did – chanting anti-TTPA slogans as we went, and taking care to watch out for the many children involved in this weekend Whaingaroa activity. We were met with a mixture of surprise, amusement and enthusiasm by the weekenders enjoying their café brunches and other locals we encountered along the way. We counted approximately three hundred participants, a decent turn out for a town with a population of around 3000.

Figure 24: Protest on Bow St, 2014.

This Saturday morning community protest exemplifies the common values including resistance to corporate exploitation of many people in Whaingaroa. Angeline Greensill's speech above also speaks to a history of protest in Whaingaroa, and a history of victories. This legacy of resistance is also reflected by Kiwi's Against Seabed Mining (KASM), a national organisation which was started in Whaingaroa in opposition to the sale of seabed mining rights by government to corporations.

Set against this wider backdrop of activism, anti-corporate resistance has emerged as a core research theme, from both the interviews and wider fieldwork. Awareness of global problems with the corporate capitalist food system was identified as a major motivating factor for many people to get involved in grass-roots activities, sparking, shaping or reinforcing their values and practices. This anti-corporate resistance reflects that of Vía Campesina's food sovereignty campaign (Wittman et al 2010). This resistance can also be linked to what has been called the 'anti-globalisation movement', or what Graeber (2009; 2011) considers should more appropriately be termed 'the global justice movement'. However, it must be noted that this link is not in any official capacity. The connection is more related to shared values and collective resistance.

This chapter explores tensions with global corporate capitalism through the voices of key participants. It then focusses on conflicts and tensions participants identified in relation to both local and national government, some of which are perceived to be influenced by corporate pressure. The final section of this chapter highlights the internal conflict experienced by participants as they strive to live in line with their ethics and encounter inevitable contradictions. Along with Seo and Creed (2002), I consider that tensions and paradoxes such as those presented here hold potential for raising awareness and further reflexive engagement with ethical issues.

Resisting global corporate capitalism

Let's talk about the spy-laws, is that an oxymoron or what? Or global warming? – Jenny.

Even though it's so simple – it's so complicated to do as well, because you're always battling the economy – Robz.

In the quotes above, Jenny and Robz both present a willingness to engage with an opposition to dominant power structures. The culture of grass-roots resistance to corporate exploitation, as evidenced in Whaingaroa, can be seen as interconnected with various other historical and contemporary movements including environmentalism, permaculture and Transition Towns, described by Liz in Chapter Seven. Corporations, particularly Monsanto, are held by participants to be particularly corrupt and exploitative. People have become informed through discussions, reading books, magazine articles, online sources and watching documentaries relating to this kind of corporate activity[2]. There is a broad shared perspective that large corporations are responsible for social and environmental injustices: exploiting workers through low pay and inhumane working conditions and exposure to pesticides; poisoning the environment with such pesticides; creating imbalances with synthetic fertilisers that pollute water-ways, destroying diverse ecosystems and eroding soil health; shaping economic and legislative conditions whereby small farm-holders struggle to operate; genetically engineering seeds which may pose unknown risks to human and ecological health; and then releasing these seeds into the environment and shaping laws so that corporations, such as Monsanto, have no responsibility for such contamination. Furthermore, participants expressed concern that corporate ownership of the DNA of seeds allows these large corporations to sue contaminated farmers who save their seed to grow it the following year. These actions, as well as the wider corporate capitalist system are held as key contributors to human-created climate change. They are considered problematic for both global and local wellbeing: as both ideological and physical threats to agricultural communities around the world, and arguably, to all of humanity as well as the health of the planet. This core understanding was reflected throughout conversations within the local Whaingaroa community as well as across the country with people engaged with food activism and sustainability. It may be appropriate to define the community, more broadly, by a shared narrative of resistance against global corporate capitalism, and more specifically by the grass-roots based food activities with which they are involved. The line of reasoning goes something like this:

1. There are major problems with corporate capitalism (including those listed above)
2. Something must be done to counteract these problems.
3. Asking the question: what do we have the power to do?
4. Focussing on the every-day and the local: what are we eating and where does it come from?
5. Doing whatever we can to resist the system and create solutions.

In conceptualising problems with the global corporate system and then living lifestyles which, to varying degrees, are based around 'local solutions', these diverse people and groups can be described as a siteless (Sissons 1999; Foote 2009) community of proactive resistance. They also appear fit loosely within Graeber's (2009) conception of the wider political left which, he states, was founded on the premise that since human beings are continuously creating and re-creating the world, there is no good reason why we – as human beings – cannot create one we actually like, presumably with more equality and less injustice. This willingness to engage with and re-shape the world lends itself to the critical theoretical perspectives of social constructionism as explained by Grant and Humphries (2006).

When exploring people's views, it pays to bear in mind that perceptions are far from static. They are continually shifting and changing to a greater or lesser degree. For example, although Cally's core values may have remained relatively similar, her focus has shifted since her student days. She reflects:

The things that I was aware of back then were bigger things rather than personal things: world peace and protests; walking down Victoria street against Vietnam; bomb tests at Mururoa and all those sort of bigger issues... and there's still all those bigger issues but I've come to realise, for me anyway, it's more about just personal practices. The personal side of those bigger issues like for me there's Monsanto there and yes I'd like them to stop but I'm sorta just down here growin' me own veg, I'm not out there occupying, I'm just occupying my space.

In this occupation, Cally is enacting her values through her daily food-related practices. When she thinks about problems with national and global politics, she sometimes feels powerless. She is not doing, or cannot do, enough to change things on that 'bigger' level. In contrast, she perceives that she does have the power to make many decisions about what she does in her every-day life. This conception of food as powerful was shared by many of the other research participants. In people's day-to-day lives conscious micro-level choices can be made as a form of resistance to corporate exploitation in the pursuit of profit. This profiteering attitude is something Kaiwaka is particularly outspoken about:

When we hosted the Organic Sector one fella said to me, 'how much can you get out of there?' and he said 'if I can't get $10,000 out of there I won't bother doing it!' My answer to that was '[even] if I can't get $10,000 out of there myself, my missus my family will get a bloody good kai [feed], we'll have a full puku [belly].' That's the main thing, we're not hungry. And he looked at me and said 'well you're not a businessman!' And I said 'no I'm not, businessmen stomp on people! I'm not that kind of person.'

This view of business as exploitative is not actually a blanket condemnation of all business by participants, but specifically targeted at those which pursue growth and profit to the exclusion of other values and with little regard for people, communities and the environment, as Jon remarks:

The corporate model – being 'for profit only' – it's just for short-term profit because it's destroying the topsoil and depleting the water levels so it's actually not even for long-term profit. The costs are passed on to the local people or the tax payers or whoever.

Along with this critique of corporations comes the acknowledgement of their immense power in contemporary global politics. Wayne points out: 'it's not kings or governments running the world now, it's corporations. They control governments, they control policies'. In contrast, Justin stated that he does not think too much about big corporations, he just tries to avoid them and focus on sourcing more ethical ingredients and products like fairtrade sugar. He reflects his experience that in the hospitality industry resistance to big corporations can be particularly difficult:

I don't like Coca-Cola, I never have, I just don't like dealing with them, they're bullies. They're so big they'll come round and say we'll give you all the fridges you want and that's a massive expense that they don't have to pay for – And they just bully you, and the problem is it's not even like it's cheap, I mean ok it's cheap to buy the big 2 litre bottles but I pay the same for a 300 ml bottle as you do for a 2 litre bottle so there's no benefit for me to sell a crappy product when I can buy what I believe is a better product, Karma Cola and it's an ethically better product for the same price. We do have the odd bottle out back cause some people they want a rum and coke they don't want a rum and cola. We don't advertise we carry it, it's just in the back fridge. We need a soda water or tonic water. I'm going through the process of finding alternatives.

In discussions about corporations and food genetic modification (GM) or genetic engineering (GE)[3] inevitably arose as issues. The feeling among participants was that GM poses potentially serious risks without necessarily bringing any significant benefits. The risks are communicated both in terms of human health and economic exploitation by corporations. Through their narratives runs a strong and coherent critique of the motives of corporations and the rationale that GM is about feeding the world. The general consensus is that there is, in reality, plenty of food produced globally and that hunger has largely been a distribution problem. These sentiments are shared by Vía Campesina and the wider food sovereignty campaign and anti-GM literature (for example: Wittman et al 2010; Smith 2003). Opinions have been informed by the participants' reading and research, documentaries. Mike is particularly opposed to GM:

I loathe it with a passion, and it's not because I'm anti progress or science it's just the motivations behind GM is not about feeding the world or high yields or anything else. It's about control of the food chain and it is a topic I've researched quite thoroughly. The more I learn about GM the, more scary I find it and we shouldn't be putting it into our food chain.

The potential health risks associated with GM are Mike's main concern, especially links to inflammatory disease and increased pesticide use but he considers the politics behind it to be 'pretty ugly' as well. He describes research linking GM to inflammatory illnesses and states that 'roundup-ready' pesticide resistant GM corn has led to a huge increase in the permitted pesticide levels, since they are based on trade and farming practices rather than on human health. Despite this, Mike acknowledges: 'one thing about GM is: it's controversial and you can have science on one side that's compelling and science on the other side that's equally compelling.' He has less of a problem with GM inherently on an ideological level, but distrusts the corporations involved:

We mess with things anyway – selectively breed... I generally don't have a problem with these things. I have a real problem where it gets into control and if you look at Monsanto's mission statement, they want to control world food. I do struggle with that. On an ethical level there's some GM use of medicines and vaccines and insulin, things like that, but it's controllable, it doesn't break out of the fence and run around in the pollen carted by bees. I'm okay with it but people should have the choice... It's got to be tested.

There's been no [government] demand for proper testing on how GM crops affect people. The Americans just say "we trust the companies to do their own research" and New Zealand says "we trust America to have got it right". I remain unconvinced.

Cally shares the sentiment that while GM could have positive effects, the way that it is currently being developed poses significant unknown risks that outweigh any potential benefits:

I'd love it to be successful, I think the ideals behind it, the idea of improving things and changing things is wonderful, I just don't think it's safe. It could happen if it wasn't all being done by people wanting to make money. I try not to eat GE food but there's no way that we can avoid it. I try to minimise it; I use organic feed for my chooks because I don't want the GE stuff. I don't want that coming in my eggs, but having said that it's not always available and chooks gotta eat, they're free range but they do need things. I don't like GE at all, and it terrifies me: the studies are so short and so inadequate and I'm old enough to remember the thalidomide children[4], and you look at the obvious things that we know about like the nuclear, Hiroshima, Nagasaki from the Second World War and we know about continuing generational problems and I can see that happening, we just don't know.

The general sentiment expressed was that GM is unnecessary as there is already an abundance of food being produced, globally, and hunger exists because of issues with politics and distribution, as Mike states:

The thing that annoys me with GM is what it claims to do we don't need it to do. We can feed the world with the technology we have. Feeding the world is not about a shortage of food, if it was how could the Western World waste 30–40 percent? How come we – I've got friends feeding cows on carrots, squash and kiwifruit for the cost of the transport? Europe's got 10–15 percent of its land set-aside to try to keep the prices up because there's an over-production of food – that doesn't tell me it's a hungry world. America's got payment in kind – they'll pay you not to produce.... We can waste because we're not hungry.... It's politics and distribution.

What Mike would really like to see in relation to GM is accurate labelling on products, to allow people the choice to purchase and consume it or avoid it. He expects that while some people will have to buy it based on price "most people, if it was well-labelled they'd steer clear." The New Zealand government has resisted calls to label GM products because of resistance from corporations. For Mike the right to choose is important and it concerns him that "we are losing our basic rights". He describes his understanding as follows:

In Aussie, the likes of Bayer are buying opposing seed companies, so you're not going to have a choice of whether to buy GM or not. If you have a choice that's fine – but where GM is dangerous is if my neighbour grows GM corn and I grow organic or non GM corn then it gets contaminated – there's no compensation for me and what's even worse is – say it's Monsanto – they can sue me for using their genes. How wrong is that? I've had a look at what Ag Research in Ruakura is doing with GM and their animals, and while I don't agree with what they're doing it's containable. We've had a respectful discussion. My position is you do what you do so long as it doesn't affect me, you put it out in the environment and can't control it, sorry, that's different.

For Robz, GM is also an unnecessary evil: "The ownership of food is the biggest for me." He does not think food needs to be made more nutritious in particular, but industrial farming methods have depleted the soil, making mass-produced food less nutritious than the wild food he prefers to eat. Jenny echoes the sentiment that producing more food is not a good reason for GM and that the control of the food system and ownership of DNA is a major problem:

Everyone knows that we have enough food in the world but sometimes governments are using [access to resources like food] to suppress people. It just feels so hopeless. There are all the issues in America with Monsanto with seed ownership. I remember reading years and years ago about them trying to take ownership of the native peoples' corn and it made me so angry – but I can't do anything about that. I can just do things in my own world.

The sentiment among the local food providers is that the corporate profit-driven nature of the GM industry is inherently problematic and has much more potential for harm than good. This resistance to GM and critique of the corporate is a strong element of the food sovereignty campaign (Wittman et al 2010). It also embodies strong elements of anti-authoritarianism which are also apparent in attitudes toward local and national governmental authorities. These anti-authoritarian attitudes are discussed in the following section in relation to local and national government.

Tensions with local and national government

The local food producers in Whaingaroa expressed a range of attitudes to governing power-structures. Some expressed strong resistance to top-down hierarchical government, and were optimistic about more democratic, de-centralised, community-based governance systems. Others saw the current form of government as somewhat inevitable, but hoped that it would be more supportive of small-scale food producer interests and human freedom in general. The undercurrents of tension with local and national governments presented here are related to legislation and 'red tape' that restricts food producers from selling their food without particular certification, only acquirable through meeting the sometimes strict health and safety standards assigned through bureaucratic processes. Although participants tended to be critical of governmental control, most upheld the belief that the role of government is to support public interests, to re-balance wealth, and to allow communities to have autonomy, wherever possible. Participants have often been active in campaigns to challenge and influence government activity, although there was a general feeling of frustration at the perceived increase of influence of corporations over governments and a shared understanding that energy may be better spent in focusing on local solutions, as such as those explored in Chapter Seven.

Just as ideological tensions with global corporations reinforce food sovereignty values as a form of resistance, the New Zealand Government is seen as being actively influenced by global corporate interests. These tensions were exacerbated recently by proposed changes to the Food Act described in Chapter Two. This national level influence is seen, by participants, to filter through to the control that local governments in New Zealand and health inspectors, as government employees, attempt to enact over local food providers. Perspectives on this vary between conceptions of government as conservative and unnecessary nuisances and more malevolent forces of dominance. These latter perspectives are reinforced through hearing about episodes in the United States where people have been judicially punished for home gardening or arrested for giving away food in public, as described by Giles (2013).

In general, participants endorsed governance structures that were more 'from the ground up, rather than top-down', and had various ideas about how these might function. Jon, who is particularly critical of the current government structure, was keen to discuss this:

You won't find many people that feel the [Regional] Council's doing a good job and there's all sorts of reasons for that. We can assume it's not the wisest use of resources – by councils and government – it's not efficient. Again, to me that comes to localisation – re-localisation. People who live in a local area know what that area needs more than anyone else. How can Mr Key [The Prime Minister] in his office know what we need in Raglan? How can our local MP who doesn't live in Raglan, know what Raglan needs? They can't... Representative democracy is a small amount of people making decisions for everybody, it's perceived as time efficient, I guess, but I really believe that the people who live in the immediate vicinity should be the ones who make the decisions for that area. Groups of a few hundred people at the most... Of course you would have representatives to meet with other groups to talk as well.

In general, the interview participants were critical of the current right-of-centre National Party Government, led by Prime Minister John Key, a former corporate banker, as Kaiwaka reflects:

John Key [who was the Prime Minister at the time] has a lot to answer for, not listening to the people, selling off all the power, and shuffled this and that up for sale, even with all the people saying no. And he just doesn't give two hoots because it's all about money. When he gets kicked out, he'll just pick up his kids and leave. They [former political leaders] all live overseas.

Participants, at various points, expressed frustrations with the local government, with regard to bureaucratic processes and neoliberal values. These have also resulted in odd tensions with organisations which rely, in-part, on local government funding. For instance, when Robz was beginning his public fruit-tree planting project there was a possibility to work with the environment centre which was running a similar project aiming to offer fruit trees to be planted in the gardens of low-income rental properties. However, he perceived their process as slower and requiring more organisation: "it just works a lot different for them." He was also not so keen on planting on rental properties where the fruit might go to waste while being inaccessible for the general public, whereas with planting them in the public domain "low income families still get access to them but they can be made sure they're not wasted and cared for and any excess given to the food bank instead of just dropping in the floor in someone's garden which no one can get to."

As mentioned in Chapter Two, the proposed changes to New Zealand food legislation presented as the Food Bill (foodbill.org 2012), raised suspicions among local food producers in Whaingaroa. These suspicions speculated that the government was acting under the influence of the United States and corporations to increase their power over food production and distribution. Tensions with the regulations of local councils and food officers can be seen in the following conversation, taken from a local permaculture meeting:

Sam: 'Health and Safety' is just a guise – It's just a way that they can justify [the Food Bill] and everybody goes: "Oh, all right, off you go, I need to be healthy and safe", but it's just a way of cracking down. There wasn't really a health and safety problem before.

Liz: The health inspector gets carried away with her role, she lets it take over. She's making it more difficult than it should be – the labelling is annoying, they want the standard nutritional break-down on our pesto, which our customers don't care about.

Robz: But isn't it crazy that, depending on how you grow your food it will have more nutritional content.

Liz: We put the pesto in [to a website analysis of nutritional break down] and it's a sort of super-food supplement. I find that more useful but the list is so long. They want you to put it on every jar. It's a new thing, only in the last two years. They're trying to make the market people come along with regular shops. You have to have two licences to handle food, one's a district one and one's a state one. It's definitely more revenue for the councils. I think it must have been a directive passed onto all the councils because I know people in other areas that have the same. At the market they are asking people to have certification because the health inspector comes around now. There's pressure on them to comply.

Louie: Why not print a giant disclaimer saying "I do it at home – eat at your own risk."

Liz: I don't think we've ever had a customer who's been paranoid about the food.

Cally: No, they probably wouldn't go to the market, they would go to the supermarket where everything's been irradiated and pesticided. I think regulations are important to a degree because if you had no regulations, imagine what those big business people would be doing. It's very hard – where do you draw that line? – Yes these people have to be regulated but you don't. I certainly wouldn't want Fonterra going regulation-free, thank you very much.

Ellen: I think as long as you're buying from the farmers' market you always can ask – what are the ingredients? For me it would be interesting to know, if there's water used, where the water comes from – this issue doesn't appear anywhere but I think it's quite important and you can't ask that of corporations.

Sam: I think [the regulations] are threats to food sovereignty.

The conversation above can be seen to reflect tensions with local and national governments, as well as the sentiment that regulations are less relevant when it comes to local food. Here other human interactions, such as conversations with market stall-holders or ongoing relationships of trust and accountability take precedence and are more significant than particular labelling. There is an undercurrent to the conversation that reflects the food sovereignty value that positions control locally and prioritises local food producers over global corporations (Wittman et al 2010; Rose 2013).

For Robz, authoritarian power structures are violent and destructive, reinforcing inequalities and perpetuating injustice and exploitation. He channels some of this resistance into his witty 'protest songs', but finds focusing on positive solutions a more rewarding and productive use of his energy and time:

I guess what I'm working towards is a very localised. For me localisation is the solution to most things. And you ask about the council and what I'd like to see – it would be very local, the more the better, because then you're really involved and you're really affected. It's personal. Its people you know. It's not these guys you see on television and know nothing about. Its people that you actually live with. So yeah with food, it would be great if every community took it upon themselves to think what do we need to live here, to eat, yea and that kind of stuff. By planting fruit trees we pretty much can see to the town's fruit needs. I'm excited about the idea of growing some grains, and we've got a harbour so keeping the harbour and oceans healthy… we're pretty sweet really – that's a nutritious diet of local, and being local everyone's got a responsibility and is affected by it so food becomes an important part of people's lives… all the pollution, and spraying from foods, you know it's easy when it doesn't go into our water ways, but having it locally, people start spraying like crazy it's going to get into the harbour and its gonna effect the whole community in quite a bad way… for people to be a lot more conscious about what they're eating and how they're growing their food, it's the answer.

The perspective that local people have a vested interest in maintaining their surrounding environment and community is particularly relevant in Whaingaroa. With clear examples of local organisations such as Whaingaroa Harbourcare and Xtreme Waste, it is easy to see that local people are capable of working together to create better systems and manage local resources. As well as dealing with resistance to corporations, and various tensions with the policies and actions of local and national level government, participants also negotiate inevitable internal conflict when it comes to making day-to-day decisions in their own lives. These relate to having strong values and principles which are sometimes not practical to live up to, especially in a climate of oil dependence and cheaply manufactured international goods. These contradictions and the 'supermarket culture' in which they thrive are explored in the following section.

Contradictions: supermarket culture and driving to the oil drilling protest

Participants identified 'supermarket culture' as a problem for local food. This was bound up in expectations about the availability and accessibility of fresh food, regardless of the seasons. As Justin remarks, "everything comes from the supermarket all year round." He and Alex try to combat this mentality by adjusting their café menu regularly to suit seasonal produce which has the added bonus of being cheaper and having more flavour. Rose (2013) discusses a similar issue relating to food boxes in Australia where people often drop out of the scheme because, they find they do not use the seasonal produce delivered to them because they are used to being able to pick and choose from a wide supermarket range. Mike has found that people's expectations based on supermarkets has affected the way they relate to his milk: "I think we've become a supermarket culture and we run into it with the milk thing because people want to be spoon-fed because they grow up with it. It's not a huge problem but it's just an interesting observation." Despite this criticism, most participants relied on supermarkets to a greater or lesser degree, albeit as a last resort for some. This highlights the active engagement in contradictions faced by 'ethical consumers' in their daily lives which often centre on the origins of food and where food waste and packaging will go. Similar contradictions with ethical food are presented in Guthman's (2003; 2008) critiques of new ethical food movements as a way that privilege is imposed on the less privileged. Facing these contradictions and holding the tensions of paradox, as discussed by Seo and Creed (2002) presents opportunities for further awareness.

The Bro, whose present lifestyle around food was partially motivated by observing the contradictions of anti-corporate activists eating at multi-national fast-food chains is also critical of ethical contradictions around some vegan and vegetarian food practices:

So many people think they can just have whatever diet they want. Want to be vegan? Go live in Southern India or the tropics, where your dietary choices make ecological sense but here if you want to be a vegan then you're wrecking the environment. They're shipping in Brazil nuts from the other side of the world, soy milk from god knows where, where they have to clear rainforests, and then there's that fucking packaging. How many animals will die 'cause you're drinking this shit... that burns up fossil fuel in every step of its production and transportation, then all that toxic shit that leaks into waterways over the lifetime of a tetrapack – 32 layers of glue and tin foil. Cracks me up, vegans look at me 'cause I'm drinking milk and eating a pork pie while they're drinking soya milk. In an ideal world I kill one pig a year and that will feed me and my family, eating meat in a sustainable fashion, that is, not very often and use every last piece. How many lives are you ruining by drinking soya milk... through climate change and toxic leaching – because it's in a tetrapack?

A similar contradiction is raised over protests against oil drilling. Activists who drive to these protests are sometimes criticised for being hypocritical. This criticism is similar to themes in the 'green bubble' discussion in Chapter Two. This kind of criticism raises questions and sparks discussions. As The Bro says:

You're concerned about climate change? It's really fucking hard to live a life where you don't contribute to climate change. I know I've tried it. I've lived without a car for over a year now, and since coming back to Whaingaroa I've had to start driving again, but it's hard. It's really hard. You have to make sacrifices and you miss out on things and a lot of it is not fun. Cycling to work at 6 o'clock in the morning in the howling wind and rain – you could be in a nice dry car while you've got the flu. It ain't fun.

There is a feeling of powerlessness in that people have no choice but to participate in a system they disagree with, ethical compromises are a necessary part of daily life and with each compromise comes critical engagement. Cally describes her reflexive and conscious interaction with contradictions, agency and activism:

If everyone was growing their own veg it could divert power (from big companies), that is the thing. It's a bit like them protesting about drilling for oil off the coast but why are they drilling? They're drilling 'cause there's demand and I'm driving into Hamilton twice a week. I should only do it once a month if I was organised. That's the personal responsibility. I mean, I'm not saying people shouldn't protest against Anadarko. I certainly do want that as well. Maybe that's the difference between how I was when I was younger and how I am now. It's become a more personal taking responsibility for my life and effect rather than trying to get "them" to do something and "them" to change". But we have these huge cities full of people that need feeding. It's easy for me to be righteous about it all but if I was a person living in a ghetto in New York I would have different options, so it's really hard.

Jon describes his own process of critically evaluating contradictions and compromise. Critical of the 'not in my back yard' motivation of some local protesters, he explores different possibilities around ethical responsibility:

If it's not happening at home we don't seem to mind as much. There's a lot of resistance, understandably, to oil exploration off the coast here in Whaingaroa. None of us wants to see that happening 'cause of the risks involved. Until it happens in our own backyard – and I feel it in myself, I haven't made enough noise about it – if it's happening in other parts of the world we don't seem to mind. And you know, someone said to me "Maybe we should just take it on the chin, maybe it's been long enough that other parts of the world have been destroyed for our convenient lifestyles. Maybe we should take some shit as well." It's a good one to open up a debate because a lot of the places which are being destroyed first are the places where people don't have a voice because they don't have as much money – they don't have the clout to make a difference to these big companies – so it's a big debate and it's one that addresses our core concerns because who wants oil spills on their beaches? In Nigeria, Indonesia, Papua, they've completely destroyed natural environments for our convenient lifestyles. It's good questions to ask ourselves. There's no solution overnight and I'm certainly not proposing one, it's just something to explore.

Jon demonstrates an openness to considering different perspectives. He acknowledges that his comparative privilege has been at the expense of environmental degradation in different, less privileged parts of the world and his acceptance of this implies willingness to take some responsibility for it. Jon, like some other participants, is critical of the global monetary system and interest-bearing debt, although he sees it as an inevitable part of his life at the moment. He and his partner have been looking for property to buy, and as much as he is resistant to the idea of having a mortgage, currently he is renting, 'paying someone else's mortgage', anyway. Robz has avoided this issue through 'land-sharing', making use of a corner of a friend's property and helping out with the gardening. Some of the other participants had access to land through personal or collective ownership. The Bro, who was renting a house-bus at the time of our interview, expressed strong resistance to having a mortgage:

I work at the roast office, and when I get sick of people treating me like I'm stupid because they think I'm just a barrista, I think about getting a real job.

But in my life that would involve me driving to Hamilton every day, and I look at those people driving to Hamilton every day and I think "None of them are happy, fuck that. Why are they doing that?" But they're doing that stuff that they don't necessarily want to do that don't align with their values to pay the mortgage. Yeah I've thought a lot about that. I've decided I don't ever want to have a mortgage... Yeah, debt man. It's control.

The Bro doesn't mind that he is currently paying someone else's mortgage: 'I know the guy. He's a friend of mine... and I'm quite happy to pay my mate's mortgage off.' The difference is, that in renting he is not chained to debt, although it also means he is not working towards property ownership. This does not seem to matter to him, as he is critical of the current systems of property law anyway.

Interviews such as these revealed tensions experienced by participants in relation to corporate powers. These tensions effect every-day lives as well as concerns over local and national government power to potentially strangle local food systems. Despite this, people's lives are interconnected with corporations and government in ways that cannot be avoided. These day-to-day contradictions seem to be faced with reflexivity. These themes examined here are also compatible with the tensions, resistance and entanglement experienced by the wider food sovereignty movement.

Although the food activism in Whaingaroa is informed and sometimes fuelled through resistance to corporate capitalism, the identities of participants did not seem to be primarily constructed in terms of this resistance. This contrasts to Foote's (2009) local ethnography of anarchist, vegan and punk subcultures, where the participants' identities were more focussed around being in opposition to the mainstream. In the 'green bubble' of Whaingaroa, the mainstream is less of a pressing concern. There is a sense that while it is important to stand up against things conceived of as harmful and exploitative, there is more to be gained in working toward positive action, in creating better models and in taking control back from corporations – by producing and sharing food, among other things.

There are many creative ways of dealing with these tensions and contradictions of strong ethical opposition to major forces within the dominant system. These can vary from outright opposition and minimising involvement with money, as is Robz's approach, to the notion of putting 'questionable' corporate money to good use, presented here by Wayne:

A lot of projects here in Whaingaroa are being funded by the likes of Sky City [a casino company], through the environment centre – they receive quite a bit of funding through Sky City. It's better that the funding is going to community projects rather than them keeping it to themselves – so some good is coming out of it – you've got to be practical about things.

Wayne was firm in his assertion that taking this 'questionable' money did not imply compromising on values or 'selling out', and was a beneficial use for corporate money. Xtreme Waste's approach, described further in Chapter Seven, is similar. In Xtreme's case the money taken would not be accepted if 'strings were attached', and this is communicated explicitly.

As Seo and Creed (2002) note, a paradox creates tension that can lead to potential transformation. The tensions and contradictions expressed in this chapter can also be viewed in this light, particularly in the awareness they generate. For instance, the uneasiness of participant's interdependence with the corporate globalised world can compel them to seek other alternatives. This is also evidenced in the stories relating how many of the community groups described in Chapter Three were formed. Awareness of these tensions fuels resistance to power structures which are perceived as destructive and exploitative both locally, and internationally. Furthermore, this shared resistance brings people together in community action such as the protest featured at the beginning of this chapter. What has developed in Whaingaroa might be called a proactive culture of positive resistance, based on ontologies of connection and creativity. These function in contrast to the corporate ontology which Rose (2013) argues is based on alienation, or Graeber's (2009) construction of the corporatized state as centred on an ontology of violence. This proactive resistance is deliberately enacted to build connections and relationships between people, to build healthier and more resilient social, economic and environmental eco-systems. The tensions and resistance of focus in this chapter can be seen as interconnected with the values described in the following chapter.

6 OTHER CASE STUDIES: URBAN AND COMMUNITY

Urban food

In this section we meet two people involved in activities that can be related to food sovereignty or food activism in an urban area of New Zealand. There are clear parallels between the values and experiences of Jono and Kora, in their urban settings and those expressed by Josh and Faith, the rural sustainability community participants at Wilderland featured later in this chapter. They are also similar to the which focus on the community of food producers in Whaingaroa.

Jono

Jono is a tenant in a rented property in central Auckland where he maintains a vegetable garden. He grew up in the 70s with a big backyard and wild area between his family's home and the neighbour's. Although he values access to land on which to grow food, his situation as a tenant is precarious. There are very few rental properties in central Auckland with room for a garden, and the inflated housing market is fuelling further development of buildings over the preservation of green spaces. I met Jono through mutual friends involved in activism. Through conversations with him, the perspectives he presented seemed to resonate with the values associated with food sovereignty and his story highlights interesting tensions associated with urban living and access to land.

Gardening is sort of becoming trendy again. The interesting thing about this garden is it belongs to a family of central-Auckland gardens that are dwindling to nothing. It's one of the last of its kind as a rental property. I made a point of moving into this flat because of the size of this garden. Because the church is next door, this property was not subdivided because they wouldn't allow driveway access through the back. There's no fence between these two properties because the same landlord owns both of them, so you get this lovely open space. That's really lovely. I feel really lucky to have this experience. It was basically poisoned land when I found it. If you look, there's a circle garden there in front of us; when I first bit into the soil I found myself digging into what appeared to be an old bed – rusty bedsprings, so I put the garden a bit further forward. It's a bit embarrassing for the old leftie movement. There was all this bloody plastic [from old buried political billboards] in the garden. This house is one of those grand old Auckland flats where all the people who've lived here have been supposedly switched-on types.

Interesting to note that when we're talking about soil/gardening that 'dirt' has the opposite meaning, everything that is dirt is clean and everything that's not dirt is not clean. There was a culture in New Zealand in various times with various different types of people or just throwing your rubbish in the backyard. The problem with being an urban gardener and trying to live an urban life is that maintaining a big garden and property takes a lot of energy. A lot of things have gone to seed and I haven't managed to keep up this spring.

Over the last hundred years or so people have gradually become acclimatised to stricter regulations – that it's normal for the government to regulate the plants people grow and for corporations to have control – quite a strong level of legal intervention – there seems to be a creeping attempt to get people to

*think that food should be controlled as well as medicine, and for the govern-
ment to be involved in restricting the way people grow and share food at a
community level. They're saying it's to protect people's health [but it's actu-
ally] to increase institutionalised power and corporate power.*

*I think all of these things are a mixture of deliberate and non-deliberate
[action], not conspiracies in a master-mind way. We know psychology has
been used in marketing to create complicit consumers but I expect that most
of these things are not that well-orchestrated: [They look] more like conspiracies in hind-sight. There are a bunch of vested interests involved in influ-
encing laws that make it look like a conspiracy and the little people – the
ordinary people – are the ones who lose out. When it comes to food the first
and most obvious thing is to get yourself parked on a property where you can
grow food, share food and save seeds and don't listen to the state or anyone
who tries to stop you. Really they can't. People just have to keep doing what
they've always done: keep seed stocks alive, grow food, and keep up with
these community, grass-roots connections as much as our time enables us,
because people-power is effective. The only real response to this state and
corporate power is a community response – people building alternative
economies that ignore or undermine the dominant power structures.*

*As much as I can, as a not-very wealthy person, I support organic, local and
fair-trade economics, trying to get my money to people who are trying to do
the right thing. The garden has played a role, there's the house up there and
the garden is like some kind of organ that keeps going, maybe the heart.
Other people have got involved at the time but mainly it's been me. It has
affected the character of the place. It hasn't had a huge effect practically,
apart from the exchange of food going between here and the house and the
compost. It provides a vibrational and aesthetic backdrop and provides an
intelligent place for food to go.*

*Urban living gives less time for gardening and I struggle to get enough time
to do as much gardening as I want. This brings us to how cities are structured. One of the reasons this kind of garden is disappearing is that it's
considered a fait accompli [a done deal]. The way that city development*

happens needs to be a lot more thought-out and sustainable. We have the opportunity to work forward and design for sustainability.

People really should "spread out" in the right way, turn unsustainable farm-land into sustainable backyards and small farm-holdings, sprawling and green and lush with lots of edible sections and good public transport systems. Every single house has to have its own water tank, everyone have solar power, significant rates-breaks for having a percentage of land in food production. If that happened, urban sprawl would be sweet. We just have to shift the model of development and the rules and regulations around that development. Huge amounts of food are going into a landfill – every single blimin' sandwich is taking nutrients out of the biosphere, essentially, and if it makes its way back into the biosphere it's in the form of a noxious gas.

My core values relating to food is a sort of socialist thing I think – I see food as one of the basic units of wealth – these days, people are made to think that money is the basic unit of wealth, but actually food is essential. The more food you have in your community, as well as shelter and water, the wealthier you are – if people and communities are in control of their food, rather than top-down insti-tutions, people and communities have power. I come from a paradigm of values that say that people power is paramount – sovereignty over food – because food is vital to life, and if food is healthy because it's well produced then it stands to reason that people and communities will be more wealthy and empowered. In that sense, the separation of food from the community and the separation of production with things shifting to big international corporations whose entire purpose is to make money – and definitely not nourishing people – that goes along with the fracturing of communities. I like my individual freedom and I believe in individuals having the power to grow food, but by being overly indi-vidualist people's power to support one-another is being threatened.

I'm not 100% against GE forever. What concerns me is that these corpora-tions started fiddling around with stuff for profit-driven reasons, disguised as healthy reasons, and then just started putting it in the food with minimal research. I suppose it's possible that it could be beneficial; it's just another string to our bow as a creature with a bit of a penchant for changing things around us in a beneficial way – but it's the way that they've gone about it, sneaking it in to everything and then there are the awful stories we hear about farmers being sued for accidentally growing patented crops. I think any intelligent person should be suspicious of what's going on and the lack of sufficient research. Surely it's obvious that there's a potential for unintended consequences from transgenic engineering. Don't put it into our diets until we know what it will do.

We're humans and we do change our environment and invent technologies to make life easier for ourselves, but we have to balance that with always keeping an eye on nature and see how that's working out. We have got very unbalanced in recent times and we're seeing all sorts of dreadful conse-quences starting to emerge. At the same time, we can't just run back to nature and become hunter-gatherers, that's not going to work. We're going to need technology, but we can keep an eye on it and keep balancing. One bottom-line way of doing that is try to invent technologies that in-and-of-themselves give back to the earth – try to make it nicer than when we came – if everyone lived like that, imagine how nice it would be. If our technologies were geared to give back it would go a long way to protect us from our own excesses.

Kora

Kora grew up in an urban environment and has travelled extensively. I met her through Kiwiburn, a small community arts festival in the North Island of New Zealand. Like Jono, Kora's perspectives and values reflect those associated with food sovereignty, as explained at the beginning of this chapter. She has been involved in a lot of dump-ster-diving food rescue activities in various cities around the world. She is particularly concerned with food waste, a concept not often considered to be a core part of the farm-to-fork food system, as explained by Ackerman-Leist (2012). A sense of injustice and outrage is expressed by many participants in response to the large amount of food that is wasted through the dominant corporate food system, and this often motivates food rescue activism. These sentiments are reflected in Kora's narrative, below.

I found out about dumpster-diving when I was in Edinburgh, and a friend was talking about it. At first all I thought about was homeless people going through the trash but then I saw my friend's booty and there was all this good food. In Scotland they don't lock the dumpsters and dumpster diving is quite common, but in NZ most supermarkets do lock them or have them behind big fences. The more gourmet supermarkets don't tend to lock them. One time we were at the one in Ponsonby and someone came out from the store and said, 'please don't make a mess'. They usually put all the bread into separate bags so you don't have to go through the other rubbish. I hope that they do it on purpose because they don't want it to be wasted. I really got into it when one of my friends came over who more-or-less lives off dumpster diving, she just went right in in the daytime and opened up the dumpster and started eating it then and there. I wouldn't do that because I would be worried about getting caught [mostly worried about having jumped a fence. Not worried about being seen to be homeless].

The thing that I care about is the wastage of food – I think of food in the same ways as: reduce, reuse, recycle – I feel the same way about my clothes. Maybe not reduce, because I like food, but avoiding waste. There's so much wastage in our world that is completely unnecessary. Even if I can afford it, I would rather reduce unnecessary waste. The produce might be coming from somewhere where they can't even eat or feed their families and we've just gone ahead and thrown their food away – it's just rude. My whole flat was into dumpster diving – I don't think I've ever gone by myself – also having a car, being in Auckland… it's a matter of having someone else with me. We were a flat of six, and four out of six, and our ex flatmate as well, we'd go once a week. We started getting raw milk with a collective. We started with 5 litres and ended up with 10 a week because my flatmate was making cheeses as well. We would give our ex flatmate a litre of milk and go to the dumpsters. We got a whole lot of hummus one time, we had to have a rule to have hummus with every meal – or you have to try this yogurt – otherwise it's just waste again and that defeats the purpose. We sometimes came across vegetables that were a weird shape and weird cheeses that I never would have eaten otherwise, maybe cranberry flavoured.

Sometimes I think about what the media are calling an 'ethical eating disorder' you think so much of what you eat, where it comes from, which company, is it wasteful, what about the packaging, what else did they put in it...? It gets to the point where I'm at a supermarket or sitting in a restaurant thinking 'can't have that because it's got that in it' and you just have to get over it. People often forget that food is one of the most important things in our lives and it's also a good way to get people to come together because it's one of the things we all have in common. With the way life is going, a lot of people are eating alone or in front of the TV – we've always eaten around the table in our family.

If [food] actually goes off quickly it's a good thing – if it doesn't go off it probably has crap in it, like preservatives. There's all these things that make sense, that are common-sense: if it smells good, eat it, if it doesn't go off it's not food. Food's from nature, but a lot of food these days is counter-intuitive. Dumpster diving is often for both political and ethical reasons, and it's resourceful – to get free stuff. The laws about use-by dates and the huge amount of waste in our country are immoral – a crime. The way the shops lock up their food waste is weird – the ownership of something that's going in the trash. They are assuming that people won't go to the shop and give them money.

Doing things consciously, with purpose and intention, is important to me. I don't want to just buy something because it's easy. There's too much stuff in this world, I don't want to buy new stuff, I can buy other people's old stuff, thinking about where things are coming from, what I'm going to do and how long I'm going to have it. I've been trying to question things and reassess things all the time. Being conscious of the decisions I make in every-day life. I don't want to fall into the trap of not wanting to know. It sounds high-and-mighty or idealist in a way but I don't want to be one of those people who doesn't consider these things. If I make compromises on my values, at least I know I'm aware of that. I don't want to look back and wish I hadn't done things that made other people's lives worse. We are so lucky to live in this country. When I was visiting Tanzania, these people sang every night after dinner, it was a time for their family to get together. These people in other cultures who have less, they can teach you so much about your life.

I don't know too much about GE, but I don't see the point when nature provides us with those nutrients that it can and has provided us with for years and years. We have enough food on this planet to feed all the people, it's just not going where it's supposed to go; it's going to the rich countries from the poor countries, rather than being balanced. These corporations are basically trying to solve a problem that they themselves created in a way that makes them more money. I don't need to eat bananas, I don't need to eat things all year round. It's really unnecessary. A lot more people are thinking about where their food is coming from, and it's not just fashion and green-washing, they're thinking about how we have been fucking the world up and trying to do things about it.

In the ultimate ideal future everyone would be self-sustainable and to be able to feed themselves and their families – everyone in the world. That would require a huge upheaval in the way that we do things now. If we started eating less meat so there was less demand then we wouldn't have to grow them in feedlots – not having to ship food across continents – bringing it back to the community, back down to normality rather than it being a chique or hippy thing to do – bringing it back down to reality. It would be cool if growing food was just normal. Changing the ideas around property and sharing fruit trees – community spirit and knowing your neighbours.

I call it 'the year I started to care'. I realised it wasn't just me in the world, I realised we are all interconnected, that was the year I got into vegetarianism. I would never force my views on anyone though, but I will tell people what I think.

Wilderland

In order to draw a more fulsome picture of food sovereignty in New Zealand, I wanted to include a case study based in intentional community. For this reason, I spent time at Wilderland, a community in the Coromandel with a focus on sustainable education.

I first visited Wilderland at the very beginning of my Doctoral fieldwork and returned many times over the following three years. Wilderland is an organic farm and sustainability education centre in the Coromandel peninsula, on the east coast of the North Island of New Zealand. It is sometimes described as a 'commune' an 'intentional community', and sometimes as an 'unintentional community' by long term residents. It was started in the 1960s, by Dan and Edith Hansen. Dan had lost mobility in his legs in an accident and required help to run the organic farm, which lead him to encouraging people to both visit and live on the farm in a community. Dan's values were influenced by the spiritual teachings of Krishnamurti which led him and Edith to establish Wilderland as both a vegetarian and drug and alcohol free space. This section provides my initial ethnographic reflections from the early visits to Wilderland and two Vignettes from long-term residents, Josh and Faith.

After braving the twists and turns of a coastal Coromandel highway, followed by a dusty gravel road and badly eroded driveway, I arrived at Wilderland for the first time with my travel-weary four-year-old daughter, Tesla. The "welcome home" sign and the shade of fruit trees brought a sense of relief. We passed some unusual looking shacks; one painted to look like a shark, and reached what appeared to be the main centre of the community as indicated by a larger building with cars parked outside. As soon as we arrived we were greeted with a hug from Faith, one of the management committee members, who took a moment to recognise me. We had met at a small festival, Kiwiburn, much earlier in the year, but as she recalled, my hair was longer then. I had also communicated with Faith through emails to Wilderland in my preparation for this visit.

I felt disorientated to begin with, aware that I had entered a different social reality. At Wilderland it is normal to hug hello, even on the first meeting. We spent some time outside the hall, and shared a banana passionfruit picked by an Israeli man, a friend of the community who was visiting that day.

Tesla played with Anna (6) and I talked with her mother Shaki. She and her husband, Avner, moved to Wilderland from Israel four years ago with their two daughters. I had also previously met Shaki at Kiwiburn. Wilderland is self-described as primarily an educational trust focusing on gardening, bee keeping and sustainability. It is also a live-in community of twenty to thirty people of various nationalities. Presently it is comprised of around twenty New Zealanders, Australians, Israelis, North Americans and Europeans. Some people come as visitors and stay for years, others just a few weeks or months, taking on varying levels of involvement in the organisation and running of the community.

We were invited into the hall for a cup of tea. The main building has a separate room at the front called the Kids' Room which is also used as office space as the internet is accessible from there. Behind this is the hall: one large room roughly the size of a small house and visibly dilapidated as indicated by worn, uneven, particle board floor. Despite this it is a particularly functional building providing a communal kitchen, library, dining, lounging area and the main centre of the community. Residents live in small houses scattered around the property but all are expected to come together every morning in the hall. Underneath the hall is the food storage room, laundry area, shower and free op-shop: shelves of free clothes that people may take or add to. Next to the hall is the workshop, used for repairing vehicles and other activities involving tools. Slightly further up the driveway is the honey house, used for storage and preparations of the honey harvested by the community.

My first impression of Wilderland is both of abundance and dilapidation. Ripening avocados drip from the trees along with plentiful citrus. Picturesque views are found in every direction conjuring notions of paradise. We observed a mix of well organised communal gardens and wild weeds amid native plants. Even many of the weeds seemed pleasant – fragrant jasmine, delicious banana passion fruit. No gorse in sight.

Faith gave me a few important instructions including "pee under a tree, poo in the loo". Composting toilets are strategically placed around the main areas of habitation. I noticed that they didn't smell too bad, although in the heat of summer with more people on site they could get a lot worse. Faith gave us the visitor's book to read and sign. This is a legal requirement, the result of council pressure on Wilderland over the past few years. That night Tesla and I snuggled up in the house bus with purple lacy curtains about two minutes' walk down a narrow bush track from the hall. We were fortunate to be able to stay there as the regular resident was away visiting family.

Ironically, I had started this food sovereignty journey with a processed cheese burger, two supermarket trips and a bakery mission on the way here. It was difficult to know what food to bring. I had been told about the no-meat rule in the communal kitchen, so I decided not to bring meat at all and settled for sourdough bread, hummus, butter, jam and regular bread (for Tesla) miso soup sachets, tea bags, rice crackers and raw milk. Faith told me that breakfast and lunch are communal and that dinner is up to people to make their own or choose to cook together. I was a little unclear on the processes involved with communal meals at this point.

On our second day we were late to rise and get organised. We missed the breakfast meeting, although I wasn't very aware of the process as yet. Faith let us know about the missions of the day and we proceeded to weed around the coriander and kohlrabi in the salad gardens near the hall. I helped Faith to identify miners' lettuce from convolvulus. The former is a spinach like green that we grow in our kitchen at home, the latter a noxious inedible weed. I helped cook lunch and then took Tesla and Anna down to the estuary to entertain them, then back up through the main garden. I was aware that the mornings are for working and that I was less able to contribute and participate in this because of my four-year-old. I felt a subtle social pressure and tried to help wherever I could. Lunch included rice, salad, hummus and fried bread. After lunch is free time. I read a bit and played with Tesla, Anna and her sister, Zoe (9).

Tuesday afternoons are reserved for a community meeting. These meetings are conducted in the hall with participants sitting on the couches, benches and arm chairs in a roughly circular pattern. Wilderland uses an 80% consensus model rather than a full consensus model that can often mean very long meetings. New participants and short term visitors are encouraged to just observe the meetings. Many of the decisions are also made by the management committee or the trust at separate meetings.

Some of the main issues arising at this particular meeting included internet use, groceries and money, gardening plans, fundraising. Many of the conflicts seemed to stem around people using too much internet or food (scarcity), or taking other people's food. The latter was particularly an issue a few weeks before when an old timer from Wilderland returned and crossed many boundaries including helping himself to other people's personal food. Personal food is kept in a separate fridge to communal food and is labelled so that when someone leaves other people know to use their left-over food. There was a call at the meeting for grocery tabs to be settled. Some staples at Wilderland are for communal use and participants can also buy luxury items such as nuts and dried fruits at a wholesale price.

At non-work times the hall is used for meals, chatting, making music (usually acoustic guitar and singing) and often juggling. Tesla chatted to Tim, one of the Wwoofers/gardening interns as he juggled, and to Edward, a bee-keeping intern who played guitar while I talked to Russel, a long-term participant, about food politics. The vegetables consumed here are almost all grown here. This time of year, October, is not the best season for fruit; the avocados drip from the trees but won't be ripe for months. On the evening of our second day after hanging out in the hall, we joined a group slug mission and collected hundreds of slugs by torchlight to be fed to the chickens.

We arose on our third day in time for a breakfast of porridge and freshly made granola at the hall. The breakfast meeting encouraged a big group of people to work in Hinahina, the main food garden. We joined in this mission and I spent an hour weeding on my knees before Tesla got bored and I carried her back up the hill to watch a movie with the other girls. I took tools down to the garden and about half an hour later Tesla came back down, escorted by the Wwoofer who was responsible for cooking communal lunch that day. Tesla promptly got bored again so I walked her back up (not carried). On the way she got a cutty-grass cut on her hand which she was terribly embarrassed by. Not wanting to continue going back and forth I stayed in the hall and helped with the cooking and washed dishes for the rest of the morning.

Lunch was flat bread, dahl, kale and silverbeet salad and rice. Simo (a long term participant) and Edward talked about dumpster diving, regaling us with their tales of good scores. Tesla fell asleep on my lap in the hall in the afternoon (not like her). Simo juggled and isolated glass balls then he made the most delicious peppermint slice with wholemeal flour, too much sugar and dark Ghana chocolate. That evening a big group of us watched a documentary on Bob Marley. Tesla sat through the whole thing and enjoyed it. She had a fever and was too tired to contribute a witty quote.

On the morning of our fourth day Tesla was unwell and slept in so I stayed in the house bus with her and took notes, well aware that I was missing breakfast and the breakfast meeting. I experienced some guilt for not being able to participate as much as I would have liked to, although I was aware that it was my own guilt and that the community seemed very understanding and compassionate overall. I contemplated whether the communal guilt was a natural way of passively motivating people. I noted that although I enjoy helping and getting things done I could also quite happily entertain myself if no one else was there to judge. I watched from the house bus as people slowly moved down towards the Hinahina garden.

On our last night Tesla and I star-gazed with Edward and looked at his collection of crystals at the Magnolia house. A small shack without power, presently home to three interns. The only space Edward has here is a small bed. Earlier in the day I talked with Andy, an older intern, originally from New York, who wants to stay here for a year in total (until April) to experience all the seasons and then move on "It's pretty austere living here with no income" he said. He wants to find a way to generate income using some of the skills he has learned here. I also met two new Wwoofers, both Canadian, and we spoke about food sovereignty. One of them has worked for an international child poverty not-for-profit organisation. On request, Troy, one of the long term participants, fire-danced for us with his poi. We sat on the deck outside the hall and watched the flaming orbs twist and twirl.

Tensions and scarcity

Wilderland survives on an annual income of $50,000 and feeds 20-30 people year round. This limited budget is largely dependent on income from money made from markets and the community shop through the sale of honey, as well as jams, chutney, fresh produce and tangelo juice. As finances are tight, various tensions arise over expense priorities including the maintenance of dwellings and purchasing of bulk foods. During the busy summer season the strain on resources means having to turn visitors away. This time of year is important as most of the money for the year is made over summer from markets, store and honey harvest. There is a much higher workload and much more social pressure to contribute. Tensions also arise over work-load and perceptions of other people's level of contribution. While Wwoofers are usually expected to contribute only four hours of their time per day to work activities such as gardening, preserving and cooking, long term residents often work long days, and some willingly contribute more time than others.

I noticed scarcity arising over particular food items – potatoes, for instance – which visitors often cooked up and ate for their non-communal meals, if left accessible. While long term participants would prefer such resources were saved for communal meals for everyone to enjoy, they talked about finding a balance while wanting to ration and not wanting to be too authoritarian. During my early visits, I avoided strain on food resources by bringing in food from outside, as many long-term and short term participants also did. This scarcity over particular resources contrasted sharply with the often overwhelming abundance of seasonal produce, particularly fruit.

'Doing shop' was generally considered by long-termers as a nice quiet break from the chaos of communal activities. Market also provided a break from the physical boundaries of the community. The experience of Wilderland is considered by many of the people I spoke with to be intense: an immersive pressure-cooker for social activity, full of emotional upheaval, excessive ups and downs and a deep sense of connection with people and place. I have experienced this pressure-cooker every time I have visited.

The following section presents two vignettes from long-term Wilderland participants. They are presented here for the purpose of providing themes and threads through people's stories that connect both with the other New Zealand-based food activist stories, values, tensions and intentions, and also with the wider themes of food sovereignty, local food, and food democratisation.

Josh

Josh grew up in a small rural town in New Zealand, before moving to the city to find work. At the time of our interview, Josh had been living at Wilderland for more than three years and was considered to be a long-term participant. At that point there were three other participants who had been living there for longer. The longest had been there five years. Josh had moved to Wilderland after becoming disillusioned with city life. He wanted to live in closer alignment to his social and environmental values around sustainability, self-sufficiency and community support. These values are reflected in his narrative, below.

I came to Wilderland from a place of not wanting to live in the city, wanting to live in a different context, a deeper context. I'm in charge of harvesting loads of different varieties of subtropical fruit: heaps of apples, tangelos and a lot of other citrus, avocados, kiwifruit, tamarillos, persimmons, cherry tomatoes, plums. I'm generally responsible for making sure that the preserving happens, we sell a bit of our fruit, we eat some of it. We have standard products that we make like the tangelo juice. Honey is our main income. I am also generally running the markets on weekends. I also do firewood, labelling and some other stuff. They kind of just came to me, there was a gap that I filled. The longer you stick around at Wilderland the more responsibility comes to you, if you want to do something you just have to wait until everyone else fucks off and then you have to do it. I live here and work here full-time and it's as related as you can get. It's hard to find boundaries between my work here and the rest of my life.

I'm really lucky to be living a life where I don't feel that it compromises my ideals, because I've got pretty high ideals and I look at modern society as being a mess and a bit of a blight on the planet. I'm feeling a little bit outside of it here and I'm doing something that is more solid and makes sense on a historical scale: a modern incarnation of a traditional way of living that sprung up in harmony with the earth. That harmony is pretty broken these days with lots of humans – we've gotten into this expansionist thing of wanting more and more where the rest of the world needs to suffer from it and the lower classes and the rest of the eco-system has to suffer. So that's the idea with sustainability, isn't it? To put things back in balance. We're not there yet, but this is as close as I've seen anyone getting. In the wider scale we are trying to get ourselves out of a financial hole with the eventual goal of becoming less reliant on finances – on the monetary system.

Money is not evil, it's just an exchange system, but the way the world has become greedy for money, with corporate interests becoming more important than people and nature, is a problem. We don't by any means want to pretend that we're separate from the world because we're part of the world, but tribes have been relatively self-reliant for a long time in history. If we're reliant on a system that's destructive, we're not really self-reliant. The biggest tensions that I've seen here have been over fundamental ideas: what do people see Wilderland as? If they clash with other people's higher ideals about Wilderland it can be a problem. Some people see the aim as primarily a professional standard of sustainable living and education. Others see Wilderland as an ongoing experiment in cooperative living and being financially sustainable. It's not as harmonious as a benevolent dictatorship, but it's better because of the participation.

When I got here there was a small group of people: four people and lots of wwoofers and then we built it up to a larger group of core people. We managed to share the load a bit more and improve a bit more and get a bit closer to the vision. A lot of people come here to escape 'the system' and what we've done is replace it with our own system. Is that freedom or not? It's a system we have created, it's a combination of all of our ideas and we have to compromise a bit. We get up and feel obliged to go to meetings and do work and we feel pressure to do it because we need to do these things and restrict ourselves in these ways. It's trust land and we are here because we agree with the objectives of the trust and if we don't live up to those objectives we're out of here. There's a system for everything here: which people are allowed to come and go or stay, which food we eat and which we sell...

We've always had half the wider community looking at us as dirty, smelly hippies, freeloaders, a blight on society: really negatively. Then there are a lot of other people who are really big fans – the Coromandel is full of people who believe in an alternative lifestyle and are very supportive of us. People do recognise us from abroad as a model of community living. We've had groups of students come over to study us. We've had thousands of people through here from all over the world whose lives have been changed. Hopefully what we do here is a model for an alternative to a lot of the negative things that are going on in the world. I would like to think that exchange of goods around the world can be at a level where it doesn't have to destroy the planet. In terms of my values, freedom is really important. There's a responsibility that comes with it which is not getting freedom at a cost to others. Self-reliance. Sharing. Respect. I want to think about the bigger picture and always use that as the guide.

Sometimes I feel like Wilderland is too demanding because the goal of it is to be something so big and powerful that doesn't have room for people to be human, feel at home, feel comfortable and relax. You've got to throw unlimited amounts of energy at it to make it work, but if we want a system that is a model for the world then it's got to be liveable. I like the idea of the four-hour workday (but it's a bit of a fantasy), the communal living thing, hanging out with a whole lot of people but being able to go home if you want to be by yourself. Communal eating is great; we look after our food really well. We eat fantastically here. I enjoy my friends here and extra-curricular things. I like feeling involved to a level where I'm useful, where I can use some percentage of my potential here, and other great things: avocados, climbing trees,...

In terms of the difficult things, sometimes it's just my mental headspace. Wilderland is intense: the ups are intense and the downs are intense, and it's weird that you can feel completely isolated in a community of loving people. It can be frustrating to feel there's an imbalance of things being done; that we have to deal with other people's strong opinions on things rather than feel autonomously the master of your own projects here. But this can be a positive thing, a realistic part of living together and compromising. Understanding that we are doing our best and that there are only good intentions here.

The ideal world, for me, would be made up of smaller scale groups, community. When you get into city-sized organisations of people there's no room for people being heard, so you get hierarchy. Smaller groups can interact with each other. Is utopia achievable? I don't know, but people in groups should have a say and a quality of life and security. Corporations don't really have a benefit for a healthy world. Networking with other communities is important, creating a network, that's the next step, that's way more powerful. Going backwards with technology might not be necessary. I think it's beautiful to advance technologically. Personally I'm not too worried about losing modern technology. The internet's amazing, as a global thing. It's one of the most important things in the world these days. It's had a huge effect on me, especially. In some ways it's still free, not the usage of it, but the information. The internet can be a model of freedom that can be applied to other things, its values or its systems, to see if it works.

How rich are we? We have so much wealth here, it's just not financial wealth. Scarcity makes people insecure, what people choose to do with that feeling makes a difference: you can just worry or you can do something about it. Abundance comes with responsibility; you can choose to waste or you can choose to take advantage of it and make sure it's used and make sure that potential is maximised. A lot of people have abundance in one thing and scarcity in another; they mine the abundance to balance it out – time into work – preserving. It's balancing what you've got with that you want. You always wonder if you're putting in enough energy to get what you're getting – because you're getting an amazing amount, living here.

Faith

Faith grew up in Australia and had worked professionally in community development and education for sustainability before moving to Wilderland. At the time of our interview, Faith had lived in the community for two and a half years and was preparing to leave, travel and live overseas with her partner. Faith's reflections on the ideological tensions she negotiates and the contrast between people's idealised values and the practicalities and difficulties of food production are particularly relevant to the focus of chapter five. These themes are re-addressed as part of the discussion in chapter nine.

I had been working in the sustainability field teaching and had gotten burnt out, so I went travelling. When I arrived in Wilderland I realised that this was where I fit and where my skill-set was valuable. My first impression of this place was of two young children who asked me: "What are you?" – which showed me that these girls were so used to diversity, with people coming from around the world. I also experienced a great friendliness and welcoming.

In the trust deed that was written before Dan passed away it says it's a place for the education of all human beings: children, young people and adults and for transformative learning. What's really needed now is more long-term people, care-taker teams to help with shared learning and retention of information. Meetings can be frustrating. Often people who are only here for a few weeks feel they have a lot to say not knowing that those things have already been said time and time again: "let's get chickens". We have problems with resourcing proper systems for chickens and there are quite strong ethical differences between people in how chickens should be treated. "Let's paint the shop, let's have a café in the shop" well, there's no electricity in the shop. It's like one of those magic eyes that you don't get until you look at it for a while – and then you realise what the lynch pin is.

Wilderland really needs a visitor centre to accommodate students so income is not so dependent on food production and can be based more on education. Sometimes things are just not very realistic. People come with a purist outlook and want everything to be completely sustainable without really realising how much work is involved in producing the nuts, grains and legumes for an average of twenty people onsite all through the year. They don't really appreciate that it's not a model of perfection, in fact it's the very imperfection of Wilderland that makes it such a good opportunity for learning. There are so many challenges, tensions, and this spectrum between the two ends of the polarity: chaos and order. Some people want to turn it into a more ordered place, other people want to make it more chaotic, which has the potential for more learning. Mostly this tension coexists but sometimes there are some conflicts. We don't have a conflict-resolution process and there's a strong tendency towards burnout with the leaders juggling too much.

I'm not fanatical about food but I do think food in societies functions better with a local focus – this dispersion of energy that creates a global culture leaves us all feeling alienated, and it's concerning that these large monopolies of corporations are controlling most of the food supply. I would like to be able to grow everything I eat – or not everything, but be able to trade locally with other people for produce, and look after the soil and the ecosystem. I have a permaculture background. Most of the food in the supermarkets is grown in a monoculture. Wilderland is a catalyst. Organic is good for your health and local is better for the planet. Wilderland tries to go all organic but there are some things (like cooking oil) that we can't afford to buy local or organic so we have to make compromises.

I spent a lot of years working in more conventional structures, making good money, but really the only thing I was interested in was land that remained completely inaccessible to me because I wasn't willing to take on a huge mortgage, so that is why I came to live in a place like Wilderland, so I could have that connection with land. We should have habitat – like animals, and humans shouldn't be enslaved to a bank in order to have habitat – without that, what is the use of money? Some people say life here is austere but I don't live an austere life at all. My life is incredibly abundant. I'm trying to cull my possessions; most of them are second hand or free. I would say it's 'simple' and I love simple. What's the opposite of simple? Complicated. Simple is much better. I have been living in a house that's just one room and it was perfectly adequate.

I think it should be acknowledged that growing one's food, even on a community scale, is a lot of work and I think it's understandable that people opt for the off-the-shelf items that are so readily accessible and much cheaper. People can buy conventional food, organic food or grow your own food. One requires huge amounts of time and energy, one requires a lot of money and so it's no wonder people opt for the conventional. I wonder if we will ever have a system where good food is not just available to people who are privileged in some way. We've pretty-much, as a culture, lost those skills. Our grandparents' generation knew not just how to grow the food, but how to preserve it and cook it. We have such an evolving culture and I used to try to think of some way to direct it, but now I'm just letting go. But I value the fact that I can live in the manner in which I choose to live. Wilderland opens doors and shows people there are options. A lot of young people feel there is no choice but to fit into the conventions we've developed as a culture.

Reflections

I was very aware on my first visit to Wilderland of the importance of participation in work and of my own limitations in doing so because of Tesla. Although I did not receive any direct or indirect pressure to help more, I felt influenced by the knowledge that other people were working, and by the culture of hard work that keeps this community functioning. Parenting in this community is challenging and there is little extra capacity to care for older people or people struggling with disabling injury or other disability.

The tensions that arose during these visits seemed to centre on the scarcity of things such as internet, coffee and bulk goods. These too are echoed above by Faith and Josh. During my early visits, tensions still lingered over a recent participant who had taken other people's food. These were all openly discussed during the meetings. Overall communication and kinship seemed to be very strong, with people seeming to genuinely enjoy each other's company for the most part. I did notice a few personality clashes that mostly came up in conversations when the third party was not there. I experienced a sense of belonging, even when we only visited for a short time. This began with the 'welcome home' sign, visible on arrival. I also found people very open, for the most part, and willing to talk. Many participants seemed to have strong political and social convictions similar to those articulated by Faith and Josh. These became obvious through conversations.

Many of the strands or values, tension and practices, and of negotiating paradox presented in this chapter are carried through the following chapters which focus on the local food providers in the township of Whaingaroa. They are also more specifically woven in to Chapter Nine, the discussion chapter.

7 VALUES AND ONTOLOGIES OF CONNECTION

A thing is right when it tends to preserve the integrity, stability, and beauty of the biotic community. It is wrong when it tends otherwise (Leopold 1949, 239).

I posit that by developing a deeper, philosophical, understanding of self and humanity through 'noticing' values and actions people can contribute to a discourse of 'hope' and the realisation of universal flourishing. Without a developed consciousness to the ways that people are with each other and with Earth, the dominant order is likely to prevail (Casey-Cox 2014, 39–40).

The values expressed by Leopold and Casey-Cox in the quotes above also resonate with the values of the participants. This chapter focusses on a variety of these values, largely expressed in relation to food ethics. These values can also be seen to relate to other aspects of life including areas of community, economy and ecology. Connectedness is key here, and Rose's argument that food sovereignty is based on an ontology of connectedness is repeatedly relevant, as is Capra and Luisi's (2014) complex systems theory.

This chapter begins with an exploration of indigenous values that are referred to in interviews. It then goes on to focus on the way that local food producers value each other. The subsequent sections go into more detail about specific personal and community food ethics, local and organic food, food waste, and finally through a discussion on the importance placed on connectedness and 'real' food. The following conversation took place at a permaculture potluck in April, 2014:

Robz: Not many people go to the community gardens around here.
Me: What would you like to see happen with community gardens?
Robz: Food, food everywhere. Free food, food without ownership. Food for people to eat.
Bill: It was provided to us for free by Mother Nature so it seems strange that we would put a price on it.
Robz: For me its localisation, knowing your neighbours and every neighbourhood's got its own garden.
Jodi: People need to be encouraged to grow and make produce and then we can get it local.
Then came a discussion about the possibility of a local food shop and farmer's market:
Liz: I think its coming, it was a maybe, just an idea a few years ago but the sale [of a building] has gone through. [The property owner will] be funding it but someone else will figure out how it will work, it will take lots of money to make it happen. He's the money-making man but these things don't happen without lots of money.
Dan: Do you think he'll charge good rates for the stall-holders?
Liz: Well, that's the big question!
Dan: I'd like to see every supermarket with a section for local produce.

Embedded in this conversation are many strong interconnected values shared by the community. When Bill mentions food being provided 'free' by 'Mother Nature' it can be seen as an example of resistance to commodification, along with Robz's ideas about producing an abundance of public food. This is contrasted with Dan's desire for supermarkets to include more local food, and the large sums of money required to set up the local food shop mentioned by Liz.

These ethical values do not necessarily stand in opposition to each other, they highlight some of the complex tensions between idealised values and practical realities. The word 'local' has strong positive connotations here, yet, like other values, it is not immune from critique. 'Organic' also generally means something good to many people who express values around 'ethical' and 'healthy' food.

Although, among local food producers there is an understanding and sometimes an experience, that obtaining organic certification can be difficult and costly. It is often not considered necessary in a local-food context, where knowing and trusting the food producers is considered both possible and desirable (Ackerman-Leist 2012).

Personally focussed food values tend to focus on promoting the health of the individual and their family, although this can be extended to wider notions of community, and to humanity in general. Privilege is often associated with the capacity to choose to buy more expensive 'ethical' foods which may contain fewer pesticide residue such as organic produce.

In exploring these values during my fieldwork I noticed three core themes: personal, environmental and social. As these are often intersecting and interrelated I mapped them using a Venn diagram in Figure 25.

Figure 25: My reflective Venn Diagram of food ethics, 2013.

Many local food providers have deliberately based their lifestyles around finding ways to access and produce organic food in a way that does not fit with conventional notions of privilege. There is also often a sense of social responsibility, an idea that the state of the globalised corporate world is so bad, that choosing better options and contributing to less destructive labour, animal welfare and environmental practices in agriculture becomes an obligation. This may also serve to ease some guilt around relative privilege. In this way, personally focussed food ethics intersect with the social and environmental, although people's priorities may be centred in one area in particular.

Leopold's land ethic (1949) critiqued traditional Western ethical frameworks that stem from the individual and are projected outwards. He proposed a framework that holistically includes the whole biotic community. This ethical structure is more in alignment with understandings of the interconnectedness of ecosystems. It resonates with the values expressed by Liz and Rick with their ecology backgrounds, and also with many of the other key participants. Indigenous Māori values[1] like whakapapa [ancestry and inter and intra-generational connectedness] and kaitiakitanga [guardianship, stewardship], expressed by The Bro and Kaiwaka, are similarly holistic and inclusive of the whole ecosystem alongside spiritual and social values.

Indigenous connectedness

Scholars such as Wittman et al (2010), and Holt-Gimenez and Patel (2009) emphasise that the framework of food sovereignty strongly supports indigenous perspectives and values. It is difficult to talk about 'indigenous' as if it is a homogenous group – although these scholars tend to emphasise, in general, the more traditional indigenous approaches to food production, in comparison with the approaches of globalising corporate capitalism. Shiva (2012) asserts that indigenous perspectives tend to be formed and informed through observation of and interaction with the ecosystems in which they evolve. She argues that intricate and diverse indigenous knowledge systems are being colonised by the intellectual monoculture of Western science, which undermines and invalidates them. This can be seen as another stage in colonisation which is ongoing and embroils us all (Shiva 2012). Both Māori and Pākehā [non-indigenous] participants were critical of dominant knowledge perspectives, especially those seen to be supported by, or supporting corporate capitalist agendas. This section presents some indigenous perspectives that may relate to food sovereignty, especially in New Zealand.

The first thing to note, when discussing indigenous people in New Zealand, is that Māori are not, and have never been a homogenous group. When the term 'Māori' is used here, it is in the broadest sense, to imply things that relate to or fit within the very general category which was invented with the beginnings of colonisation. Differences between iwi [tribes] did emerge briefly in the course of this research. As The Bro notes, 'There are quite some radical differences' between his iwi, Tuhoe, and many others. These include differences in creation stories and cultural practices. He describes his central values as follows:

It's an interesting thing, eh? I've a whole list of values, but some of them can be conflicting. For example, the value of hosting, but also being hosted, and being a good guest. I've struggled with this in the past, especially when I had more rules, like I don't eat meat, or inorganic, or whatever. You start spending time on the marae [Māori community centre] and there's this value of manākitanga [hospitality, generosity, care and respect]. And it conflicts with my ideas about how I would feed people and what. So these values come up against each other and you have to make judgments and trade-offs all the time. So now I eat whatever's put in front of me because it's an expression of manākitanga, not necessarily what I would eat at home, but it's macaroni cheese with sow-crate pork [not free-range], but as a good guest I'd observe manākitanga. Kaitiakitanga [guardianship]. Probably whakapapa [ancestry] is the most important concept or value behind my approach to food. These days whakapapa has been dumbed down to this simple notion of it's who your parents and great-grandparents are. But I reckon whakapapa is actually a more fuller concept about the journey of all things through time and space. All things have whakapapa. A rock has whakapapa, snow has whakapapa, stars. But yeah whakapapa, and whanaungatanga [relatedness], would be the two most important values. And the two go hand in hand, you know, it's almost hard to tell the differences, like having a relationship and that requires knowing whakapapa. So these days I'm not so precious about what I put in my mouth. I'm relatively comfortable eating the sow-crate pork and macaroni and cheese on the marae [Māori community centre] because I know what is involved in making sow-crate pork. Even though its horrifying, I know what I'm eating, what I'm putting into my body, the sacrifices or compromises that have been made, what's going into it. Whakapapa: I'm always trying to understand the full nature of where things have come from, how they were produced. And naturally that lends itself to eating locally.

The Bro's strong emphasis on whakapapa, relatedness and relationships resonates with the ontology of connectedness described by Rose (2013), and the complex systems theory of Capra and Luisi, (2014). In describing his own personal ethics around food, the Bro expressed that traditional and ethical values sometimes contradict each other in practice.

Food sovereignty is also said to both value and support the contributions of indigenous people (Wittman et al 2010; Hutchings et al 2013). This can be seen in the work of Te Waka Kai Ora and in that of their local Whaingaroa member, Kaiwaka, who is both a valued member of the community and also supports the work of other local food producers. The values he describes are also reflected in Te Waka Kai Ora, as he describes:

This is what we're made of eh? The whakapapa [ancestry, connectedness] of your kai, the wairua [spirit] of the soil and the whenua [ground], the mana [integrity, prestige] and the mātauranga [understanding] of the people, and te āo turoa, [the natural sciences] in the garden, how things grow, how they perpetuate, and the mauri is the essence of life... and by practicing all this you give rise to pure projects. To join Te Waka Kai Ora you have to know your whakapapa, know where you stand in your tribe and you have to get up and speak for your tribe. We believe that when we are born we are born with two umbilical cords. One is cut from mum but the other umbilical cord goes straight to the Atua [God(s)] and you don't have to cut it, or know that it's there – but all you have to do is touch it and the touch comes into you and that touch is when we are playing with the soil. That's when we're connecting with the Atua, and we're putting something lovely back in there, so he doesn't want it to die, he wants the world to flourish with all that.

These indigenous values were not only reflected by the Māori participants, but also to varying degrees by Pākehā participants, many of whom shared a reverence for indigenous ways of doing things, as Liz reflects: "Māori systems are amazing because they distil values and principles into proverbs and a lot of them are environmental, they're metaphors, like about a bird in a forest but they're actually about people." The mana that Liz and Rick have within the community is evident in the way other people talk about them, as The Bro states:

They've got really solid ecological principles as well. They just have a much more practical understanding of this permaculture and sustainability thing: actually listening to the land, and being able to give it what it needs you to know. There's nothing more spiritual than having dirt under your finger-nails. Or knowing the name of the pig that I'm eating right now, and I know the name of his parents and I weeded the field that fed this meat. I can tell you of the plants that grew in that field that turned into this bacon. That's spiritual.

Both Liz and Rick are particularly positive about their experience with Māori governance structures in comparison with more Western oriented organisations, as Rick explains:

Lizzie and I sometimes will take a project to our community board and they'll say 'It's too expensive, why do you want our money for this?' It's quite negative and they're restrictive in time and they've got a structure with the chairperson at the top and he's not supporting it. Whereas you go to the marae committee and there's total respect for your space, they let you talk about it, they listen, they've thought about it. There might not be an instant decision, there might be multiple visits, but it's honourable and it's a really good system. It's really different from the one that's in our business world and other government structures.

Indigenous values also shape and inform food production practices, especially for Kaiwhenua Organics who are committed to tikanga Māori, as Kaiwaka explains:

We grow by the cycle of the moon. On the new moon we're starting to grow all the food that grows above the ground, when the moon's coming up. That's Rongo Mā Tane[2]. When the moon's waning, dropping down, that's when you grow all the food that's under the ground – that's Haumia Tikitiki[3]. So that's when it's dropping down to darkness, giving all the food under the ground kai [food], then when it hits the bottom it's time to give all the food above the ground sustenance. Then the sun comes and makes it grow even more – so they all work in synchronization together – just waking up in the morning and watching the dawn. That's one of the things people miss these days: just getting up early in the morning and looking at the sky – with what's up there, the clouds, what's up there today? My grandfather used to do that all the time.

These ontologies of connectedness, including recognition of and respect for Atua [Gods], can be seen to relate to different aspects of life, and are particularly tied into food ethics. The following section explores some of these ethics in more detail.

Valuing each-other

Food sovereignty reflects the valuing of local food producers. While it may be in the interests of the local food producers I interviewed to be personally valued, it is also evident that they value each other, and local food in general, to the point where competition is actively avoided. Jenny describes the lengths she went to in order to avoid being in competition:

In setting it up, I didn't want any competition with anyone. I didn't want any conflict so I looked at the bakeries and they don't do sourdough bread, and I had a talk to Bronwyn at the Herbal Dispensary and gave her a couple of samples but she was quite happy to keep supplying the Hamilton bread and because I was starting in such a small way, in small numbers that I wasn't really a threat. All the bakeries were happy about it.

These perspectives also reflect Rose's (2013) analysis of the ontology of connectedness as integral to the food sovereignty movement:

Just as alienation forms part of the capitalist rationality in an ontological sense, it is connectedness which lies at the core of the food sovereignty ratio- nality, which is aimed at healing the ecological and social rifts. In its prac- tical manifestations to date, I regard food sovereignty as constituted by three foundational 'pillars', namely: redistributive agrarian reform, agro-ecological methods of production, and (re)localised and democratised food systems. Each in its own way contributes to the healing of the ecological and social rifts; and integrated as a whole they express the ontology of connectedness. (Rose 2013, 11–12).

The food values presented in this chapter is informed and motivated by resistance to corporate alienation and exploitation, as well as by a deep sense of connection. Personal and political values are influenced by multiple factors in this community which can be defined by shared ideological strands. These values seem to be influenced by the tensions covered in the previous chapter. These combine with, and sometimes contradict personal, familial and other cultural values. Caring for people and the environment is central to people's values, as are notions of human freedom, responsibility and respect. The ontology of connectedness reflected by participants seems to be informed by observations of ecosystems, indigenous knowledge systems and intuition. The understanding of human beings as part of ecosystems, rather than separate from nature, is key here, as is the agroecology concept of basing agriculture on ecosystems. This is most visible in the prevalence of the 'permaculture' term and its practice within the community.

Notes of connectedness and creativity are evident in the narratives and are contrasted with opposition to the violent exploitation and disconnection of the corporate capitalist system, as Kaiwaka illustrates here:

As people we just have to come together and live together and fight the battles together – not apart. Hey, Māori and Pākehā own New Zealand. But at the moment corporates do and by the time they give it back to us we'll have nothing, eh? And we'll have to start again, get rid of everything that is here, clean the land of all the poison and start again and be pure again and then never go back there again. Learn from it!

Kaiwaka's notion of ownership, expressed above, goes beyond the Western concept of private property and includes values of kaitiakitanga [guardianship, stewardship], and the responsibility for cleaning up pollution. In this context his imagination is focussed on envisioning and moving toward sustainability and health. Along similar lines, permaculture principles can be extended to the way society and culture are interpreted, as Liz explains:

We look at society like an ecosystem – a reminder that social manifestation is a beautiful thing and is unique. Culture is the blossoming of a set of social interactions in any one place. With nature there is no wrong or right. When we're observing in our community we have to look at things we can see as well as things we can't see.

This perspective of society as both "like an ecosystem" and as part of wider ecosystems, interconnected with the environment: the soil, air, water, plants and other living things has been a recurring theme throughout this fieldwork. This ontology is also consistent with Shiva's (2012) conception of indigenous knowledge and food systems as complex, interconnected and diverse. These knowledge systems can sometimes clash with the dominant Western sense of environmental protectionism adopted by government departments, as Rick reflects in the quote also presented in Chapter Four:

I was working for the wildlife service, specialized in endangered species, so designing reserve systems and realising the need to be holistic in the management. Everyone was focused on predator control, but I've seen examples especially in the Pacific where bio-abundance is actually an alternative to predator control. If there is heaps of food and no competition then animals can coexist. I was given an opportunity in '85–'87 with another guy who was interested in permaculture to write a management plan for a reserve in the King Country so we tried to integrate some permaculture ideas, particularly designing a system of young and modified forest with plantings of exotic trees with things like plum and apple and the wildlife service in those days thought that was outrageous, planting exotics in the nature reserve. I had a little bit of a frustration that many of the projects which I worked on at that time were really focused on recovery of the individual, the ambulance at the bottom of the cliff.

Rick also ran into trouble with his support for getting indigenous bird populations up to a harvestable level. This clashed with the conservationist perspective of 'fencing off nature'. As Rick points out, harvestable levels of indigenous species are actually higher than conservation level.

Personal food – community food

We are the food we eat, the water we drink, the air we breathe. And reclaiming democratic control over our food and water and our ecological survival is the necessary project for our freedom (Shiva 2005, 5).

As described in the previous section, and in the quote above, food ethics tend to relate to various kinds of personal, social and environmental concerns. All these concerns are connected with resistance to corporate exploitation and moving towards better, fairer, healthier and more sustainable alternatives. On a personal level, there is both an emphasis on 'good' food which is 'nutrient dense', fresh and nutritionally complex, as well as a resistance to things such as pesticides and processed foods which are often considered to be detrimental to health. Social concerns are often around exploitation and human rights, due to recognition that many of the world's commodities, including food, are produced by people in varying levels of unacceptable labour exploitation. To try to avoid this exploitation and promote more just working conditions, effort is put into deliberately purchasing fair-trade imported products where possible. Environmental concerns are largely enacted through minimising 'food miles' by consuming food produced closer to home, supporting known sustainable food producers and limiting waste and packaging as much as possible. Animal welfare is also a major factor in contemporary food ethics and labels like *free-range* and *cruelty free* are becoming increasingly popular (Mason and Singer 2006; Curry 2011). The focus here is also on minimising unnecessary suffering, a value which has also been reflected in some of the interviews.

These ethics have largely been informed through critical engagement with available information about food systems, through books, articles and documentaries around food and through conversations. Justin has also found that being involved in Conscious Consumers[4] "actually makes it a bit easier to become aware of what we can do to make things more sustainable." This has influenced the packaging they try to use for takeaway products, which is predominantly biodegradable. They recycle as much as possible with Xtreme Waste and try to encourage people to use recyclable coffee cups. Their interest in sustainability also extends to sourcing 'sustainable fish' from a list published by Forest and Bird. These efforts come with financial challenges as well:

Being a café, price points our markets quite low. We're not a restaurant and sustainable fish tends to be higher end so it makes it less affordable, like free range bacon... blue cod is really expensive [to buy in], snapper's not sustainable – so it's trying to find the balance. I get confused 'cause there's a couple of lists floating around and some of them contradict each other, so I just go with what Conscious Consumer says on their list which is the Forest and Bird one. I've got my suppliers working on that.

Relying on the expertise of an organisation like Conscious Consumers means that Justin can avoid being overwhelmed by too much information, and can focus on running the business. This organisation is establishing itself as a sanctioned conveyer of trust as organic certification can be, as described by Ackerman-Leist (2012). This is one way of resolving some of the tensions that arise from feeling overloaded with information and not having the time or specific expertise to navigate it.

Mike has found that, as a local food provider, his interactions with customers has influenced his perceptions on ethics and increased his understandings of what things are important to people:

One of the good things about dealing directly with the public, which not all farmers do, is it keeps you in touch with what's important to the consumers – animal welfare and the environment and the integrity of the product. We don't want residue drug or pesticides in our milk, we want to be sustainable. People and animals have been treated fairly along that path.

In this process, ethics are continuously being enacted and also developed in relation to new information and practical realities.

Personal life values interact with environmental, social and economic values. When I asked interview participants about their values some talked primarily about food, the community or the environment and others talked about more abstract virtues. One of Jon's core values is 'do no harm':

Only take what I need. I feel I've grown to learn that I don't need to like what everybody does as long as I can accept that they're free to do it if they choose to. There's a difference between acceptance and liking and I don't think it's necessarily possible to like everybody or everything they do but I acknowledge their right to do so as long as they're not harming. Use as little resources as I can to a reasonable point where I'm not stressing myself out or limiting what I can do in the community. It's a bit of a balance that we all trip over quite dramatically in our teens if we really care about the world. And just looking for opportunities to do things differently and encourage others. They can do whatever they want; they just have to find creative ways to do it.

This process of separating one's values from judgements of other people is something that Jon ascribes to emotional maturity. While Jon continues to enact his values in the work he does at WOK, and in the wider community, the space he has created has facilitated more connectedness between different people in the community:

Even more than I hoped – chance meetings at WOK of two people doing their own shopping and it's really lovely to see a relationship blooming all of a sudden and people realising that they have something really strongly in common that they didn't realise and sharing, exchanging details and just walking off with a big smile on their face. That just makes my day. Community links, it's massively about that too, also it's a community network, email-wise. I have 85 people on my mailing list. Also, more and more I'm realising it can be a really good template for people achieving – accessing organic food more cheaply so I'm going to see what I can do to spread this around.

This development and proliferation of 'healthy', functional local food systems is a key part of rebuilding local food systems (Ackerman-Leist 2012).

Some food ethics are played out in the form of boycotts. Among the local food providers of Whaingaroa these can take the form of the specific avoidance of particular foods for particular reasons as in the case of Cally deciding to stop buying quinoa:

I try not to think about it really the whole ridiculous thing of food flying round the world sometimes going somewhere and getting processed and sent back here. You know the whole thing to me is just absurd and has to stop. I hate what it does to people, I'm not gonna buy quinoa anymore when I've run out. The fashionableness of quinoa has now meant that the people who live there can't afford to buy it – they just grow it and sell it. In South America, I forget where exactly, 'cause it's all fashionable and so good for you the price has gone up so much that they can't afford to have it for themselves and so their diets are degenerating cause they're using other things.

Similarly, Mike and Mady boycott products with palm oil, and avoid using it on their farm as supplementary cattle-feed, 'because of its impact on the rainforest'. Mike also avoids purchasing herbicides and heavy antibiotic use and would do so even without organic certification as a factor. These, along with anything containing GM ingredients, he describes as 'the no-go zones for us'.

For people who run food-related businesses, enacting their own food ethics has the added challenge of balancing profitability and good business sense with what foods are in season. As Justin points out, the current movement towards free-range and sustainable and local farming practices has developed from older, re-industrialised, farming practices, "but then it's newly really popular among people who can afford it 'cause it is a thing of being able especially somewhere like New Zealand where we don't have those established old communities". Free-range farming is intended to provide a better quality of life for animals as they are given more outside space rather than being confined in small cages as in intensive farming methods

(Singer and Mason 2006). Although this is also commonly believed to produce healthier and more superior animal products, it is a point where the ethics of valuing animal welfare and human health cross over. For Justin and Alex, in their home as well as in sourcing ingredients for their cafe, this is an important issue and one that must be negotiated in line with the practical economics of running a business:

I absolutely feel that [free-range] is very important, it's a 'catch 22', I wanna do free range but it doesn't balance out, 'cause the cost of say free-range bacon, if I was to pass that on to the customer I wouldn't sell any bacon – it's one of those things that we're working on.

'Free range' appeals to him because of his concerns for animal welfare and also because his experiences with free-range eggs have shown Justin that they are of superior quality: "Lovely and yellow, they've got a nice flavour to them and they hold together, they're nicer to cook with, they're not watery and pale or pasty, so it's a better product."

The Café that Justin and Alex run is part of Conscious Consumers, which provides badges to member cafés and restaurants that meet specific standards for practices that are considered more 'conscious' or ethical. The badges are awarded in three categories: Community, including 'local' and 'generosity' (donating excess to charity), Smart Waste, including BYO containers, recycling, eco-packaging, composting, eco-cleaners, and Ethical Products, including free-range, fairtrade, sustainable seafood, vege/vegan, and organic. Justin explains how he got involved in Conscious Consumers:

I was running a group of cafes in Hamilton for about a year and a half and they approached us there and said 'would you like to be Hamilton's first café's in the area under Conscious Consumer's?' We sort of started the ball rolling then and then when I moved out here I just thought, well – I quite like what they are doing and they were going through a lot of changes at that stage as well, they were changing the badges I think and the requirements to meet the badges, and it's taken a long time, it's been two years and we're still not quite where we wanna be, but it's not as easy as ticking a box.

Justin says the Conscious Consumers programme appeals to him because it reflects the way he and Alex live at home and their values. It provides an incentive to learn more about different areas, for example, more sustainable fish, and also generates some public interest and awareness over food ethics.

Just as the food sovereignty literature emphasises that people should have the right to safe, healthy and appropriate food (Wittman et al 2010), so too is this reflected in the voices of food providers in Whaingaroa, as Liz describes here:

For me, I believe people should have the right to quality healthy food. We shouldn't eat food with dangerous chemicals in it, and if we can't and then the only way is to have our own food production systems then so be it. But it's also crazy to drag food thousands of miles around and using refrigeration to give it a long shelf life, but we should be eating more seasonal local healthy food, enjoying the seasonality of local food. It's better for us, our bodies are designed to do that. We should pig out on one thing, like avocados, and then move on to something else. It makes you more attuned to your environment, gives you that feeling that you are more a part of a biological system, whereas with supermarket purchasing you're not, you can just get whatever you want. There are no seasons.

This strong focus on the local also reflects the values of the food sovereignty movement (Wittman et al 2010; Rose 2013). The concept of a 'right to food' is interesting because it transcends, or contradicts individualist values and neoliberal assumptions that human beings are essentially selfish (Graeber 2001). Robz also echoes this sentiment of rights which he perceives as conflicting with the dominant economic system:

Everyone should have the right to be warm and dry and fed no matter what they do or don't do for a job, just basic rights which we don't really have, we're kinda borderline, we're pretty much there doing it without money but we're kind of always battling the system in a way. Even though it's so simple, it's so complicated to do as well because you're always battling the economy I guess.

Wayne extends the right beyond people, to all living things. He sees working towards food sovereignty as a gradual process in which places like Whaingaroa are leading the way. These examples demonstrate that the concept of the 'right to food', which is part of food sovereignty ideology, is strongly reflected in the community of food producers in Whaingaroa.

Local over organic

At its best, an appreciation of beauty can inspire a sense of belonging. 'Rootedness'… where we have to wait a season for vegetables, years for fruits, and decades for nuts and timber. We can become local in our long and patient waiting… [A unique cultural dish can be replicated but] diminishes in authenticity with every mile it travels beyond a given boundary. These local specialities convince us that local foods are therapy for our culture's chronic transience (Ackerman-Leist 2012, 8).

Although the local food providers of Whaingaroa generally support the concept of 'organic food' they are also critical of the 'organic' label, especially with regards to highly processed and industrially produced organics. These are often transported vast distances, accruing many food miles. Organic certification is seen as a costly and time consuming process which is particularly difficult for small-scale producers. Certification can also be seen as a way of out-sourcing trust, as Ackerman-Leist puts it, certification institutions become "sanctioned brokers of trust" (2012, 13). Participants are critical of this disconnection. While they seek to avoid using synthetic pesticides or consuming food which has been exposed to these, they would rather support local producers, with whom they can establish trust-based relationships. There appears to be an understanding here that the notion of 'organic' is more about what *isn't* in the food. It does not particularly account for nutrient density or sustainable land use. It serves as a place-holder for trust in a food-system of multiple disconnections, a sentiment that is shared by Ackerman-Leist (2012). Liz and

Rick went through a process of getting organic certification for their small farm some years before. In their experience, the process was time consuming and did not seem to add value to the food they produced and sold within the local community, where trust was already established. They let the certification lapse, while continuing to farm using organic methods, and did not experience any loss of value for their products.

Mike has first-hand experience of the trials and tribulations involved in organic certification, and also knows other farmers on either side of the certification situation. He describes another local organic farmer who cannot feed his pigs food scraps if he wants to stay certified "so he can't make any money on them because he has to buy in feed." Another local farmer who is not certified can buy in "cheese that's gone wrong from Fonterra really cheap as feed for his pigs." Mike had been certified organic for twelve years at the time of the interview. As mentioned in Chapter Four, he and Mady were in the process of reviewing whether they wanted to stay certified.

We can still follow the driving principles without being certified and it will probably make our life a lot easier. The paper trails and the loops you've got to go through are just pretty demanding. The actual auditing itself is seventeen hundred and fifty dollars but we use compost that's 30 or 40 dollars a tonne dearer than the same product that's not certified, and when you're using two or three hundred tonnes of that a year it erodes the premium we get. If we make a new fence it can't be in tanalised timber so you've got to use more expensive options. All those things are adding up. I probably spend an extra two or three weeks a year in the office – that's not where farmers want to spend their time. There's a lot of compliance anyway but with organics and auditing you have to have a paper trail for everything – everything – and some of the rules are getting silly: if we have to dust with a bit of magnesium to top up the levels, and that's typical for New Zealand pasture in the spring, because the rules are made in the States we can put magnesium on their feed but not on their grass. Now in New Zealand grass is feed. We get by because we're feeding hay or silage in the spring and we put it on that, but it mustn't go on the grass.

Mike and Mady had gotten just through a recent drought by drying off [halting milking] their cattle early. Mike says the organic principles and deep-rooting pastures used on the farm have helped them through the drought, although it was easier for the farmers who did buy in feed like palm kernel. Mike says while he and Mady would not have bought palm kernel, he could have bought uncertified silage from neighbours, but to stay certified he would have had to buy it from Hawkes Bay or the South Island, an unjustifiable expense in a season when most cows are not being milked. As Mike says: "We're just up against rules that are getting hard to live with."

Ironically, one of the reasons for potentially choosing to let their certification lapse is that the rules around organic certification are beginning to "cross that animal welfare line. We can treat cows, but then you have to get them out of the system." This means slaughtering cows that might otherwise live longer lives once they have recovered from illness. Another reason Mike states, that organic certification can interfere with animal welfare, is that farmers are slow to buy feed during droughts, "even when they should have". For Mike, integrity is important, "probably more important than whether you're certified organic."

Even for those not directly involved in the difficult processes and rules around getting certified, organic is not necessarily the answer. As Jon states:

Really organic food isn't the answer either. I think the only solution is small, localised everything[5]. I can't see that any other way is sustainable in the populations of however many billion people we've got on the planet now. I think we need to do everything on the local scale as much as possible and only the bare essentials should be sent anything more than say 80km.

For many people interested in eating safe, nutritious, ethical food, an absence of pesticide use and caring for land is more important than certification, as is the local factor. Sometimes these values compete and become confusing, as Cally describes:

Food needs to be good for you and so the organic, or in my case, not so much organic it's just not non-organic, you know, it's not sprayed. I don't think that's good for people. Over the last 10 years, more and more, I've become aware of the food miles stuff and all of that and also fairtrade. The three things for me are organic, fairtrade and local... oh and seasonal which goes with local I guess.... Sometimes I'm a bit torn about what to buy when I'm buying things 'cause they don't always match up. I don't usually buy any fruit or vegetables that are grown outside New Zealand, other than bananas because I'm addicted to bananas... preferably the closer to where I live the better. When I buy bananas, I buy the fairtrade ones if I can get them. If it can be grown in New Zealand, or if it can be grown in Whaingaroa then I'll buy that or if it can be grown in Waikato you know it's just as close as possible without being totally neurotic about it.

Here Cally describes some of the compromises and contradictions she faces in negotiating her 'local' food values. Although the distance that food travels is often taken into account when it comes to 'local food', it is a much more complex topic than just food-miles. Ackerman-Leist (2012) explores the intricacies of the local food concept:

Local is not just about a circumference from where you live or a town boundary or 'food miles'. It isn't an arbitrary stretch of land or geography. 'Local food' is one of the top environmental and social issues of our time... it could be that we've come to the realisation that food, human health, landscape and local economies are the common interests that we all share and recognise on a daily basis. Perhaps it is because the costs of our current food systems are manifesting themselves in our physical well-being, the patterns of our daily lives, and the ecological integrity of our planet, all in ways that we can no longer ignore..." (Ackerman-Leist 2012, 3.)

This conceptualisation of 'local' as not entirely based on physical proximity, but as interconnected with ecosystems, economics and the relationships of the people involved resonates particularly in Whaingaroa. For example, Jenny says that she would like to eat more organic food but it is not affordable on a limited budget.

A lot of the organic food is more expensive and that reflects all the work that's gone into it but it's just not affordable. I'm not a foodie at all. I just eat when I'm hungry. I think what I would like would be more facilities to grow my own food at home: more fruit trees, bigger garden, beehives. It's important to eat locally and support the local growers. Even though technically I'm very poor I prefer to buy some local produce and ethical produce and I'm prepared to go without on some things as long as I'm buying proper food.

This inaccessibility of 'organic' food can alienate people from holding it as a central value. There is a sentiment expressed by participants here that actually 'organic' was just normal food one or two generations before, but that the combination of cheap industrially processed foods grown with synthetic fertilisers and pesticides – as well as the 'middle-class' marketing of 'organics' and the expense involved in certification are all contributing to this problem of 'organic' food not being accessible for many people. As well as this, supposedly 'organic' food produced using intensive farming methods, where the soil is not cared for, is considered to be less nutrient dense, less ecologically responsible, less delicious, and more expensive.

While the price issue of 'organic' food acts as an incentive for some participants to produce more of their own food, it also combines with other values and resistance to corporate alienation to prioritise the local. Wayne says he would "rather keep it more local." As someone with many years of experience with organic food production he is aware that it can be a lot more labour intensive and less productive, but he is critical of pesticides:

There's a lot of hungry people in the world and organics can be a lot more labour intensive and less productive so if we were to suddenly just stop using chemicals and switch to organic farming methods then production potentially could take quite a decline – food prices would go up and get more out of reach for people in more lower income houses. So there is a balance there, but also you have to be mindful of the overall picture, that what we're doing is poisoning the planet. So we have to take some initiative today to have a future for everyone tomorrow.

He would like to see more people choosing to support local food producers to keep the profit within the town to stop it going off-shore. He also sees local food systems as interconnected with trust and accountability: "If the individual producer has some values they will take pride in what they're doing and not try to cheat others. There's more accountability when you know the people."

The Bro says he had avoided drinking milk for years, "Half the reason why I wanted to start drinking milk again is so that I could talk to dairy farmers, so I could go to the farm gate, buy milk and you get to talk to people." He sees only a slight benefit from drinking conventional organic milk, produced by corporate bodies, in that there are reduced pesticide residues, however: "you're still supporting a big corporate monster whose aim is to extract as much milk from the land as possible using whatever means necessary." Organic certification is not high on his list of priorities:

I could buy organic olive oil that is all certified etc, that comes from Italy. Or I could buy Village Press which comes from Hawkes Bay. And sure they use a few pesticides, it's not organic, a few chemicals here and there, but I can get in my car and I can drive to Village Press and I can talk to the guy who grows it and I can say, 'I like organic food and do you need to use those chemicals? There are alternatives'. I've done that. But I can drive there and see. Who knows what they're doing on those groves in Italy? They could be using propane torches for all I know. But I know the guy who owns Village Press, he's a nice guy, you know, he's got a family.

This emphasis on relationships is similar to that reflected by Acker-man-Leist (2012), as is the tension of local food miles not necessarily being more efficient. The additional driving for food may actually use more energy than bulk transportation in some situations. Ackerman-Leist (2012) specifies that local food is not just about existing relation-ships, and that one of the most compelling reasons to engage in it is that it requires the brokering of new relationships which can help to build local economies as well as foster healthy ecology: "We are consciously making the choice to build new economic relationships, rekindle traditional ways of doing business, support those in need, and even invent new technology-based social networks that can, rather ironically, link neighbours" (Ackerman-Leist 2012, 10).

The Bro described a local small-scale permaculture grower in the 1980s who used to sell his produce through the local supermarket. The management refused to put the organic label on it because, at that time, it was undesirable. However, "now you call something organic, you can charge premium for it and people come running, and no one trusts conventional food either. I don't trust organic food either myself, I only trust food where I've looked the grower in the eye." These relationships and the trust and accountability involved in local food systems relates to the ontology of connectedness, described by Rose (2013).

The centrality of relationships and connectedness when it comes to local food are also reflected by Ackerman-Leist (2012) when he describes the local food discussion at its best as an "expression of caring" (5). This caring can relate to human beings and communities as well as identity, economics and wider ecology. Trust is something which can be built between people through conversations and inter-actions, rather than outsourced to third party certification processes. Justin reflects the importance of trust and accountability in relation-ships with local food providers:

At least if it's a New Zealand company I can ask some questions, and say 'Can you tell me about this product because I'm interested?', like my free-range egg lady. I said 'oh, can I come and have a look at your farm' and she goes 'yeah', and it's just beautiful and that's really cool to see – how the chickens actually roam around and it's just like her photo on the website said. It's just big paddocks with chickens in them and that's choice.

As Justin points out, supporting local food is considered to be good for the community: "if you're supporting the local producers and suppliers that's got to be good for Whaingaroa and the area." He considers it to be good for the local economy, and says that the product is also fresher and seasonally better. He currently sources salad greens from Kaiwhenua as well as locally caught seafood and oyster mushrooms from a local grower. The most challenging thing about local food, other than the price, is the difficulty in getting a consistent supply: "Whatever fish they've got – flounder or something and I need 20 a week. They might only have 12 on Thursday and it's hard for me to list a dish if I can't get consistent supply". The café sources free-range eggs from across the harbour and uses coffee roasted in Hamilton, because of an existing relationship and so as not to compete with the locally roasted coffee which is apparently fair-trade and organic but not certified as either: "They're not big on that, they don't see it as important they know they do it and they can prove it but they don't want to go through the process. That's their style." I commented that this would make it hard for Justin and Alex to get their Conscious Consumers badge for coffee. He agrees and added that it also makes it harder for the coffee roasters to market because the labels are becoming more and more important to customers.

As Ackerman-Leist (2012) points out, 'local food' also faces ethical contradictions: "Big trucks, ships and trains are almost always more efficient than farmer's pickup or consumer's car" (Ackerman-Leist 2012, 13). So while closer proximity seems to be less wasteful, it may not always be. This is one reason 'local food' must not be looked at simplistically. Exclusive focus on food miles can also mask other huge energy sinks in the food system involved in food production and storage as well as issues with waste (Ackerman-Leist 2012).

Waste not want not

The elements of a food system most within our control often tend to be those parts of the system that are closest to home, and they are also among the most energy-consumptive components found between farm and fork (Ackerman-Leist 2012, 35).

Another primary consideration around food ethics centres on waste, both in terms of packaging and bio-degradable 'food rubbish'. Ackerman-Leist (2012) asserts that reducing waste is a critical link in creating resilient local food systems. His perspective of farming being about energy flows echoes the paradigms of permaculture and agro-ecology which are also reflected among the local food providers of Whaingaroa. The general feeling here is that packaging should be minimised and food 'rubbish' separated out and composted. Although rubbish is somewhat ubiquitous in contemporary times, it wasn't so long ago that it was a non-issue, as Rick describes:

I'm old enough to remember the 1970s, we'd go shopping and there'd just be tin cans, glass and waxed paper, we recycled the cans and glass and burn the paper. Plastic really wasn't an issue.

Avoiding excess packaging is one of the reasons Jon started WOK in the way that he did: "We can save a lot of packaging if we order 5 kilos of rice. Not only is it cheaper than if we order little 500gram bags, but then it's just one sack instead of tiny little bags and the sack can be re-used for all kinds of things." Rick describes some of the work conducted by Liz and Xtreme Waste towards raising awareness on this topic:

Liz last year did an audit of the waste bags to see how we were getting along, 'cause we're up to 76 percent diversion of the total sole waste stream. As a result of finding that out, a great number of bags contained organics food waste, and paper waste. So that led to the introduction of a trial food waste collection for 100 homes, which was really successful. As time went on, Liz and a few of those people, saw the volume of food waste, so they started to purchase differently. Even working at the tail end of dealing with waste had quite a transformation of people in terms of their behaviour in supermarkets. Instead of getting two for the price of one, they started to become aware of their amount of food waste, became disgusted by that and started to re-use the food and buy less.

This can be seen as an attempt at transforming supermarket culture where everything is purchased in packets and easily discarded. Jon described his take on this initiative:

There's been an organic waste diversion trial at Xtreme Waste in Raglan recently. It's a way of retaining the nutrient loop within Raglan so food-scraps from your kitchen go to Xtreme Waste and get composted into mulch or raising mix which you then put back on your garden and they get composted again, so instead of throwing your scraps into the landfill we're re-cycling them again. You can compost at home and that's good too, but doing it on a larger scale, nearby is probably a lot more efficient.

According to Liz, similar practices have seen a drop in food waste as a result of providing the facilities for separate collection. This system is not promoted as an alternative to composting, in fact, as Liz says: "for many years Xtreme Waste and WEC have encouraged home composting, lots of workshops, advice and support." But while some Whaingaroa residents are engaged in composting and worm farming many are "just too busy or not into gardening. There are quite a few reasons why people don't."

A similar system has been implemented in another small New Zealand town, but in a different way, as Liz explains, for them:

It's in the rates, without any consultation they said 'you're having this food waste collection and if you don't comply you could be fined.' So they came in with that very government style, totalitarian, just do it. Xtreme Waste would never do that, it's not our style. We're from the bottom up.

Despite not implementing fines the participation in Whaingaroa has been comparable:

Using a different style, encouraging people, making them aware that they are doing good things for themselves, the planet, for Xtreme Waste, that there are lots of driving factors. People are motivated for different reasons, for example you'll save money, you won't have smelly rubbish. Then we went and talked to people at seven months into the trial. We went to a random 35 percent of households to find out why people did not participate, and why they did. We didn't have a lot of money, so we had the choice of auditing the rubbish bags or going to talk to people. I thought we'd get more from talking to people. Most of the people who had come on board were the ones putting the rubbish in their bags. The ones who weren't participating, mainly, were composting. It showed us that we had picked up those ones who weren't composting. There probably were around 5% who were still putting food in rubbish bags. I can see as the bags come in. It's cool that some people have used the service still, I've given them information during the trial; they've got the equipment, so they can jump on and off the service for free.

The success of the food waste collection has led to plans to extend it, with support from the council. For Liz, this is a tool for behavioural change, shifting people's perspectives around food and waste.

I asked Jon whether he thought a centralised food scraps programme was a better option for people who are already composting their waste at home:

It depends on a lot of things: if they're got time, if they're doing it well or if they're just doing it haphazardly because haphazardly done compost is not good for your garden. It's nitrogen rich and not good for anything else. It creates an imbalance in your soil over a period of time, also some people might be concerned about rodents. It depends on every situation. That reflects laws and regulations, you can't have one law or regulation for everyone – it works as a framework but not for every situation because every situation's different.

Liz would eventually like to see everybody composting of their own accord, maybe in neighbourhood composting stations with expert composters who can take all the compost for the street. Although, she notes:

They'd have to be within the health regs, so they couldn't get too big within the urban area. Or maybe a park where there is a food forest – wouldn't it be awesome if there was a community compost which then went onto the food gardens? You see little opportunities; once people start seeing or experimenting with a new idea they come over quite quickly.

Rather than just hearing about it or being told. Like with the food forest for a long time, there were blocks there, people said that the children would slash the tress down, but its fine! It's just opportunity. It's great to make a good compost product to sell at Xtreme Waste, we've got lots of green waste to make good compost, and in that there lies an opportunity, if we had more, a town-wide collection, then we could make a lot of compost. Then there is a chance for a grower or two to have enough really good quality medium to grow a significant amount of food, organically, without having to bring in extra.

Another waste awareness-raising campaign in Whaingaroa is Plastic Free July. This campaign originated in Australia[6] and has been take up by the local environment centre. It takes the form of a voluntary challenge. People who chose to participate in it avoid purchasing anything containing plastic for the entire month. 'Plastics Anonymous' meetings are held weekly at the local pub, as a kind of support group for the challenge and as a social event where people can discuss their latest plastic troubles and confess any indiscretions. This campaign has been so popular in the community that a local supermarket and the Herbal Dispensary have brought in special plastic-free products including toilet paper – and repeatedly sold out of these. The supermarket has begun stocking a particular plastic-free toilet paper year round. This product is branded as environmentally friendly as it is made from a by-product of the paper industry. The supermarket have also provided a bin, during the month of July, for people to leave plastic wrappings in. Although many plastic-free participants choose not to buy anything with plastic in the first place, this bin may provide an intermediary for the less-committed and can be seen as an awareness raising tool. Cally, who has participated in Plastic Free July, describes how her various values can sometimes conflict:

It's really hard – when we had the Plastic Free July thing and people are saying oh you know you can get cheese without wrappers on if you get cheese at this speciality shop [in the nearby city of Hamilton] and I'm like: ahh it's still one use plastic almost; it's one use oil 'cause I gotta drive there and drive back I mean what's the...I'm adding to it you know...it's really hard you know sometimes.

A local librarian has taken being plastic-free to the next level by avoiding it from one July to the next. In the entire year she managed to accrue only a very small bag of rubbish containing assorted items such as the packaging from a gift sent by a friend and several receipts, which appear to be paper but are actually printed on plastic. From casual conversations, the hardest thing she experienced was not being able to purchase wine, as the screw-top bottles are lined with plastic. She got around this by drinking wine purchased by friends. This extreme case is held as an example by other members of the community, as Mike describes:

I'm watching this lady in Whaingaroa doing a year without plastics and I'm quite interested because with us, even though we're careful, the frigging plastics and things even our newspaper and magazines come wrapped in plastics – so much of the stuff you get is two layers of plastic and even some of the organic fruit in the supermarket comes in plastic and I've spoken to them saying organic buyers don't really want plastic and they say 'oh I didn't think of that'.

Jenny decided not to offer bio-degradable plastic bags with her bread for Plastic Free July, as she usually serves the bread in brown paper bags anyway, although she has found some customers would prefer no packaging at all: "I have some people bring their own recyclable bag and they don't want a paper bag, they just say: put it in the bag, and I don't see what's wrong with that."

Food needs to be real: decommodification and reconnecting

Echoing the food sovereignty focus on de-commodification of food, there is a strong emphasis within the participants' narratives on reconnecting with 'real food'[7]. Jenny, who styles herself as an 'opportunivore' because she avoids processed food, but is not a fanatical 'foodie' says she has always thought 'food needs to be real':

I think that around bread it's interesting that some people say "I like your bread but the crust's too hard" or "It's too strong" and the whole concept that the bread that you buy in the supermarket is the right bread – that it's real – but if you see bread that's not perfectly formed and on a shelf and not packaged up in plastic, that it's somehow not as good. I always thought that food needed to be real and the more removed we got from it the less real food became – you know you dig up potatoes and oh wow! Yet there's not the same reaction when you just pick up a bag in the supermarket. There's no respect for food now. The young people just eat food and throw it away. A lot of my bread is bought by mums and they say "my son just loves it" and I'm not a bread-evangelist but I think kids just recognise real food. There's several mums who just say their kids won't eat anything else and I think it's not because my bread's totally amazing. I think it's because kids have this instinct about real food.

She describes this reconnection with food as part of a bigger movement, rejecting processed corporate food:

I think there's a huge swell coming – lots more people have chooks now in the back of the garden and it's okay now, whereas a while ago it wasn't. In the 80s and 90s it wasn't common, even in a rural area, to have a house-cow. I like it – when you go out and milk the cow – it feels more real. People have become too disconnected from food. When you grow your own potatoes you know all the work that's gone into it and you get potatoes and you feel so proud and they taste so good. Not everyone can do that but you can do little things. You can grow parsley in a pot, or coriander. I think it's coming back now. Even gardener magazines are more food and family oriented.

Food is constantly present in Cally's day-to-day life as she grows and prepares it. She is keenly aware of labels like 'organic' and 'fairtrade', but, like Jenny, does not consider herself to be fanatical:

I'll go out to dinner and eat whatever's there but I try to be aware of that as much as possible. I mean it's just part of my life, you know it's not a side-line, it's definitely an integral part of everyday life really… Yeah I think the whole modern food system to me is – the ad on TV for Burger King or something the other night I mean the burgers that they showed looked like the pretend ones that you put in a little kids doll house, like they're so plastic looking – like food isn't really food anymore. I really think that yes it's lovely to have pineapple or it's lovely to have some tropical fruit when you live here but it's just such a waste of world resources we have to learn to eat what we can grow locally. I hate the whole Monsanto sort of corporate takeovers.

Although this 'real food' sentiment was echoed by most participants, it was called into question by The Bro. While he personally values 'real food' he challenged other people's conceptions thereof: "How do people define real in terms of food? Is it real because it conforms to some notion they have in their head of how food traditionally was produced?" This demonstrates that while members of the community are interested in questioning conceptions around food values, that the concept of food as 'not just a commodity' is reflected in the community: 'disconnection' from food is perceived as undesirable and problematic and 're-connecting' is important, as Jenny says:

Food is a thing we all need. We have to have it and we have to think about it, but I think in the cities, especially overseas, people don't have to think about it. It just appears somewhere and disappears somewhere, but I think we should all be composting. We should all have worm farms. We should all be aware of where the food we don't use goes. It can be just as valuable as a waste product. In reality – in a little place like mine – nothing is wasted. The only stuff I throw away is plastic.

This centrality of food to people's lived experience, as Jenny describes here, is what makes it an interesting and multi-faceted lens through which to understand wider social, cultural, economic and political issues. Through such a lens the corporate capitalist ontology of alienation can be seen as reflected in people's alienation from their food resulting in the apparent disconnection that was evident to many participants. Justin describes a similar disconnection from food, which he perceives as troubling:

Driving through to Matamata there's massive fields out there. They grow asparagus there and you just see these guys: paddocks of brown dirt, just bent over. It's crazy and it's something that a lot of people just think of as coming from the supermarket in a bunch.

Cally, too relates this disconnection to corporate capitalism, and describes her enactment of food ethics as a process of personal responsibility:

I guess what it boils down to is that I feel that food should be a lot more personal than it is, you know, food is what you put it into your body, it should be a lot more personal, rather than dictated by corporate international multinationals. What have they got to do with my breakfast? I don't want them in my breakfast. But it's personal responsibility, taking responsibility for yourself.

These shared perspectives of reconnecting with real food echo Rose's (2013) acknowledgement of the multi-dimensional and multi-functional nature of food and agriculture, as well as its various interconnectivities across the various spheres of social life. This connectedness, he argues, is the background for the food sovereignty framework's ontology of connectedness.

For participants who recognise the alienation of the globalising capitalist system, connectedness must be re-claimed. Wayne describes this reconnecting process as one of intentionally creating different 'impressions' or perspectives on food, life and reality:

We have these impressions from the media about what we should want: big car, big lifestyle. These things aren't sustainable, so what we really need is to create different impressions, of a more holistic lifestyle, eating organic food, then that's a lot better. So these people living in Whaingaroa, their perception is a lot different, their impressions are a lot better. Some ignorance has been removed.

From his experiences, Wayne thinks the township of Whaingaroa has a much higher population of people who are aware of such issues and are therefore actively trying to live more ethical lives.

Food choices based around ethics are not immune to critique here. The Bro describes the contemporary trend towards quirky dietary requirements as a form of disconnection from food:

I always say to people there's no clear conscience. You're either a predator or a competitor. All these people who have these quirky dietary requirements. I get the medical reasons. Mostly its urban people who have little connection to the growing of their food. I don't know any vegan who grows all his own food. I don't grow my own food. I try and at least choose to eat things which potentially come from horse-riding distance from where I live.

Despite the evident differences in perspective of what constitutes 'ethical' food, the concept of connectedness was a common thread throughout the interviews. Here, Madi also describes connectedness as important, and alludes to connections between food, status and identity:

People being connected with their food would be a good start. It tastes so much better that way. It naturally changes your choices of what's on your plate, your appreciation for it. I think that the way that we eat is dysfunctional. A lot of people use food, what they eat as a kind of status that they want to claim... It's really interesting – the roots – the patterns around people and how they are eating.

Overall the ethics of the food providers in Whaingaroa reflect the food sovereignty values around social and environmental justice. Among these similarities are experienced contradictions, many of which are actively acknowledged and which sometimes become opportunities for creating personal and wider community change. Participants expressed varied perspectives on what values they considered to be more important: animal or human rights, personal or environmental health. Overall, these differences are reflected upon both individually and through conversations, perhaps opening up spaces for the transformation potential of paradox that Seo and Creed (2002) describe, and/or perhaps in ways that reaffirm ethical identities. The food ethics presented here seem to arise out of genuine concerns over social and environmental exploitation and the desire to avoid harm as much as possible. This awareness of wider ecological relationships is a core part of the ontologies of connectedness intrinsic to the framework of food sovereignty (Rose 2013). The tensions and contradictions described in chapter five and the values and ethics presented in this chapter are further examined in the following chapter in relation to the solutions-focussed practices they have inspired both within individual lives and in the wider community.

8 FOCUSING ON SOLUTIONS: COMMUNITY ECONOMIES AND ECOLOGY

*We **are** the food we eat, the water we drink, the air we breathe. And reclaiming democratic control over our food and water and our ecological survival is the necessary project for our freedom (Shiva 2005, 5).*

We are privileged to live at the most exciting moment of creative opportunity in the whole of the human experience. Now is the hour. We have the power to turn this world around for the sake of ourselves and our children for generations to come. We are the ones we've been waiting for (Korten 2010, 283).

Dreaming is not only a necessary political act, it is an integral part of the historical-social manner of being a person. It is part of human nature, which, within history, is in permanent process of becoming...In our making and remaking of ourselves in the process of making history – as subjects and objects, persons, becoming beings of insertion in the world and not of pure adaptation to the world – we should end by having the dream, too, a mover of history. There is no change without dream, as there is no dream without hope (Freire 1992, 90–91).

Just as Graeber (2009) positions the activists of focus in his work as operating from ontologies of imagination, Casey-Cox (2014) positions imaginative thinking, dreaming and self-reflection as potential resistance to the dominant order. This resistance could potentially "dislodge the somewhat normalised mantra and myths of an order that many have internalised" (Casey-Cox 2014, 108). Along with Casey-Cox (2014), I take inspiration from Freire's positioning on dreaming as a necessary political act. Similarly, many participants value exploration of possibilities, re-conceptualising ideas and experimenting with different models for living.

When I asked The Bro what he would like to see happening in Whaingaroa he responded: "It's already happening, just more of the same." Similarly, Jenny expressed pride in her small bread business as well as the desire to see more small-scale local food initiatives:

I just feel proud that I'm producing a good product and it doesn't bother me if some people don't want it because lots of people do want it and I feel proud that I'm producing a good food for our local people. I wish we could have a whole little alley of shops like this… cheese or herbs. It could happen.

Justin also expressed a strong desire to see more local food in Whaingaroa:

I really, really, really wanna live or work somewhere where there's a fresh food market. You know, like that guy that's got the yellow trailer across the road? If there was just something like that where all the little producers could come together and just have a stall – once a week or… I would love it every day. I would just love to be able to go: 'Okay, what are we going to have a special for today?' and go to the market and go 'Oh look, there's some lovely scallops!' or something.

This desire to see more local food can be seen as part of a deliberate choice to 'focus on the positive'. Rather than putting a lot of energy into frustrations and resistance of the corporate system and the alienation it engenders, these local food providers are concentrating on what they can do themselves. Wayne expresses this sentiment in the following quote:

Trying to stop a powerful company like this is not really practical, so the only practical thing I can see is that every individual has to make a choice to stop giving such power to those corporations and then naturally these things will change. ... Like: "let's get rid of Monsanto," well alright then, get rid of Monsanto. How are you going to do this? You can't just whinge about the problem, you have to have a solution, otherwise things won't change.

To understand the focus on solutions in the practices of local food producers in Whaingaroa, it is helpful to have an understanding of permaculture, just as it was relevant in Chapter One in explaining my methodological approach. Permaculture is similar to agro-ecology which is prevalent in the food sovereignty literature (Holt-Gimenez and Patel 2009). Both are systems of knowledge and practice which are based on ecosystem function and can be applied to agriculture. These systems were also mentioned briefly in the previous chapter in relation to values, they have particular relevance to local practices and initiatives in Whaingaroa. The strong focus on ecosystems here also ties in with Shiva's (2005) argument that ecological security and ecological identities are our most basic and fundamental. This sentiment certainly rings true among the participants.

Permaculture systems are designed from 'pattern to detail' meaning that there is clear visioning, dreaming and imagining involved, as Liz explains: "Permaculture is a lot to do with patterns – always look for patterns." The patterns in nature are treated as examples of flows and cycles upon which human systems can be based. Embedded in permaculture is the emphasis on integration over segregation, and the idea that reciprocity is rewarding. In the permaculture course they teach, Liz and Rick and the other guest teachers emphasise the value of community and strong social networks. As Liz explains: "Consensus building takes time but usually produces a really solid outcome – more than democratic [voting] process." There is also a strong value placed on diversity, both socially and ecologically. These values will be seen to be integral to the practices of individuals and organisations described in this chapter.

This deliberate permaculture focus on small localised solutions will be explored throughout this chapter, firstly, as a kind of community activism or direct action as seen in the example of Xtreme Waste, and secondly, in relation to the personal food choices of participants. Community building will then be discussed, followed by an exploration of how tensions that arise in community might be resolved.

We just did it anyway: Direct Action and Community Practices

Direct action… is a matter of proceeding as one would if the existing power structure did not exist. Direct action is, ultimately, the defiant insistence on acting as if one is already free (Graeber 2013, 233).

Although organisations like the Whaingaroa Environment Centre work hard to maintain relationships with governing bodies such as the local Council, an argument can be made that most of the food sovereignty related activities in Whaingaroa happened in spite of the council and national regulations. This can be seen in the following statement where Jon describes how the Whaingaroa West food forest was set up:

It was really just a group of us saying 'there's a big grassy area here. No one uses it'. I walked around all of the local area asking people if they used it and 'Did they think a food forest was a good idea?', and there was a 99 percent approval. It was an area which was virtually unused, surrounded by suburban houses to benefit and to keep an eye on the food forest. The Council were fine at the start and then came at us – could we cover ourselves for litigation if anyone injured themselves by slipping on fruit? We just did it anyway. As is the case with the Council someone probably assumed someone else had said it was okay, and anyway, it's not known for sure who owns that land because the IHC building is there and they think they asked the Council to look after it now the Council think they own it.

The story of Xtreme Waste, the local recycling centre, is a good example of this kind of 'we did it anyway' approach. As mentioned in Chapter Six, waste or rubbish is intimately connected with food –

both in terms of food packaging and in terms of biodegradable materials. As Rick explains, Xtreme Waste was started by a small group of locals and has a strong community focus:

Xtreme Waste was set up by a group of six individuals who had the opportunity and it was all set up by consensus decision making and even now we have a flat structure of four managers and some people say it's inefficient, but it means that two managers can be away and there's still enough knowledge to keep things running and make decisions. It's not an individual business it's a community business.

The site of Xtreme Waste was previously a rubbish dump, before that it was used for sewage processing, as Rick describes:

There was a night cart system. A truck would come around, after dark and pick up your barrel of shit, bring it up here, tip it out and then they'd grow watermelons and sell them to the tourists – which was a great idea.

The dump landfill which was developed on the same site was considered an ecological problem as toxic leachate was contaminating the water systems leading into the harbour. It was finally closed in 1998 and rubbish was collected and sent to another landfill. There were no recycling services and some members of the community, including Liz and Rick, began to agitate for more ecologically-minded systems. This was at a time when recycling was not particularly common in New Zealand and it initially encountered some resistance in Whaingaroa, as Rick describes:

The community had to go through a bit of a process and people were like 'I don't want that rubbish near me' and 'what's all this stuff about recycling and zero waste?' It was a concept that didn't have many practical examples around the country at that time, but we thrashed this out as a community. We had several meetings and lots and lots of radio shows and Chronicle articles about 'What should we do?' – so the community did quite a lot of research and went to visit the other recycling centres in New Zealand at the time, brought back the best of their business plans. The Community Board got really passionate and the Council gave us a year's contract and so

Xtreme Waste was born. It wasn't a group imposing it on the community, it was the community forming a group to focus on the waste issues – so it was a real need.

The project began with a handful of volunteers picking up cardboard recycling in unregistered vans. This eventually led to the securing of the old dump site and a temporary contract to handle the refuse and recycling for the township area, but the struggle with the District Council continued and they refused to fund recycling services.

Whilst the need for a recycling centre may have been real for the community, it took a while for the district councillors to understand the need for prioritising community-based business over simple cost-effectiveness. Rick explains that this led to some proactive community activism:

After the first year the Chief Executive [of the local council] rung up and said they had found someone else – a multi-national company – who could do it cheaper 'And they're going to be doing all the waste for the whole district' so, 'Sweet as, thanks for your help and don't turn up on Monday.' This was before broadband internet. The Council only had three telephone lines for phoning in and out. The community here was so pissed off that they had been told what to do – especially after a year of work – that they rung up to abuse the CEO and kept it up for three days – brought the Council office to a grinding stop. They couldn't use the fax machines or anything. So he rung up and said 'Screw you guys – you can have your waste'. He [the CEO] was really good at campaigning in the media. It was about attack. We avoided that and said we were really looking forward to a long relationship with him, so that really pissed him off. We avoided conflict and were just working on the positive all the time. At the time there were a lot of people unemployed, and young people with nothing to do so we saw that as a resource – we focused on giving people jobs. We are conscious as a business – we often make decisions that cost us money as a business but employ more people. We pull toxic batteries out of the landfill instead of sending them to someone else's community to deal with. We weigh the decisions up and balance the economic decisions.

This deliberate focus on solutions has led to around eighty percent diversion of waste from landfill from the area. Rick estimates that with full implementation of the food and organic waste system a further eight percent can be diverted, meaning that only eighteen percent of the township's refuse will be sent to landfill, although the eventual aim is for one hundred percent diversion. Over the twelve years Xtreme Waste has been running approximately 152,000 cubic meters of waste has been diverted from landfills. This will have contributed to a reduction in landfill gasses and carbon footprint. The organisation has also worked with Whaingaroa Harbourcare and planted trees to ensure there is no longer any leachate into the streams and harbour: "There were no eels in the streams before, but now there's full biodiversity," Rick notes.

Aside from these ecological successes, Xtreme Waste also provided numerous social benefits including facilitating community access to resources that would otherwise be buried in a landfill. The organisation employs 26 people part-time, and over 100 people have gone through the system, receiving a reference and often training. Xtreme Waste also provides an education programme for schools and marae to further facilitate recycling and awareness around this. Rick also notes that being involved in the management of a community recycling centre has contributed to feelings of kaitiakitanga [stewardship] for many of the employees who come from the area, as well as a sense of rangatiratanga [sovereignty]. He comments that "Whaea[1] Eva [Rickard] used to talk about: It's not a political movement, it's about what's between your ears, it's about making up your mind based on your values and principles and getting on with it – and doing it."

Xtreme waste has yielded a variety of economic benefits for the community. An informal survey conducted several years ago indicated that 70 percent of the income from the organization stays in Whaingaroa, amounting to approximately one million dollars which moves around the community three times before going back into the banking system, as Rick explains:

Rate payers every year in Whaingaroa pay about $420,000 for all the services we provide. We turn that into about 1 million dollars' worth of activity that goes around 3 times, so we turn that 420,000 into 3 million dollars' worth of activity – so that's a really good investment. It's a 1:6 ratio for the community. We're living in Whaingaroa, we don't have shareholders anywhere else, so there's no syphoning out to make other people rich.

Wages are paid throughout the winter which works to balance the seasonality of activity in Whaingaroa. As Rick says: "If we can free up 10,000 dollars every week into the system then it goes around and around. It's about redistribution of wealth."

In order to survive, Xtreme Waste has had to be flexible and diversify. As a charity they can be both a partner to the Council and also access funding from non-governmental sources, which helps when facilities need to be upgraded. Rick explains his permacultural perspective on economics: "You can keep pouring money into something – but if a bucket's full of holes you will have to keep pouring and pouring. It's about plugging up the holes." One example of this can be found in the provision of two different sizes of refuse bags, regular and small. Whaingaroa is currently the only community to offer these options, which Rick says is about "Honouring our old people who are resourceful and conscious of waste and don't use much, and also they can't carry those big bags anyway." Under the previous Council collection scheme ratepayers were paying a flat rate for two big bags of refuse every week. This current system is more designed for people to pay for what they use. As people have to buy their own refuse bags it also encourages them to recycle more and to be more conscious of their waste-related behaviours.

In terms of business solutions, Xtreme Waste has developed education programmes which they offer to businesses, focusing on how to cut down waste bills. They have set up recycling services for farmers and they have also developed a recycling-oriented mini-skip business, which is especially useful on construction sites. Xtreme Waste workers will drop off two or three small skip bins so that offcuts can be separated out into reusable materials. The skips are free for metal, ten dollars a kilo for wood and more for waste.

Building on this educational focus, Xtreme Waste have a contract with the Council to provide Zero Waste education to all the schools in the district. Over the past ten years this has included working with two hundred and ten schools and forty thousand students. On top of this, they have operated educational tours of the Xtreme Waste site to over four thousand people including politicians, school, and university groups. With such a success story, it may come as no surprise that the Auckland Council is now planning to set up similar community based recycling centres in the Auckland region. The first of these is already underway in Waiuku.

The direct action enacted by Xtreme Waste has not stopped at focusing on the continuation of the organisation. In fact, it has gone much further. Rick describes how the organisation has used a variety of creative tactics to 'lobby' business:

A few years ago the yogurt companies refused to put a recycle symbol on their containers, so we sent them 1000 containers and said we'd send them 1000 every month. They said 'a 1000s not much'. We said, sweet, there's 40 community groups in NZ who will all send you 1000.

The company quickly changed its practice and included the recycling symbol on packaging. Similar unconventional protest tactics were employed to lobby a government minister who made a decision to get rid of reusable glass milk bottles in the South Island, as Rick describes:

In New Zealand you can send anything to a Member of Parliament. You don't need a stamp, just put their name on it and put it in the mail. 1000 milk bottles in the mail. It's a great way of lobbying!

In that instance there was an election before this activism could have its full effect. Xtreme Waste leaders have not been deterred. They consider that the responsibility for disposal of waste should lie with the company who creates it in the first place and therefore encourage 'product stewardship' where the cost of recycling is paid in the price of purchase. This idea has not been popular with New Zealand governments so far, as Rick explains: "Our government is scared of imposing regulations on businesses because that's a relationship they want to protect but then it's the consumer who has to pick up the bill."

Xtreme Waste has also successfully lobbied New Zealand's largest dairy company, Fonterra, after the company introduced white opaque 'UV-proof' plastic milk bottles with no recycle stream, creating excessive unrecyclable waste. Rick explains:

We'd been giving them a hard time – after a few Herald articles they got uncomfortable – they came down and asked how they could help: 'give us $20 grand so we can build a new stainless steel trough – you guys have developed a new milk bottle and created more work with no premium. So we said: We'll challenge you to set up a new market for these in 12 months – not an export market, a New Zealand market: a manufacturing market.' Incredibly they did – they make irrigations and piping out of this plastic. Bloody good on you Fonterra for setting this up in New Zealand.

Xtreme Waste has also put pressure on Fonterra, over the excess landfill waste created by the 'tetrapak' packaging used for their 'milk in schools' programme, in which school children may regularly be given milk. The small community recycling group has challenged Fonterra to set up a tetrapak recycling plant in New Zealand. An early experiment is evidenced along the side of the recycling sorting shed at Xtreme Waste in the form of silvery wall materials made from tetrapack which has been compressed with gentle heating. Rick notes that the material is not wearing well but is positive about working constructively with businesses such as Fonterra to create better recycling outcomes: 'We'll work with you and try to find a home for tetrapak.' This relationship is viewed as a kind of partnership, however, it is important for Xtreme Waste to maintain their independence, rather than feel it is under coercive power from bodies from which it receives funding. According to

Rick, that is always a clear part of arrangements, as they are negotiated.

Foods We Eat

Although it can be argued that people always fall short of reaching aspirational ideals, overall the local food providers are in the habit of 'practicing what they preach' in terms of lifestyles and food consumption. This can be viewed as a kind of everyday 'direct action' (Graeber 2013). This also relates to the permaculture principle of 'small slow solutions' and can be viewed as part of the enactment of personal food sovereignty (Dowling 2011). Most participants attempt to grow the majority of their fruit and vegetables or source produce locally rather than purchasing from supermarkets. Supermarket produce is generally considered to be less ethical, because it is usually either imported from overseas or trucked around New Zealand, wasting fossil fuels unnecessarily. Conventional non-organic produce is also considered to be a health risk because of the pesticides used in its production. Furthermore, the taste of supermarket produce is considered inferior to that which is produced at home, or grown in small-scale organic production. Grains and legumes are considered more difficult to grow in sufficient volume and are often imported into New Zealand, although Jon tries to source things as locally as possible and stocks some New Zealand grown pulses.

Mike and his family usually drink their own milk, although at the time of the interview he had dried the cows off because of two successive droughts. He poured milk into our cups of tea from a carton of conventional organic milk purchased from the supermarket. He described their usual sources of food:

We're good for milk and soft cheese and butter because Mady can make that, and we don't do the hard cheeses because of time. Hard cheeses are hard. Then we've got our meat: sheep, pigs, beef, so we're well set up, that's home-kill. Going back to our own food, we've got quite an extensive veggie garden. We've got orchard trees, some from my dad's days, and we've planted a lot, citruses kicking in, stone fruits are kicking in quite nicely, because it's very hard to buy good fruit. The supermarkets' are crap. You buy apples that look good and some are organic and they're floury, and you have your own home-grown apple and it's great – nothing like it. So we're not self-sufficient, but we're quite close to it. We sometimes have a meal where everything on the plate is home-grown, except say, salt and pepper, but we still have to buy some of our food in. We belong to WOK, we get as much as we can through them and then we top up at the supermarket. At WOK we get bulk flours – organic flours – pastas, tins of tomato for sauces out of season. We're doing more preserving but we don't seem to get enough for the whole year. Mady's mum helps a lot so I think we can lift our game a little. We'll treat ourselves to things like corn chips from WOK, and the dried goods, oats and things like that. So plan A is as much off the farm as possible, plan B is from WOK, and plan C is supermarket and if I could kick the supermarket into touch I'd like to – nothing personal, but it would be nice. With local food and Whain-garoa, our weakness would be grains but it could be done. We know we can grow maize or corn, it grows well here organically. Way out on Aotea [nearby] they used to grow wheat. There are farmers in the Waikato growing barley. You might not be able to have everything.

The current lack of locally grown staple foods including grains and legumes is seen as a barrier to fully enacting local food values through daily eating practices. Wayne has overcome this, to some extent, by growing his own lentils. His market gardening skills have been put to use in producing enough lentils for his personal consumption. Other locals have expressed interest in the possibilities of community grain crops. Due to the climate, some foods cannot be grown in Whaingaroa, particularly tropical crops like mangoes and chocolate. Jon sees these as luxuries that people will eventually have to live without, in the face of peak oil as well as global economic and environmental crises. Other participants expressed interest in the possibility of rekindling trade by sail with the Pacific for goods that cannot be produced here[2].

Like Mike and Mady, Cally and her husband also grow a lot of their own food:

We grow a lot more now, it's a bit silly really, we grow a lot more now that the kids have gone. I home-schooled them all so I didn't really have the time or energy to grow food too much. I mean, we've always had a garden but we're growing more now. Last year we went for about five months when the only things we bought were treats; everything else out of our garden. I've never been much of a winter gardener. I don't seem to have much success with anything except broad beans, which I love, but each year I'm trying to expand a little bit more. At the moment: garlic, onions, peas, sweetcorn, courgettes, cucumbers, pumpkins, lettuce, spring onion, herbs, tomatoes, New Zealand spinach incessantly – you can't not grow it once you've got it – capsicum, eggplants. Then we've got ducks and chooks for eggs and we've got a lot of fruit trees, apples and plums and peaches and hazelnuts and, yeah, can't really think... nashis... so quite a lot of that... and honey.

Jenny, too, tries to grow as much food at home as possible, including meat. She sees this as an enactment of her values around food being 'real':

I try to grow as many veges as I can – at the moment maybe 40% of my food: all the veges and some fruit and some meat – I don't often buy meat. I'm not vegetarian but I feel that if you've grown a beast on your farm, and you've looked after it, and you've killed it humanely – I sort of feel like the deal's okay. I'm not into buying cling-wrapped polystyrene meat at the supermarket. It's not real. You have to respect it.

Land ownership can certainly be seen as a kind of privilege, one that many people are excluded from. While some of the participants own land on which they can grow food, or else have access to family owned land, quite a few do not. For these participants, access to land comes through informal arrangements based on relationships with landowners, through the openness of land-owners to share their land in a more communal way, or through community gardens which can be seen as a kind of 'commons', a concept explored in further detail in the following chapter. Wayne, Robz, The Bro, and Madi, are all able to grow food through relationships with land-owners.

For Wayne, vegetarianism is a central part of his personal food sovereignty, and is a way of enacting his food values on a daily, practical basis:

I stopped eating meat four years ago and I definitely think it's a lot cheaper to be a vegetarian. I eat at least 80% organic and I don't spend much money on food but I grow all my veges, so the food that I do buy is just from WOK, it's pretty small, maybe a bit of cheese, some pulses.

The Bro, too enacts his values through food choices, and has negotiated shifts in these values and practices:

You can still have a lot of control over food and you can exert influence in that way. I don't even think that much of that has to do with the dollar. I haven't drunk milk in years and half the reason why I wanted to start drinking milk again is so that I could talk to dairy farmers, so I could go to the farm gate, buy milk and you get to talk to people. I think about that all the time, and how I choose to buy food or serve up food, 'cause you know I run a catering business which is kind of run on Māori and permaculture principles and people think that I only buy organic or that I have all these rules when it comes to food, and I've come from that, like I used to be a strict vegetarian and only ate organic and I was quite proud of that and then I read Michael Pollan[3] and realised how fucked up big corporate organic is and how it's actually owned by big corporate conventional agriculture so anyway.

In negotiating similar value-based tensions, Madi finds her choices are influenced significantly by the situation she finds herself in:

I like to eat out of the garden, so that often looks like eating the same thing often, which I'm really happy with. If I've got the choice, stuff growing in the garden, then find that I am eating raw, lots of green, sprouts and fruits. There's nothing that I won't eat, I've been in situations, for example I would opt not to do something, like sailing in the Pacific, if that meant that I would have to eat really old food, low quality or fish, which I had never had eaten before. I was raised a vegetarian. I like the luxury of making raw cakes and things but I'm also really aware that Brazil nuts come from Brazil and like there is only one nut on each fruit which people use so casually.

For Robz, focussing on solutions involves planting as many fruit trees in public spaces as possible, as well as food foraging and sharing knowledge:

...learning about wild foods and medicines and going around and doing teaching about wild food, just so people have that wisdom. It's nice to be able to have empty cupboards but not have to worry about it 'cause you just go – and in ten minutes time you can have a bucket full of food, really nutritious food. And you know even on a bike, wherever we are, there's no fear 'cause you know that there's just all this food and we know exactly what it is. It's a really nice thing to carry through life. So I'm trying to spread that on to other people, especially young kids, like teenagers. I'd like to take a group of three or four young teenage people and camp over; have a fire and just show them how I live and forage, and just plant that seed: 'Hey guys there's this option too, before you get yourselves in debt at uni or feel pressured to be something out there.'

Over the winter Robz and Matai ate a lot of cleavers, dock, puha [sow thistle], dandelions and wild carrots: "You can eat the greens as a cooked green and just cook the carrot, steam it or cook it, boil it." When I arrived to interview Robz, three-year-old Matai began telling me about plantain, that it was good for cuts.

On timing and 'we don't really have meetings'

At the permaculture course I attended in the autumn of 2014, Rick explained the absence of local permaculture meetings in Whaingaroa:

We've [local permaculture community] been spending so much time together on shared projects that we don't really have meetings – it makes you wonder what a meeting's for.

Despite the high number of people interested in permaculture in the community, at that time, no one was specifically organising meetings, although people were meeting and sharing information through various shared projects. Since then, Robz has started monthly 'Permy Pot-lucks' hosted by different members of the community at different properties. These meetings have sometimes been combined with working bees, socialising and information sharing.

Over the following summer, the prevalence of Permy Pot-lucks seemed to dissipated as people in the community are often either busy with summer work or away on holiday. This illustrates the particular seasonality of Whaingaroa which is reflected in social gatherings, as Liz explains:

If you want to get people together you have to do it at the right time, not in the summer when everyone's too busy. Now is good [autumn], and winter but you have to be careful because quite a lot of people go away in the winter months. They work really hard in the summer and then take the time out in the winter; sometimes people go away for a month or two. Potlucks are good in the winter and other kinds of events might be good in the summer but you've got to be aware of the cycles of your community.

Being aware of these cycles and flows within the community is an important part of a permaculture perspective and must be taken into account when organising solutions-focussed projects.

Timing is of particular importance in terms of wise energy use. Large projects are seen to have natural ebbs and flows of activity as Rick explains:

Timing of community projects is important, for instance, with Xtreme Waste. Our landfill closed and pretty much overnight we had to work out an alternative, but with something like the harbour, I've been working on that for twenty years, and it's not likely that it's going to be finished in the next five years. I've pushed it hard a couple of times and it's gone nowhere, but it hasn't stopped. You can't unnaturally push it; it's a waste of energy.

Liz used the 'Transition Towns' project as an example of this. When the idea of transitioning to a post-fuel-dependent system was first circulated in the township it gained a lot of attention, but since then many interested parties have become busy with other projects: "And it's easy for people to say 'that's flopped' or that it's not happening any more but it might be chugging away at a lower level waiting to come back." It can be noted too, that many of these other projects are interconnected with the wider Transitions Towns[4] values such as building community connectedness and resilience:

When we were introduced to Transitions Towns, and we looked at it, we realised we were already doing it. What was interesting was this exercise of doing an inventory – that was quite a powerful exercise to look at all the community wealth we had.

Focussing on solutions is seen here by participants as something that must be lived out as coherently as possible in every area of life, despite the contradictions encountered. It is not enough to join a particular environmental group or support a particular charity. Rick reported a similar sentiment among the locals in Fiji:

In Fiji, the Forest and Bird and member organisations would try to hook the Fijians into joining their groups and the Fijians would say: "Why do you do that? – You live unsustainably from Monday to Friday and then you join an environmental group and do some tree planting on the weekend." They would prefer to integrate sustainable activity into day-to day life.

Community building

There is a commonly held understanding within the community that contemporary corporate capitalism, along with a history of colonisation and industrialisation, has created social disconnection and that there is much work to be done in 'community-building'. Healthy communities are considered to be those with strong connection and shared celebrations.

Mike describes how the milk he sells from the farm gate has been a win-win situation for his farm and for the community who have the choice to purchase his milk. The opportunity to buy unpasteurised milk has also created 'milk groups' within the Whaingaroa area and also in Hamilton, of people who take turns to drive out and collect milk for the members of the group, saving time, effort and petrol. These kinds of groups help to build ties within the community as people get to know each-other and make connections which are reinforced through other associations. Similarly, Jon describes WOK as a site of community building:

Also it's really been – even more than I hoped – chance meetings at WOK of two people doing their own shopping and really lovely to see a relationship blooming all of a sudden and people realising that they have something really strongly in common that they didn't realise and sharing, exchanging details and just walking off with a big smile on their face. That just makes my day.

Aside from providing a space in which customers can meet, WOK works in other community-building ways, providing local growers like Liz and Rick, and Wayne, with guaranteed sales for their fresh produce. This arrangement is similar in function to a Community Supported Agriculture [CSA] structure, in which participants invest in the production of local farms and receive a share of the produce, often in the form of a 'veggie box'.

The Whaingaroa Creative Market is another site of meeting, especially for the stall-holders who are regularly there. Trading is common between stallholders and informal, mutually beneficial systems have developed, as Jenny describes:

I haven't known Liz and Rick for that long, I've known of them for a while, and at the markets people were buying their pesto and they said: 'We'll try Jenny's bread' and they were coming to me and saying 'Is there something good to go with this?' and I was saying 'Their pesto'. So in the end we just said let's just go side-by-side and we can support each-other better that way. The garlic [sold in her tiny shop on their behalf] is non-perishable – well not really perishable and it's a bit of passive income for them and it just sits there and I don't have to do anything extra on my part.

For Wayne, starting the community garden at the police station was also a deliberate attempt at community building:

People are afraid of the police, there's a bit of a barrier up – but they're meant to be protecting our community and if we're afraid of people who are supposed to be protecting us there's something wrong. So one of the goals is for people to get to know the police and for the police to get to know people.

He also sees the local time-bank, described in Chapter Three, as a community building tool, which has the capacity to link different people who would not otherwise meet.

Despite the strong focus on 'community' for a lot of people in Whaingaroa, there are no intentional communities in the area. The Bro reflected that intentional communities are complicated and require 'a bunch of rules'. There are only a few people he would consider buying land with, including Liz and Rick:

They are some of the most emotionally intelligent people I know and that's why. So you wouldn't need to write all this policy and rules, you'd just be able to talk everything through... I'm not sure the values are quite the same, but that doesn't matter, the ability to go through the process is the most important thing... there are lots of Māoris who have the same values, but I couldn't buy land with them because I can't talk to them, or have the hard conversations with them in a constructive fashion.

Justin also values 'community' and sees sourcing ingredients from local producers as part of that:

I just think it's a good thing for the community, if you're supporting the local producers and suppliers, that's got to be good for Whaingaroa and the area. I mean, when I say 'local' I kind of mean Waikato, it's a bit restricting otherwise. I think it's economically better for the community, I think it's a good thing to support your neighbours and generally the product is fresher and seasonally better.

He also describes a sense of community among cafés with similar values. People involved in these cafés can 'bounce ideas off' each other and share information. Justin says he enjoys going up to Auckland for a bit of research with other ethically focussed businesses.

When Kaiwhenua Organics first started, Kaiwaka did not want to connect with the wider community, but soon found that local food has a way of building community connections, regardless:

I didn't want anyone to come up here when I was first here, it was our little place. I never thought that it would connect us into the community. When I went into the chemist, the lady in there said 'I grow the same salad as you but it doesn't taste the same'. So I said 'What do you do?' She sprays her hedges and I say 'I don't do that!' I use a tin on a hot day to kill weeds. Then you can put a kai in it straight away. It's all natural. You don't have to wait thirty days for it to dissipate into the soil. Rick and Liz have told me a lot: black plastic, put some rocks on it – kills off all the stuff underneath. It's all about understanding the cycles. 'Flower goes to seed, that's seven years' weeds'.

Community building here is interconnected with sharing knowledge and providing support. For Kaiwaka, his work is about setting an example, not just in Whaingaroa, but for wider Māori communities:

This place is our release; it's a way to disconnect from the system, but say: 'This is what you should do'. We can stand on our own two feet. If you fellas took a leaf out of our book and set up every block of land this way, we'd be able to support our own communities, grow our own kai. Everybody else can be fighting, do what they want. We'll just look out for our community and we'll be happy. And then we can teach others how to do that. Kaiwhenua is leading the way for Māori to go back to their land and work their land – have a diverse effect on everyone. The garden does that.

For Liz and Rick, with their ecology and permaculture backgrounds, community and culture are constructed as both like an ecosystem of different flows and cycles, and as interconnected with the wider environmental ecosystem. Despite this holistic understanding, there are still corners of Whaingaroa that they do not feel connected with, as the following conversation, which took place at a permaculture course, illustrates:

Liz: I never go to The Club [social club] in Whaingaroa, I don't know about the social structure and the networks. Even though I live here, there's lots of parts of the society in a small town, there's always work to be done to stay connected in some way. People used to say to me: you know everyone in Whaingaroa. No, no I don't. Even though it's a small town there's lots of people.

Louie: My granddad will go there every day at four o'clock for his 'drinkie-time'.

Rick: They only allowed women to be financial members about 5 years ago.

Liz: My values don't align with some people, but they're a part of the fabric of our community. There are the darker parts; it's easy to sometimes pretend they're not there. We have a drug problem in Whaingaroa. It's hidden but it's still there. Some people come here and think it's beautiful and it's all about being healthy and surfing, but it's really good to acknowledge without putting a judgement on it, necessarily.

Observation is an important part of permaculture, which, as a system, can be applied to community. From observations, understanding can develop which has the potential to lead to transformative action. From years of observation, Liz relates a profound appreciation for the richness of the local community:

When I look at Whaingaroa I just find it amazing because we do seem to have – and I've never looked at another community through the same lens – but there are so many creative and talented people here. I hope that I would feel like that if I lived in another community, and that's because of things like bartering, shared learning and celebrating people's differences. I hope, if I lived in another community, that I could be as celebrative of the social wealth as I am here.

This notion of social wealth is explored in more detail in the following chapter focussing on community economies.

Resolving tensions

During the permaculture course in April 2014 I asked Liz how the inevitable tensions that emerge in communities can be resolved:

Through celebrations: you've got to celebrate everything that's going on, instead of focussing on what's not being done. Just keep celebrating what the achievements are and obtaining that yield. When we start not working well at Xtreme Waste it's because we've not taken the time to celebrate. In a functional community there will already be lots of ways of doing that – rituals for celebration – but in a less-functional community you might have to create activities or find some tools to bring people together. Even a themed party is so much more interactive than a non-themed party.

In Liz's experience, local celebrations help to ease tension. This could in part be explained by the abundance of energy and resources often involved in celebrations which ease tensions of scarcity (Stuart 2009). As Rick states: "If there is heaps of food and no competition then animals can coexist." This can also be seen as relevant for human animals.

Alongside producing enough food to avoid scarcity, Wayne advocates resolving tensions through disrupting supermarket culture:

I'd like to see more people in their own houses producing food for themselves. People are so dependent on the supermarkets. It's very much a turn-key lifestyle and if the fuel runs out what are we going to do? We are all reliant on external things. We are not really reliant on ourselves, and Whaingaroa's got a low income for a lot of people and if people are producing their own food it's better for everyone. With the markets, you have to pick the stuff and then you're banking on hoping to sell it, whereas when you order it you're not wasting produce, although a lot of excess produce can go to the food bank. That was the main idea with the community garden too – to donate stuff to the food bank.

Planting community fruit trees can also be seen as part of this attempt to create an abundance of accessible food. These may be small steps, but locals are optimistic about them, as Justin says: "The little pockets that are growing, they can get a strong footing and start making a few more waves."

Another important consideration in observing community tensions and their resolutions centres on the transformative potential of crises. This can be seen in the example of Xtreme Waste being set up after the town dump had closed, and also in the formation of Whaingaroa Harbourcare after the harbour became noticeably polluted and also. These two organisations emerged at a similar time, as Liz explains:

There was a real upwelling of frustration, in the community, it was definitely linked to the work and getting together of the people, and the work Helen was doing with the catchment. That fired up people's opinions.

This can also be seen further back in the history of Whaingaroa, mentioned in Chapter Three, with the transfer of the previously confiscated Te Kōpua airstrip land to be used as a golf course and the subsequent protests led by Eva Rickard, which Rick links to the evolution of other local initiatives:

I think there are also connections through to Whaea Eva and the land, because it was at a time when the local and national government were not representing the people, making really terrible decisions with severe impacts on rural communities, and things were really economically very differently in Whaingaroa. Small shops closed in the winter time, people were leaving. Whaea Eva made a stand, saying 'No! We know what is best for our community', getting that land back and then for the whānau being so generous giving that land back for general community use: the campground, the skate park, the air strip, and then developing Te Kōkiri for training, small engines, sewing, wood working. It was such a generous gift.

Liz also links the leadership of Eva Rickard to both the community development in Whaingaroa as well as her own personal identity:

She always said 'Don't wait for other people to do things, just do it yourself if you believe in something, if you believe in your heart that something's right or wrong, that's tino rangatiratanga [self-determination] – in you as a person', which was really helpful for me as a Pākehā to understand what that truly meant.

This history of activism, and the inherent sense of self-determination can be connected to contemporary environmental and social activism which is lived out through a variety of activities carried out on different levels. These include daily food practices, public fruit tree planting and community gardening. This activism is also evident through the operations of organisations that provide employment, strengthen community connectedness and environmental awareness, and which work to lobby government and large corporations to change their practices.

This chapter has focussed on demonstrating the deliberate and proactive focus on solutions in the community in Whaingaroa, and the management of paradoxes and contradictions by individuals and the community. This can be seen as driven and informed by resistance to the exploitative corporations and restrictive government regulations described in Chapter Five. This focus is also guided by the values explored in Chapter Six. The following chapter will further explore social economics in relation to the community.

9   LIVING ECONOMIES

If you have difficulty understanding the Wall Street logic, which is taught in economics and finance courses, it may be because you are in touch with reality (Korten 2010, 36).

Life, not money, is the measure of real wealth (Korten 2010, 18).

Here is an excerpt from a discussion which took place during a Permy Pot-luck in Whaingaroa in 2014:

Jodi: Markets are also trading, between the stalls.
Liz: Swapping.
Jodi: Yeah.
Liz: That's the fun thing at markets is all the internal trading that goes on.
Jodi: People need to be encouraged to grow and make produce and then we can get it local.
[Discussion about potential developments with local food in the area]
Liz: I think it's coming, it was a maybe, just an idea a few years ago but the sale [of the Foursquare building] has gone through… [Name omitted] will be funding it but someone else will figure out how it will work, it will take lots of money to make it happen. He's the

money making man but these things don't happen without lots of money.

Dan: Do you think he'll charge good rates for the stall-holders?

Liz: well that's the big question.

It has been one of the great surprises of this ethnographic project that economics, previously a topic of little interest to me, has emerged as one of the most fascinating areas of the community of Whaingaroa. To grasp this, one must adopt a fairly 'organic' understanding of economics to begin with. The diverse economies described by the feminist theorists who write under the name Gibson-Graham (2006) are helpful here, as is the foundational work of Marilyn Waring (1988), in taking note of the myriad forms of unrecognised, yet important, labour that is being carried out in every community. David Graeber's (2001) work on the anthropology of value goes a long way towards contextualising diverse understandings of economy, wealth, and meaning through various cultural frameworks. These understandings will be drawn on in this chapter in order to better understand the complex and interconnected community economies of Whaingaroa, along with notions of 'the sharing economy', 'living economies', and 'the moral economy'.

In understanding the intricacies of economics in a community like Whaingaroa it is helpful to first understand that economies here are deeply interconnected with culture. Terms such as 'moral economy' have been employed for several decades in relation to peasant communities in order to illustrate this interconnectedness (MacRae 2016). This concept, of the 'moral economy' will be employed in this chapter, along with reflections emanating from Ostrom's (1990) work on communal governing of the 'commons'.

In the food sovereignty literature, the broader understandings of economics are linked to the concept of 'agrarian citizenship' (Wittman et al 2010; Rose 2013).

Agrarian citizenship, says Wittman, 'goes beyond traditional or liberal conceptions of rights linked to individual property, production or possession'. Instead, it proceeds from an 'ecological rationality', not an 'economic rationality', and 'recognize[s] how the political and material rights and practices of rural dwellers are integrated into the socio-ecological metabolism between society and nature'. (Rose 2013, 99)

This too is relevant to ontologies of connectedness, wherein complex systems are recognised (Rose 2013; Capra and Luisi 2014).

The concept of 'social capital' can also be seen as relevant here, although it is a concept that has drawn criticism for its apparent connection with capitalism, particularly neoliberalism, as Gibson-Graham (2006) comment:

A new language of 'social capital' has emerged as promoted, for example, by the World Bank... The detailed concepts developed for many years by economic anthropologists to describe the performance and meanings of diverse transactions have been displaced, their specific significations decontexualised and reinterpreted as elements of the bonding, binding and linking relationships that constitute 'social capital'. Dumped into this grab bag category, they are represented as bland relational ingredients of social cohesion or lack thereof... The choice of nomenclature in which the term 'capital' is liberally attached to certain social relations (as well as to the other four dimensions of the sustainable livelihoods framework – natural, physical, human and financial), cannot be seen as innocent. The capitalocentric assumption is that the social relations addressed by these concepts are 'investments' that can eventually be monetised, exchanged and used to generate profitable returns (Gibson-Graham 2006, 58).

The term 'social capital' was used by participants in the process of my fieldwork in order to indicate the value of immeasurable social things. Most notably, Liz talked about it during the permaculture course in April 2014 along with the idea of 'community wealth': "Make sure that we're building it and not plundering it." In this context, the terms are being used in an obviously anti-capitalocentric sense. 'Wealth' is being reframed as something, not only more complex than financial capital, but as something more important than money. This view resonates with that expressed by Gibson-Graham in the above quote, despite their rejection of the 'social capital' term.

Also relevant here is Elinor Ostrom's (1990) Nobel Prize winning work demonstrating that 'the tragedy of the commons' is not inevitable and that community groups can effectively manage shared resources. 'The tragedy of the commons' refers to a common theory in economics whereby resources or spaces held in common are overused and not cared for by people, acting in their own self-interest. This is generally taken for granted by economists who either argue that the State must protect public property and manage its use, or that it should all be privatised. Key to Ostrom's (1990) argument is that some individuals have broken out of this 'trap' whereas it remains problematic for others:

This leads me to ask what differences exist between those who have broken the shackles of a commons dilemma and those who have not. The differences may have to do with factors internal to a given group. The participants may simply have no capacity to communicate with one another, no way to develop trust, and no sense that they must share a common future. Alternatively, powerful individuals who stand to gain from the current situation, while others lose, may block efforts by the less powerful to change the rules of the game. Such groups may need some form of external assistance to break out of the perverse logic of their situation. The differences between those who have and those who have not extricated themselves from commons dilemmas may also have to do with factors outside the domain of those affected. Some participants do not have the autonomy to change their own institutional structures and are prevented from making constructive changes by external authorities who are indifferent to the perversities of the commons dilemma, or may even stand to gain from it. Also, there is the possibility that external changes may sweep rapidly over a group, giving them insufficient time to adjust their internal structures to avoid the suboptimal outcomes. Some groups suffer from perverse incentive systems that are themselves the results of policies pursued by central authorities. Many potential answers spring to mind regarding the question why some individuals do not achieve collective benefits for themselves, whereas others do. However, as long as analysts presume that individuals cannot change such situations themselves, they do not ask what internal or external variables can enhance or impede the efforts of communities of individuals to deal creatively and constructively with perverse problems such as the tragedy of the commons. (Ostrom 1990, 21)

Xtreme Waste provide a clear example of a group of individuals who have broken out of the trap of 'the tragedy of the commons' as do other Whaingaroa food activists represented in this book. It is impossible to determine all the complex and interlinked variables involved in why this is the case. However clues can be found in the presence of several of the factors Ostrom mentions in the above quote. There is a general sense of shared purpose, particularly around betterment for the community. There is also a strong sense of trust built into the many interconnected relationships in this community.

Political economist Jessica Gordon Nembhard (2008) also offers some illuminating reflections from her work on community-based economics:

Those of us who study the economy from the grassroots, from the point of view of the "have nots," and of sustainability, are learning that a commitment to economic empowerment and economic justice is essential to long-term economic stability, particularly the revitalization of depressed areas and the protection of our physical environment. We are learning that a better understanding of collective assets and non-traditional resources contributes to finding and implementing alternative strategies that reach and benefit those that "the market" has failed. We are also finding that practicing economic justice is necessary to the maintenance of democracy. If we want affluent communities of people living dignified, happy lives, creating sustainable wealth for all, and participating positively in civil society, then we need a new economic paradigm — a revaluation of our economic principles, goals, and practices (Gordon Nembhard 2008, 271).

According to Gordon Nembhard, democratic community-based organisations "operate according to a set of principles encompassing equality of participation, collaboration, profit sharing, and cultural and ecological sensitivity" (2008, 272). She argues that the 'value added' through democratic economics builds better quality of life for more people as well as economic stability. This occurs through self-management, empowerment, community asset development and democratic participation.

Korten's (2010) work on 'living economies' draws ecological principles into the realm of economics. As first presented in Chapter One, he describes the organising principles of healthy living systems as follows:

1. Self-organise into dynamic, inclusive self-reliant communities of place
2. Balance individual and community needs and interests
3. Practice frugality and reciprocity
4. Reward cooperation
5. Optimise the sustainable capture and use of energy and matter by adapting to the specific details of the microenvironment
6. Form and manage permeable boundaries
7. Cultivate diversity and share knowledge
(Korten 2010, 147)

Each of these can be applied to aspects of the developing community economy in Whaingaroa. It can also be seen to support a myriad of healthy societal and environmental functions. These principles can be seen to be contributing to a basis through which participants, like Liz and Rick can begin to tell what Korten (2010) might call authentic stories of liberation. The principles of healthy living systems are evident in the social, environmental and economic practices of the community of food providers that were the key participants, as well as in local organisations such as Xtreme Waste which were founded on permaculture principles. As mentioned in Chapter Two, the national organisation for permaculture in New Zealand is closely connected with the Living Economies Educational Trust. These organisations share similar perspectives in which great importance is placed on 'the margins': the wisdom and experience of older people is valued and unemployment is treated as a valuable resource. As with the term 'social capital', in many instances the discourses of alternative economics walk a fine line between the words associated with neoliberalism, capitalism and the reduction of diverse meaning down to quantitative measures. However, there is a sense that these words which mean 'value' must be reclaimed in order to have discussions about that is important – that the lexicon must be re-contextualised and that difficult conversations around value are an important part of developing alternative economic thinking. Understanding this radical economic paradigm is vital to understanding the diverse living economy presented in this chapter.

Rich lives, small wallets: social capital and social commentary

One of the most remarkable things about the local food providers of Whaingaroa is that many of them live on relatively low incomes and yet, for the most part, enjoy what they describe as particularly rich lives. Much of this phenomenon can be explained by people having different priorities, as Kaiwaka explains:

I'd rather have a garden full of kai than a wad of money! When that money wall falls down, we can eat our kai; they can't eat their bloody money! But it's really hard with just three of us. To try and keep the gardens weed-free 'cause the weeds suck the sustenance out of the earth. You take two steps forward, and one back. A saner man would have given up a long time ago. We've got the passion for this job. It's not about the money.

The economic values here can be connected to those of the voluntary simplicity movement (Elgin 1981), which advocates frugal and sustainable living, in opposition to globalising capitalism's incessant drive for productivity. Robz's deliberately frugal, if unconventional life with his infant son, Matai, is a clear illustration of such a philosophy in action:

I feel very rich and I'm way below the poverty line. We live a life that people dream of, spending our summers just cruising around: in the mountains, in the bush and then come back to Whaingaroa, beautiful Whaingaroa... just having a life, owning your life. I guess money buys you time. We could live without a dollar but that would be a full-time job pretty much, to get all that food, all that nutrition. It would take a lot of planning. So the little money that we do have. Fifty bucks a week or so buys us a lot of time, a lot of hours. We can buy a bag of spuds, buy a bag of flour. I think of other ways to make money, but I'm happy enough taking the kids down to the stream and in an hour or so I've got four days-worth of food.

This philosophy with its focus on sustainability, sits well within the paradigms of permaculture and food sovereignty.

For Wayne, who draws a lot of his personal philosophy from yogic teachings, living a simple life is about shifting away from 'materialist delusions':

So many people are stuck in a job they don't enjoy – it's an endless cycle for them. In the Yogic and Buddhist traditions it's called Dharma, which is your life purpose – what you should be doing in your life – in the sense of what your job should be – try to find what you're good at instead of just being in a job that you don't really enjoy but you do it just for the money. It's better for everyone to do what's in our individual natures. It's my nature to be good with plants, so I should work with plants. It's simple. I enjoy working with plants and it's very nice. It takes some time to be aware of this developing. So many people don't really know. They've got this wrong perception that it's all about competition and putting the self first, no equanimity for everyone. It's our perception that has to change. People are living such delusion: 'I can't have this... I must have that to be happy'. It's a trap. People who move to the big city working such long hours in a job and it's a big concrete jungle, and you get your happiness through buying things with the money you earn – it's just a cycle – you've got to work more and to buy more stuff to make you happy. It's just a never-ending cycle like that. Move to Whaingaroa where people have a different perception of things or go away camping for the week in the bush – you realise you don't need all this stuff. It's quite nice, but then you come back and your perception is more material again.

Although one might read Wayne's quote above as insulting to those who are just struggling to make a living, his comment on 'putting the self first' is not directed at people living near or below the poverty line. Wayne, who is on a very low income himself, is critiquing the idea of what is often promoted as success in dominant discourse. Embedded here is almost a 'situationalist' type of critique similar to that reflected by Graeber (2009). This suggests that under neoliberalism even the winners ultimately lose because they destroy the world and have nothing to show for it but soulless money and unending discontent. The game is so flawed that 'even the prize is bad'. It is the sunken feeling of winning the monopoly board game only by making everyone else depressingly broke.

The local food providers in Whaingaroa provide good many rich stories showing that an economic system based on counting dollars and transactions is incredibly limited and inaccurate. Although Jenny is arguably worse-off financially now than before she started her bread business, when she was dependant on a benefit, her life is now richer and more satisfying. She is critical of the way the welfare system treats people, and is relieved not to be dependent on it anymore:

I'm making less than I was on the dole, but at least I'm independent, and I really hated that whole experience of being in the welfare system. It's just appalling, and although I'm really grateful for WINZ for giving me the grant, the general culture of the organisation – which is a representation of our whole society, I think – the way you're treated is really bad, but there's not a lot of work where I live [rurally] so I thought I'd just have to make it happen myself.

Despite earning less money now, with her local bread business, than she was previously receiving on a benefit, she finds the satisfaction from her business very rewarding, as well as the social aspects:

It's very social. That's the surprise part of it. I didn't intend to be part of this street network. Some people have flatmates – flatties – well we're shoppies. There's four of us. We spend a lot of time out here [on a bench seat on the main street of Whaingaroa] passing comment on society. We should have our own social comment page – very high-brow, 'Whaingaroa styles' – but we're always happy and we're always nice. It's been a real unexpected bonus – getting to know people. It's of huge value other than the monetary side. I never think "oh dammit, I have to go bake". Sometimes there are other things I want to do... This part of it has been an unexpected bonus – this camaraderie and sitting out here. We call this our office. Staff meeting! Theresa – get here or put in an apology!

This camaraderie, and the entertainment and sense of purpose Jenny has as a result of her tiny bread shop adds to the richness of her lifestyle in a way that could not be purchased with additional funds. While living on a benefit was socially isolating, despite having more money, she is now able to do things that she generally enjoys while earning enough through her efforts to 'get by'. This kind of diverse wealth is difficult to measure.

The Bro too, shares a different perspective on wealth based on comparing value across time and space:

I guess it depends on how you define rich, you know, I don't drive a car so anyone who drives a car is rich to me... This dude, he comes into work and always tries and have these big deep conversations... He was talking about how, I dunno, some crazy bullshit about how scarcity is having an effect on human development and evolution, and I'm like, 'do you think you live in a scarce society?' and he's like, 'Yeah, resources are getting scarce... and the cost of everything and they wind the cost up and wages don't go up blah-de-blah.' Then this guy pulls up in a car and I'm like 'bro, that car, what is that? 120 horsepower?' And he's like, 'aw it's like 135', and I'm like, 'really?' and I turn to the other guy and I say, '200 years ago, who do you think it was that would be able to afford to own 120 horses? 'Cause this guy he owns 120 horses and he drives it. Where you going?' And he's like "I'm going to Hamilton to do the shopping,' and I'm like, 'this guy's taking out

120 horses to do his shopping' like really... do we really live in a resource poor environment? Fuck no! We just waste our resources on shit.

The Bro's perspectives have been informed by experiences of acute material poverty at a level uncommon in New Zealand:

We live in an unequal world, eh? I spent like a week or not quite a week living with a family, six people: two grandparents, four grandkids. The parents were in prison for selling drugs because that's all they could do to make decent money, in the Philippines... Six of them, they live on the side of the road in two pallets, pushed together with a bit of tarp strung over the top of it, and that's their home, that's where they live. So now when I look at people in this country and they're like, 'I've got no money and I'm poor and stuff', I'm just like, 'Come on, what are you talking about? You're fat'. Seriously. I mean, if you've got fat on your body you're rich, mate. You take anyone from any society over the whole history of human civilisation, and they'll look at you and they'll think that you are a rich person, because you've got a bit of fat on you. It's interesting that we live in a society today, where being fat is a negative thing... that's because materially, we're ridiculously rich, rich in calories – empty calories. So you eat more and more, and it's like that's a bad thing. For most of history, carrying a bit of fat was like: 'Fuck bro well done, you're a good hunter, how did you manage that? You're rich.' Isn't that weird? And now it's all backwards, like poor people tend to be fat and rich people tend to be skinny. 'Sweet' has become flattened out, sweet used to be a really full word eh? You still see people using it like that to an extent, you're so sweet. It used to be a really full word and now it just means saccharine... sugar.

These perspectives can be read as personal counter-narratives to that of mainstream consumer culture where having more money and accumulating possessions is seen as desirable in order to lead a good life. Here 'a good life' is prioritised over having more money and property, as Wayne explains:

Whaingaroa, for a lot of people allows a low income but a good lifestyle. I think the 'only middleclass can afford ethical food thing' is a load of rubbish. I stopped eating meat four years ago and I definitely think it's a lot cheaper to be a vegetarian. I eat at least 80 percent organic and I don't spend much money on food but I grow all my veges, so the food that I do buy is just from WOK. It's pretty small, maybe a bit of cheese, bit of milk, some pulses. It's your lifestyle – the way you live – that dictates how much you're spending on your groceries each week. I guess poverty in a material sense, but that's more idealistic from a Western mindset – you want the big car and the big flash house – but that's not sustainable for this planet. We all need food and shelter, it's necessity for the maintenance of the body, but the ultimate goal of life is not to have a Ferrari.

This sentiment, in various forms, was reflected in many interviews and in observations in general, despite most participants not being vegetarians. Some participants reflected on their experience of past practices in times of great economic hardship. These difficult times when excesses are cut back, "might be a good thing" according to Mike:

I remember back in the mid-80s with Rogernomics[1], we had no more money, it was just survival. I remember that whoever was going to town would get the other person's stuff and it wasn't all bad. I mean, when there's enough then it dies out – it's kind of sad – the fuel prices aren't enough to actually change behaviour. You hear a lot about the price of petrol because we're all reliant on it, but you could argue it's actually too cheap.... but it's not a very popular argument. I used to take the kids down to wait for the school bus – a great percentage of cars commuting to Hamilton, but in a fuel crisis, perhaps not. I've often thought a bit about Cuba and when you cut them off they become self-sufficient. If we had a real fuel crisis – if fuel was valued at what it's worth we'd probably be on 10–15 bucks a litre because we're using it all up and we're not leaving any for future generations but when it's not there you find other ways. My dad grew up in England and fought for England and I've got a bit of an issue about freedoms because he fought long and hard to deal to Hitler and when he came back he was broke as, everything was rationed, and he made an old Austin A40 run on pig shit with a methane burner and people knew when he was coming to town because it smelled terrible, but he could get around without any fuel vouchers and I reckon we could do it – with Kiwi ingenuity. It would actually be better for us.

Mike's reflection that people become less wasteful, and try to be more resilient by producing more of their own food in times of economic and resource scarcity is echoed by Johanna Knox (2013). In her book, *A Forager's Treasury*, Knox comments that anecdotal evidence suggests the peaks of foraging in New Zealand coincide with times of economic scarcity, notably during the world wars, the great depression and the oil crisis of the 1970s. There is a sense of irony apparent here, in that it takes a crisis for people to act, and that while there are plenty of resources available people will continue to be wasteful, despite presumably having the capacity for foresight. In some ways, the stories gathered during my fieldwork suggest a different kind of class of 'rich-poor people', people living in varying levels of what could be described as financial poverty, and yet abundantly rich in other forms of wealth: social, recreational, time, educational, community agency, quality food and various other ambiguous manifestations of wealth. This is largely due to various kinds reciprocal relationships and ideological reasons that present a radical shift from what Wayne calls the 'treadmill for mainstream society'. Tensions do emerge in Whaingaroa, as they do in Wilderland, around scarce resources and high food prices, however these, too, present a paradox. Food, like petrol, can be seen to be both too cheap and too expensive. Too cheap, because the 'real' cost of production is cast off onto the environment, or outsourced overseas in unfair labour conditions, and yet too expensive for people suffering the most from social inequalities and living in poverty. In the following section we bring some parallel analysis to the food values and tensions under a social economic lens drawing on the economic literature mentioned above.

Social economics and the sharing economy

In his paper examining the moral economy in relation to Balinese rice farmers, Graeme MacRae (2016) explores the way that contemporary rural economies have been "de-moralised" and disconnected from their socio-cultural contexts in which moral dimensions are located. He found that, despite the tendency in mainstream economics to delineate in terms of markets and equations, in reality the trust and friendship between farmers and those representing businesses was of major significance, and the break-down of these friendship relationships also meant the downfall of the business relationships involved. This resonates with stories gathered from the community of food producers in Whaingaroa, and also with the wider food sovereignty movement (Rose 2013). It supports the argument that is evident from an anthropological perspective: that social and cultural factors are interconnected with economics, despite the difficulty in measuring them.

Like Mike and Mady's farm, Xtreme Waste has a focus on sustainability, not just in terms of environment, but also financial, social and community. Rick calls this a 'quadruple bottom line' and explains that the social nature of the work place makes working at Xtreme Waste more enjoyable than more mechanised work places, as Rick explains:

Hand-sorting is the most efficient way of sorting. Our product is 100 percent pure and we get the best premiums in the world for recycling. It's about brain and hand – making a conscious decision. We've got an unemployment problem. We shouldn't be honouring the fact that we're industrialised and developed systems that take jobs away from people. These guys love working, they work as a team – so many jobs these days you're isolated on your own – but these guys love it and take it in turns to run and drive and are involved in any aspect.

This resonates with the balanced job complexes and participatory economics described by Graeber (2011). It also relates to Korten's (2010, 170–171) organic analogy for economics and his assertion that the monetary system is to modern economics what the circulatory system is to the body. Each of Korten's organising principles, noted above, can also be applied to aspects of the developing community economy in Whaingaroa. This community economy can also be seen to support a myriad of healthy societal and environmental functions, as is exemplified in the case of Xtreme Waste as described in chapter seven. These principles, along with those of permaculture can be seen to contribute a basis through which participants like Liz and Rick can begin to tell what Korten (2010) might call an authentic story of liberation.

Another concept that may be relevant here is that of 'collaborative consumption' and 'the sharing economy' as framed by Botsman and Rogers (2010). Coming from marketing and business management perspectives, these authors explore the contemporary rise of collaborative business structures such as Air BnB and car sharing networks. These business models have, however, been criticised by sociologists for promoting further neoliberalisation (Walker 2015). These kind of critiques, similar to those of ethical food presented by Guthman (2003; 2008), highlight a paradox: in attempting to move away from dominant models, and in experimenting with different models for consumption, the problematic nature of the dominant system may be either replicated or may be made worse. This is not necessarily the case, and as Botsman and Rogers (2010) point out, the move towards more collaborative practices has the potential to reduce consumption, for example, the existence and increasing accessibility of tool libraries means that not everyone needs to own a hand-held drill (when what you really want is the hole in the wall, not the drill itself).

Jon describes the collaborative and mutually supportive relationship his food hub has with local food producers and the wider community:

Well, there are local people who've got a permaculture farm who grow quite a lot of organic food and teas and things like that and it has been an outlet for them that they can be guaranteed to sell a certain amount. I can let them know on a Sunday evening and they bring it on a Tuesday so that's a guaranteed sale rather than putting it in a shop and hoping it sells. It's nice to have an immediate outlet. There's other people who grow macadamia nuts or whatever and I just give them a bell every now and then when we need some more and they bring them down. It's really nice to be able to support local growers whenever I can. The spray-free orchards in Hamilton, getting local-ish only 50ks away, high quality food that hasn't had any chemicals on it for

*decades. In terms of more wider effects I guess – more community building
in that more people see more of each other more of the time. People share
ideas and recipes and flu cures with me and I can spread that around. I've
realised that I'm a bit of an information gatherer and disseminator.*

Alongside financial transactions, there is unquantifiable but prevalent
gifting, swapping and trading, especially of surplus foods. This often
occurs at markets between stallholders, as Jenny describes:

*Quite often at the market people come up and say: hey, do you want to swap
a bread for this, or I go up to them and ask to swap a bread for that. Often
you do need money, not just three bags of carrots, but if I need carrots it's a
win-win situation. I always feel, not quite humbled but quite chuffed when
people are excited because they think they're getting a good deal for my
bread.*

Wayne started the community police station garden with the intention of giving away produce to the local food bank which is open two
afternoons a week, so when he has the time on those days, he will
pick vegetables and deliver them. Justin also mentioned giving away
surplus from the café by donation to the local community house,
although not all food is suitable for donation.

*We had leftover cakes and muffins, 'cause they have meetings Mondays and
Wednesdays or something, so if they wanted they could have it for their
meetings. We are just trying to figure out a system that'll work 'cause obviously if we can sell it… but because some food that's perishable you can't
give to them. There are certain things that you just can't sell the next day
they don't look the best or whatever. You're running a bad kitchen if you're
giving too much stuff away, wouldn't be profitable. The food bank is one I'd
like to look into.*

During the interview he also mentioned an exchange he had made
with my brother, who is a hunter, of the café's old freezers for a pig.
These kinds of casual transactions can be seen as a lively part of the
informal economies of rural New Zealand communities, alongside
sharing fresh fish or surplus garden produce. They are also part of

traditional and contemporary Māori manākitanga [care, generosity and respect]. The same brother has also gifted pigs to the local Marae for tangihanga [traditional Māori funeral ceremony].

In an economic climate where small-scale market gardening struggles to compete with large industrialised farming, growers like Kaiwaka and Lynn at Kaiwhenua Organics are interested in providing education as another income stream and also as a way of sharing their skills and passing on knowledge. Kaiwaka explains how they get in touch with marae to run gardening education projects:

What happens when we do the Kai Māra [food garden] projects? We say 'ok, we've got X amount of funds, and that will be enough for X amount of maraes'. So you go out and look for X maraes and ask them if they want gardens. So I just ring them up, introduce myself. The majority of people have heard of us, we've done 40 marae already, soon it'll be 55 marae. And they're really enthusiastic.

More recently a nearby polytechnic ran a gardening course at Kaiwhenua. However Kaiwaka and Lynn were not pleased with the outcome as the only financial compensation they received was for driving people to the gardens from the Whaingaroa township. Kaiwaka and Lynn had suspicions that the organisers had accessed Māori funding, yet they restricted the cups of coffee their students were allowed. As Kaiwaka said: "That's not good manākitanga" [care, generosity, hospitality].

Another common educational exchange prevalent in both Whaingaroa and wider New Zealand occurs with the hosting of wwoofers. Mike describes the reciprocal relationship experienced with wwoofers:

We have wwoofers. We haven't advertised lately because of the little people [their young children], but we still get some through contacts and it's a good social thing. It's a lucky dip, you get some exceptional ones and some ordinary ones but it's good when the good ones work out and you get something from them and they get something from you. A lot of my travel to different countries was to stay with wwoofers – all of France was wwoofers. It works out quite well. They can be a lot of fun and it brings a bit of culture to the place.

Liz and Rick also host wwoofers and more long-term 'interns' who have the chance to learn a variety of skills and work in exchange for food and accommodation. Wayne also describes the garden manager at Solscape as "basically an intern – he's learning a skill-set – he's working a set number of hours, he's provided with accommodation." These reciprocal relationships can work well because what is being exchanged – work for food and accommodation – are things that would usually be expensive to purchase for both parties. By not having to pay as much for labour in a formal economic way, farmers are able to have less involvement with the formal economy.

Land sharing is another reciprocal arrangement, which tends to be more long-term than wwoofing and does not usually involve providing accommodation. It can also be seen as a way for people who want to grow food to have access to land while avoiding a large mortgage. In this sense there is a democratising capacity to land sharing which is dependent upon land owners being open to having other people on their land. This openness is generally developed through personal relationships, although the internet, in its vast democratising capacity has made it possible for landowners who are looking for a reciprocal land sharing arrangement to make contact with people who are wanting to have access to land to grow food[2].

In Robz's land sharing arrangement, he and Matai have been able to provide themselves with accommodation by building a series of little structures on the corner of the land that was not being used for anything other than growing a few pine trees. The trees assist with shelter and Robz assists with work that needs to be done on the property. Although he did not know the land owner for long before moving there, his occupation of the land depends upon maintaining that relationship, which has not been a problem. It did take Robz a while to find suitable people with land that was close enough to town to bicycle back and forth, and that people were willing to share. With such an arrangement in mind, when he first moved to Whaingaroa, Robz tried putting notes into the letterboxes of people in suitable areas, but eventually only found access to land through friendships he built.

Prior to coming to Whaingaroa, Robz had been living in the Far North, on land for which he had a 'rent-to-own' type of arrangement. To find this land he and his former partner had put an advertisement in the New Zealand organic magazine: "young family looking for land. Rent to own or similar". They had several responses from people in a variety of places, including the Coromandel, and went to visit each place before deciding to settle in the Far North in a house bus. Robz says that although that situation suited a young family, with the break-up of the relationship he felt isolated and wanted to be living in a community atmosphere, and so for this reason he moved to Whaingaroa. Because of the relationships he has formed here, lack of land ownership has not been an issue for Robz:

I've got friends in the Far North in Kerikeri, very awesome people, they were saying how it's such a middle-class concept. Just 'cause to live off the land, you've got to own your land outright you know, you can't live off your land and work. I guess permaculture is a full time job so it's not applicable to people that don't have the access. So mine's kind of a free community service where you don't need to own any land you just use land, just use anybody's land who's happy for you to do it. There's always going to be people who are happy you know and there's always going to be people who are trying to, who do have land to run, in that bracket, who always need help so if you've got some skills. Lenny is making this a permaculture property. I'm helping him out, he's really grateful to have the help, we're really grateful to have a home.

A recent global food crisis (Wittman et al 2010) has been associated with higher food prices. During the course of my fieldwork I had a brief conversation with a supermarket teller about the rising price of food "Yeah," she commented, "The price of all these things goes up" she gestured at my shopping, "but do our wages go up? No." Despite this apparent food price crisis, The Bro argues that actually, from a long-term perspective, food in 'developed' countries is cheaper now than it used to be:

Yeah, people don't even spend that much money on food anymore, I forget the actual statistics, but the percentage of peoples income that they spend on nutrition has dropped over time, now it's some ridiculously small amount, but we pay so little for food, people always complain about how organic food is really expensive and I kind of agree with that but actually we've gotten so used to having cheap food. We're putting the true cost of our food on the ecological credit card that our children and our grandchildren are gonna have to pay. People don't actually pay that much for food these days, especially over the 20th century with the green revolution and stuff, the cost of food has gone down and down and down and farmers go broke, broke, broke. So it wasn't a consumer choice thing. It was actually realising that so many of things that me and mates in that scene didn't like in the world, were actually beyond our control.

Participants expressed concern over the high price of certified organic food. Kaiwaka says one of the reasons they started their garden was because of the inaccessible price of organic food: "We went to buy it and – oooh why is it so dear?! Why? They didn't pay anything for a poison?" This highlights one aspect of the counter-intuitive nature of industrial food, which requires large quantities of water, oil and synthetic fertilisers to produce and yet is cheaper than less processed, locally produced foods.

Jenny has found the price a restrictive factor, which has prevented her from purchasing speciality flour:

It's all New Zealand ingredients. It would be nice to be able to buy specialty flour from mills but the price just takes it right out of any economy. People often want organic but it would be up to $10 a loaf. I can't do it for that. The rye flour comes from down south and the white comes from wherever they source it from.

That the flour she uses comes from wheat grown in New Zealand is important to her, as it is more local. This is another example of how the morality around local food influences economic decisions.

Mike talked about the well-known American Farmer, Joel Salatin of Polyface farm, describing him as "as close to a mentor as anyone I've had". Mike has heard Salatin speak in New Zealand and also visited his farm:

He's got a fantastic operation, I've seen his operation. The level of integrity is incredible, the level of productivity is incredible. Nothing goes off bulk to a factory, it's all local and he doesn't do organics, but he's adamant about being GM free. He's not bringing in fertilizers, he brings in grain that the chickens eat and they go across the grasses and eat bugs. They've put a lot of poo on instead of fertilisers. And that could work for us, but it won't work for us organically because the amount you'd have to spend – you probably don't want to spend $40 on a chook – on a chicken to eat.

This quote illustrates the interaction between moral and economic values, as well as the way that organic standards can be restrictive as the price of maintaining them does not match the market price of food. In this way organic certification has a complex relationship with the moral economy as experienced by local food providers.

The Bro describes the food situation in New Zealand as relatively empowering compared with many overseas situations:

With food in this country, you still have a lot of control over where your money goes and how you decide to eat. It's not even to do with spending so much as how you decide to eat and who you decide to do it with and how. I think you still have a lot of control over that, because we're an agricultural nation.

The high price of organic food can be mitigated by personal gardening. As Wayne points out, growing fruit and vegetables can be much cheaper than buying food: "I know many times when I've had no money I've been glad I have a veggie garden," although it requires both time and access to land.

The concept of reciprocal gifting economies, as described by Graeber (2001) is also relevant here, as illustrated by Robz:

I find when you spend your life you know giving a lot without expecting stuff in return, that's when you receive so much in return... I don't necessarily get that in return in Whaingaroa, but once we're on the road, when we're on the bike that's when karma comes into place I feel. Cause that's when just amazing things happen, randomly people just help us out so much, it's like 'oh yea, cool'. Universe's way. So I don't know, I kinda feel instead of putting money in a bank, I'm putting good deeds in... working up quite a bit of credit. You know I'm definitely not expecting to get anything back from it, but by not expecting that, from experience, you kinda receive quite a lot back, especially in a small community you know, and when someone's doing quite a lot for the community and people acknowledge that and want a help out a bit as well. Yeah, I find that a lot. I guess it's also about when you need help, it's there. When you're travelling you need probably a lot more support than if you're here. I mean, if you're here and you want to build something then that's creating that need and people can come in and help but if you're travelling and people are saying 'oh have this' or 'share this food' 'you can stay here' or whatever because you can't carry everything with you.

Fairtrade and a living wage

The concept of fairtrade[3] as well as other food values as enacted through 'conscious consumption', as discussed in Chapter Six, can be seen as linked to the moral economy. Interestingly, fairtrade has come under criticism from various angles, notably from free-market economists critical of artificially inflating markets. This is a peculiar criticism, considering that the market in this context is functioning in relation to consumer demand, as markets are apparently supposed to do, according to these same free-market economists. In fact, one could argue that this is actually an instance of markets functioning particularly well. Perhaps the discomfort for free-market economists is that there is a moral aspect to the economy here, that they find difficult to grasp or graph. Ironically, there is a sense of moral outrage presented by proponents of the free-market, that morality should play any part in economics. As Mason and Singer (2006) state:

Pro-market economists accept consumers paying $48 a pound for Jamaican Blue Mountain coffee. They don't object to corporations that blatantly use snob appeal to promote their products. So why criticise the decision of some consumers to pay $12 for a pound of coffee that they know has been grown without toxic chemicals, under the shade of trees that help birds to survive, by farmers who can now afford to feed and educate their children? There is no economic – let alone ethical – reason why people's purchases must be driven exclusively by self-interest rather than a desire to help others... Of course it is true that fairtrade coffee will not raise the returns to all coffee growers, but it is a mistake to think that because a proposal cannot solve a very big problem that it cannot do any good at all (Singer and Mason 2006, 148).

Mason and Singer conclude that if you buy imported commodities such as coffee, chocolate, bananas, tea and sugar, it is better to buy fairtrade. Although other critics of fairtrade have argued that it is ineffective at what it sets out to do, analysis has shown that the economic benefits for farmers are unassailable, although wider education and health benefits are uneven (Arnould, Plastina and Ball 2009).

In the context of Whaingaroa, the moral economy of fairtrade is alive and well. Participants prefer to buy fairtrade products where possible. The local coffee roaster, Raglan Roast, is said to only import fairtrade coffee and has established relationships with farmers in several different locations. Raglan Roast is well known for its low priced coffees, despite this, the margin on coffee is still quite high as a local barista for the business, explains:

Yeah, the coffee trade is an interesting thing. I can see a sustainable equitable coffee trade. We're so rich in coffee, people can afford to drink three cups a day. And I know the only way people can afford to drink three cups a day, is because we oppress the people growing the beans. Obviously Raglan Roast is *signed up to fairtrade and all that kind of stuff and we contribute money to a development fund, and we do what we can within the limits of the system set up. But really when it comes down to it, a 70kg of green beans is ten bucks. We can roast that and turn that into hundreds and hundreds and hundreds of dollars' worth of coffee. And that's 10 bucks for us to buy it, so fuck knows what they're paying the growers... There are things about Raglan Roast that I really like. They're really focused on delivering a product to people at, in our economy, a reasonable price. It really galls me when I go to other places, when I know they are paying the same price for beans and they charge another half... a flat white with us is $3.00, and you go somewhere else and its $4.50. That really galls me. Partially because I know how much it costs to buy a sack of beans, so you guys are ripping – not only are you ripping the growers – but the customers too.*

Despite the high profit margin, this barista appreciates the honesty of the people involved in running this local business, and that they don't 'trumpet' about their contributions to charitable funds for education. The relative affordability of the coffee beans does not necessarily make them less valuable, as the following example describes:

Little things like the young fella who works there, one of the first things we make him do when he comes in in the morning is fill of bags of beans for sale, bags and bags of beans, and he always spills them. I think he's only sixteen, and when you're sixteen you don't have proper hand eye coordination or something. And [the boss] is always horrified when beans get spilt on the floor. But the thing is he never says 'that's costing me money!' I remember the first time it happened, when beans got spilt on the floor, and he was like, 'Do you know where that bean comes from? That bean was grown on a mountain in Peru, and people do this than this, then they carry it on their backs for 50kms.' The economic thing is there, but it's more like: 'Don't you understand how much sweat and time and effort has gone into getting these beans to this cafe, just so you can chuck it on the floor?' I kind of like that... It reminds me of, when that Mexican agronomist went to the corn belt of America and he cried when he saw all the corn on the ground at the corn silos, 'cause it's just a commodity, there's nothing special about it, there's so much of it, it just drops on the ground and people walk all over it. And where he comes from they have a God, and his sole role is corn. That's how important it is. So I kind of like those things about Raglan Roast. But obviously it's not my model for a sustainable food related business in Whaingaroa.

This illustrates that the concept of the 'moral economy' as described by MacRae (2016) and has decommodifying potential, as it broadens the scope of economics to include values other than financial. This decommodification can be connected back to the food sovereignty principles outlined in Chapter Two.

Like 'fairtrade', the concept of a 'living wage' is widely used in New Zealand, and can be seen as relevant to the moral economy, as Jon illustrates here:

Now I've got a family I need more of an income, so that's part of my motivation. I'm also going to need some advice about this, from someone who's more experienced in this kind of thing, about how to do it in other places and make sure I benefit from it too, financially. I've done so much for free for so long and I really love doing it but now I've got a family I need to change my focus a bit. I'm still happy to do things for free as well but I need to be paid well for what I do and I feel like when one is experienced in what one does – which I must say I'm only beginning to be – it's only been five years – but one deserves to be paid well and it makes me sad to see people who are really good at things and have been doing it for 20 years getting paid 15 bucks an hour for it. It's not right. That's a beginner – you know, someone just leaving school being a hammer-hand fair enough – but if you're experienced at what you do you deserve to be paid well for it no matter what it is.

This quote and Robz's quote above highlight a paradox between giving things away for free and fair pay. This runs parallel to the tension between the idealised and pragmatic perspectives presented by many participants. For people who are self-employed, earning a living wage means applying good business sense.

Good business, added value and being practical

Markets work best within the framework of a caring community. The stronger the relations of mutual trust and caring, the more the market becomes self-policing. The need for formal government oversight is minimal (Korten 2010, 45).

Alongside the emphasis in the community on voluntary simplicity and moral economic practices, there is also a strong emphasis on 'good business sense' and its practical application. For the small-scale food producers represented here, 'good business sense' means producing and selling enough food to stay afloat and preparing for 'bad weather'. It is also about maintaining and building relationships within the community. It often means reaching compromises between values and cost-effectiveness. This section of the chapter explores the crossover of conventional and moral economics.

For Mike and Mady, with their modest dairy farm and principles around sustainability on multiple levels, it makes 'good business sense' to grow their local market for milk. The milk they sell from the farm gate earns them a lot more than they receive from Fonterra, and the price does not fluctuate according to the market. Because of this, they have invested time and money into implementing systems to better serve their local customers and keep organised:

We've gone from supplying milk to five or six locals to a few people in Hamilton and a few in Whaingaroa to around about 150 families now. We used to spend a lot of time in the evenings bottling and had people ringing up all the time. While it was working it wasn't working well, so we put in a purpose-built vat and we put in each morning what we feel we will need each day – to a pattern – and then people can bring their own containers and fill that themselves, and that's been working well, but even that's started to out-grow the systems we've had in place so we're just putting in new systems. We have software to manage internet payments and all that sort of thing because everybody was getting themselves into a different system and it was hard to monitor – some people pay weekly, monthly, six monthly. Mady's just upskilling and putting software in place that can be more efficient and reduce the time. We'll try to expand what we're doing because it improves our viability.

Another part of becoming more resilient in the face of a volatile market is having diversity of production and therefore a variety of potential income streams. Alongside the milk, Mike and Mady are broadening their farm's production:

When you're a 120 cow farm, which is really small by modern standards with a full time labour unit, you've gotta do something a little smart, so for us it's added value, yes, there's obviously some work involved, as with anything worthwhile in life and it does give the local community an option. Raw milk is not for everybody but for those that want it, it gives them a choice and I would defend that choice 'til the end. We're planting feijoa hedges – 300 trees. It's a triple aspect to the feijoas. They're a fantastic shade and shelter tree, hardy so you can't easily kill them, and they're a grafted variety so they fruit well, early, medium and late varieties. So apart from the shade and shelter for the stock it can be a potential cash crop that we can also sell at the milk shed, especially if the kids want help with their university fees. If all else fails Phoenix and that with the juices want organic fruit and you just have to work out if it's worth it with the cost of harvesting, having someone pick them up. Plan D is they're great stock food, so we shouldn't really lose on them. Then we've got our meat: sheep, pigs, beef, so we're well set up, that's home-kill. We supply other people and we're looking at doing a bit more of that, again, to add value and not be so vulnerable to the ups and downs of the international market place where you can get $4 kilo one week and $8 next, whereas if you set the price sometimes you'll be up a bit, sometimes you'll be down a bit on what the international market is doing but it's nice and level. So you're not exposed to the ups and downs so much.

For Mike the 'value-added' aspect of offering milk for sale by the litre is good for business. Rose (2013) notes this kind of small farm diversification and focus on valued-added production is on the rise in Western countries.

The diversification mentioned above is part of the fabric of many small local businesses. It indicates that broad and holistic thinking, balanced with ethical values is also a key part of being practical when it comes to local food livelihoods. For Jon, thinking and doing things differently from how he envisions a conventional business might function is a major part of his approach:

Thinking outside the box and doing things in a different way: 'How can I..?' rather than 'I cannot...' – setting artificial limits on yourself. Some of the time I'd think was it a silly idea or 'Will people support it?', but we really didn't know until we just did it. Also organic food is such a fast-growing sector as far as I understand and it will continue to be and it continues to grow during a recession and I found the recession didn't really have an effect on whether people bought organic food or not. It sends a message to the mainstream corporate food system of the 'profit-driven-only' that less and less people are interested in that model. Unfortunately the vast majority of people are, just because of financial pressures more than anything else. It would be interesting to see, if money wasn't an issue, how many people would buy organic. Because as many people are aware chronic diseases and life expectancy are all heading the wrong way in the so-called 'developed' world, and I should mention that the corporate model – being 'for profit only' it's for short-term profit only because it's destroying the topsoil and depleting the water levels, so it's actually not even for long-term profit and the costs are passed on to the local people or the tax payers or whoever.

As indicated here, Jon's business practices with WOK are deeply interconnected with his other values. By eliminating the overheads like the high rents involved in running a conventional shop, he is trying to provide organic food at a cheaper rate than is accessible for most people, however he is aware that it is still prohibitively expensive for many people who are struggling. This is an ethical dilemma for many people who are concerned about food ethics.

Being practical, for Justin, means making sure the café is making a profit, because otherwise 'It's just not worth it':

My issue with the free range is the bacon, I can't justify, I mean no-one is going to buy a side of bacon for seven dollars, I mean I wouldn't. It didn't matter where I would be eating I wouldn't do it, so I can't expect my customers to.

The expansion of ethical consumption has driven the prices down in a way that reflects conventional economic theory, Justin explains:

The more and more people that buy free range or organic the price does come down and more and more people are becoming aware, suppliers are becoming aware of it and it is making it easier to find the source and that sort of stuff. It's getting better and better but that is still, no one's got a bottomless pocket so you find that balance. I mean, there's a lot of greed – unnecessary greed, you don't need a whole chicken for a family of four, you can break it down and use it. If you buy an expensive free range chicken or whatever or fish or whatever it is, you don't need to use it all in one go.

This attitude of 'finding a balance' and treating food appropriately demonstrates a different level of connectedness to food, reflecting food sovereignty's focus on decommodification and its ontologies of connectedness. Rather than a chicken just being a commodity, it is valued more and the process of its preparation and consumption, as well as its disposal is given more attention in relation to wider ethical factors.

"Good business" as described in this section, reflects practicality when it comes to profit margins as well as broader and deeper understandings of interconnectedness. As Rick explains, these can be related to permaculture and are also part of the foundation of Xtreme Waste:

These are the connections to the permaculture principles and design of Xtreme Waste, using local resources, closing the loop and having zero waste. It's all very much an extension of the permaculture design. If we can, even if it is more expensive we purchase locally, without spinning the economic value on the community.

Jon also described permaculture as an important feature in his business and his attitude to community, particularly regarding the concept of 'closed loop' systems:

So I grow my food in my garden, I give the veggie scraps to Xtreme Waste, it comes back from Xtreme Waste [as compost] and goes back into my soil again. Time loops – the time bank in Whaingaroa – I help you in your garden for an hour, you help Bob carry a box of something for an hour and Bob helps somebody else and that somebody else helps me pick my apples for an hour so we're all spending the same amount of time doing things but we're helping each other. Money loops, there's a local group set up to reduce interest payments going out of Whaingaroa something like $30 million a year goes out of Whaingaroa in payments – people's mortgages, loans. Community banking, you all put money in there and anyone who needs to use it for something uses it for that thing and arrange to pay it back at a certain way but don't pay interest. We pool our money so that everyone has power to use a four or even five figure sum at short notice that we might not have by ourselves. I haven't used it for myself yet but I'm putting money in. I'm finding it really interesting and really challenging and encouraging. It's a group of us who aren't afraid to try new things. People will put up their car as security in case something happens, but that said, it is also entirely trust-based.

Many of the 'good business' values presented in this section are not especially remarkable. They fit comfortably within a conventional economics framework. The more remarkable thing is that they also fit comfortably within 'moral economy' or 'living economies' frameworks as well. Here, the diverse values that people hold are balanced with practical application and the contradictions which emerge from simultaneously being interconnected with the dominant economic systems and strongly resisting some powerful forces within those systems. Just as tensions in the physics of engineering a kete are points of the very force that hold its structure together, the tensions of paradox here can be seen to hold the narratives together, both on an individual level, and in a wider construction of collective shared values and identity.

10 DISCUSSION: COMPLEXITY AND CONNECTION

"Are you almost finished?" Robz asked me during the third year of this research.

"It's a slow process. I might be finished next year."

"And will it change anything?"

"What do you mean?"

"Will the people who have power – will they do anything differently?"

Taken aback, I explain to Robz that what I write will contribute to a body of literature, and that other people may reference it, and that is what happens with academic documents, usually. I add that sometimes policy-makers take notice of research, because it's possible, but also because I want to be optimistic

– My fieldwork reflections, 2015.

In this final chapter I revisit the various strands of theory and ethnographic material, to discuss key themes and bring them together in a summary. Of particular focus here are ontologies of connectedness and tensions of paradox, first described in Chapter One in relation to the work of Capra and Luisi (2014), Seo and Creed (2002), and the other key theorists described there. These theoretical threads can be seen throughout this book and are reflected in the narratives of every participant. Both strands are also manifest in critiques of the global corporate food system as alienating. Similar critiques also arose around what is considered by some participants to be a specifically narrow Western view of the "environment" and "nature" as either resources to be exploited or as something to be boxed off and protected – separate from the realities of daily life. This can be seen, particularly, in the stories of Kaiwaka and The Bro, as well as Liz and Rick's reflections. These ontologies of connectedness align with Shiva's (2012) view that indigenous perspectives tend to be complex and interconnected with diverse forms of knowledge and food systems. Rick's observation that indigenous perspectives of harvestable levels of native animals are higher targets to aim for than a baseline conservation level set by the relevant government department illustrates one conflict generated from different ontological perspectives. Through this lens the ontology of alienation, described by Rose (2013) upon which the globalising corporate capitalist system is constructed, offers little possibility for transformation of its own destructive practices. In contrast, ontologies of connectedness provide myriad nodes for connection, re-construction and for focussing on solutions.

To return to the kete kai [food basket] metaphor introduced in my researcher positioning, this chapter is the tight weaving at the end. The integrity of the kete is tied together by this process, folding strands back over each other, and tucking them tightly underneath so that they don't unravel. The discussion here is a similar process of rounding and reconnecting with earlier strands of stories. The values, tensions and practices described in the earlier chapters present different coloured strands. These are plaited into a handle with which to hold the contents.

Returning to the beginning

The research presented in this book began from sparked interest in 'free food' or 'food democratisation'. However, an inability to separate free-food from broader food systems and a lack of literature on these matters at the time, led me to explorations of the notion, framework, and wider global movement of food sovereignty. I intended to question the relevance of 'food sovereignty' in a New Zealand context and to explore if and how the food sovereignty movement might be being enacted, both in Whaingaroa and wider New Zealand. To this end, I intended to answer the following questions:

1. What are the culturally and situationally specific ways that food sovereignty is enacted in Whaingaroa and other parts of New Zealand?
2. What motivates people to get involved, and remain involved, in food sovereignty-related activities?
3. What are the possible linkages between these local groups and other New Zealand and global initiatives with a similar focus on food sovereignty?

On re-reading these questions the 'answers' I might now provide seem circular, obvious, and repetitive. I discovered many value-based links between research participants and those of food sovereignty. In relation to question one, my analysis has focussed much more on similarities in values, and how they are enacted in the lives of participants, than on what is 'culturally and situationally specific' in this community. Yet these values may also be seen as necessarily context specific. In Whaingaroa the particular cultural history of the area is a key strand in this book. This can be traced through from the inspiration provided by the leader and community activist Eva Rickard, and the respect for Māori values that is shared by many within the wider community, including most of the research participants, which influences the culture of the community.

The culture of food sovereignty in New Zealand comes across through the narratives of participants, and yet it is not something that can be described easily. These narratives also indicate that, in relation to question two, values are central motivating factors in the lives of these participants, leading to active negotiation of contradictions arising in their lives, and also to very deliberate 'focussing on solutions'. Values, and their associated tensions and practices, are also key connecting factors, which can be identified in relation to question three. Shifts in research focus, as identified in Chapter One, mean that these questions now seem oddly fitted to the substance of this research, not so much because they don't fit my initial expectations for the research but because I did not know what expectations to have to begin with.

The shifts in my research reflect not only the in-depth understandings shared by a group of articulate, politically aware participants, but also influences from the literature, my supervisors' perspectives and the understandings gained through participant observation in a range of community practices. Over and above the changes in perspective and focus, my *aspirations* for my research have progressively focused increasingly on the telling of the stories gathered through this ethnographic process. There is a kind of paradox at work here, in that whilst I began my study intending to tell a particular story of interest to me, that focus shifted towards telling other people's stories. I felt a tremendous sense of privilege in hearing the rich and powerful stories I gathered, and the fascination they stirred broadened and shaped this research in a way that surprised me. Similarly, I started with no interest in economics, only to find the economic aspects of this study the most interesting to focus on. This, in my reflection, is the benefit of the kind of ethnographic process of discovery I was encouraged to adopt, where the theory is worked retrospectively around the fieldwork material, rather than a typical sociological process of matching qualitative material to pre-determined theory to discover if it fits.

Theoretical reflections

Just as alienation forms part of the capitalist rationality in an ontological sense, it is connectedness which lies at the core of the food sovereignty rationality, which is aimed at healing the ecological and social rifts (Rose 2013, 11–12).

Ecosystems, both as a model for better understanding complex systems and as a basis for an underpinning theoretical perspective, are key to this book. As Shiva (2005) points out, indigenous perspectives and agricultural models tend to develop alongside, and in deep interconnectedness with, their local ecosystems. The globalising corporate food system, in contrast, presents many levels of disconnection from indigenous ecosystem models. In the narratives of the participants there can be found a common thread of searching for and creating connectedness. Here Rose's (2013) dichotomy of the food sovereignty framework's underlying ontology of connectedness, pitched alongside corporate multinational capitalism's ontology of alienation, is particularly relevant. Similarly Graeber's (2009) ontology of the imagination of activists is juxtaposed with the ontology of violence he associates with dominant power structures.

In order to explain the complexity of 'ontologies of connectedness' relevant here, an ecological theoretical model has been adopted, along the lines of the 'systems view' organisational theory of Capra and Luisi (2014). Their rejection of dominant Western 'mechanistic' ways of understanding the world has also been relevant in illuminating the perspective of participants who, each in their own way, are looking for models and solutions complex enough to address at a small-scale local level the numerous multi-faceted crises humanity is facing globally. Casey-Cox's (2014) reflection that ecosystems include a delicate balance of organisation and deep dependency, as described in Chapter One, is also relevant to understanding the communities and organisations of focus. This also relates to Catton's (1982) assertion that an ecological-based framework must be adopted in order to address the demands of the multi-dimensional crises brought about by over-consumption.

Strong intrinsically located value systems underpin the participant perspectives shared in this project, including the view that human beings are part of, rather than oppositional to or separate from, nature. As such, we are always embedded in and are part of wider eco-systems. These perspectives of connectedness also resonate with Shiva's (2005) resistance to the concept of 'ownership' of life and the rhetoric of 'ownership society' in which living beings are given no intrinsic value and no integrity. She argues that the commons are the "highest expressions of economic democracy" (2005, 3). Participant narratives also echo Shiva's (2005) construction of the movement against corporate globalisation as one toward 'Earth Democracy' and the intentional shift from "vicious cycles of violence" to "virtuous cycles of creative nonviolence" (Shiva 2005, 5). Manifestations of the latter can be seen in examples such as that of Xtreme Waste and the other examples of 'focussing on solutions' that were an intentional focus of my fieldwork.

The holistic paradigms that Hutchings et al (2013) associate with both Māori and non-Māori organics sectors, despite both being based on different epistemologies, can be seen as another example of ontologies of connectedness. The shared intrinsic value these both place on ecosystems, soil, biodiversity, and animal welfare, can also be related to the narratives of local food providers. The difference in epistemologies can be connected to the diversity Rose (2013) identifies in the broader and inclusive campaign for food sovereignty. Seo and Creed's (2002) theorising of the potential power of paradox is also particularly relevant in understanding the tensions encountered by participants between their strongly interconnected values coming up against tensions and contradictions. Seo and Creed's (2002) suggestion that the paradox holds potential for further reflexive engagement, which can be disruptive to the status quo and facilitate further changes in action, will be discussed in the following section of this chapter.

Connecting tensions and paradox

I've a whole list of values, but some of them can be conflicting. For example, the value of hosting, but also being hosted, and being a good guest. I've struggled with this in the past, especially when I had more rules, like I don't eat meat, or inorganic, or whatever... but as a good guest I'd observe manāk-itanga – The Bro.

Contradictions and tensions are frequently encountered by participants, who articulate strong ethical values, while navigating the complexities of the contemporary food-scape. In the quote above, The Bro explains how some of his values interact. Manākitanga, the practice of showing care and respect for hosts, is a more important value for him than upholding his specific ethics related to the food they share with him. This is one example of how, in attempting to live lives that do not compromise ideal values, tensions are highlighted and sometimes resolved. These may also be magnified by perceptions based on ontologies of connectedness, as well as experiences of connectedness to food, land and community. Jono's story, presented in Chapter Two, of finding political billboard plastic buried in his garden, which came from previous national elections and supported progressive and environmentally focussed parties, is one such paradox between lofty ideals and practical ramifications. Josh's reflection on living at Wilderland illustrates another:

I'm really lucky to be living a life where I don't feel that it compromises my ideals, because I've got pretty high ideals and I look at modern society as being a mess and a bit of a blight on the planet... There's a responsibility that comes with it which is not getting freedom at a cost to others.... Abundance comes with responsibility; you can choose to waste or you can choose to take advantage of it and make sure it's used and make sure that potential is maximised.

One key barrier in Wilderland's development described by several long term members of the community is the lack of visitor accommodation. A large 'visitor centre' is a continued long-term goal to remedy this, however there are significant financial barriers in the process of its completion. The perceived lack of accommodation and aspirations for facilitating bigger educational programmes are a source of tension, particularly for long term participants. This chapter demonstrates the value in addressing contradiction and conflict in its potential to raise awareness.

Tensions of privilege and deprivation

The 'green-bubble' discussion in Chapter Three, in which tensions of privilege and poverty arose regarding the establishment of a 'two-dollar' shop in Whaingaroa, provides rich material for exploring paradox. The accusations of 'green bubble' hypocrisy from those who saw ethical consumption as a kind of privilege clashed with the views of the idealistic, plastic-avoiding sentiments of the original post and those defending it. These tensions are a good example of Seo and Creed's (2002) notions of paradox and how challenging discussions such as these can lead to greater awareness of different lived experiences. While these were not readily acknowledged in the discussion, conversations sparked here continued to explore these ideas outside of the online forum. However, the shame experienced in relation to catching sight of their often-invisible privilege made more public conversations difficult for some people.

During the online 'green-bubble' conversation one person argued against 'hypocrisy', claiming that being a 'conscious consumer' meant being actively aware of contradictions while trying to live as sustainably as possible. This relates to the Chapter Five discussion of supermarket culture and the paradox of 'driving to the oil drilling protest'. There seemed to be disagreement over what perspectives were more relevant – the current reality experienced by those living in deprivation or the progressive ambitions of those wanting to affect more positive change. The attack-and-defence dynamic in the 'green-bubble' conversation allowed little room for empathy, compassion and resolving tensions, although it did contribute to awareness which continued into people's lives.

Contributors to the online discussion who experienced deprivation openly refused to feel guilty over other people's ethical considerations. This raises a pertinent tension in relation to ethical consumption: it is often more expensive to be 'ethical'. This generates a positioning of wealth privilege and moral superiority. It seems appropriate that those who cannot afford to participate in ethical consumption reject the notion, since those who are already burdened should not be made more burdened by situations which are beyond their control. In some ways, many kinds of contemporary activism can only be carried out by the wealth, time or educationally privileged because some kind of abundance of these resources are necessary in order to contribute the energy required for activism. It seems appropriate that, given the many serious intersecting global crises we face as a species, those who do possess these spare resources use them in whatever way they can to affect positive change towards social, economic and environmental justice. There is an opportunity here to turn some of the narratives around privilege away from guilt and shame, and instead focus on potential to affect positive change.

Tensions of abundance and scarcity

Tensions between abundance and scarcity resonate in many of the participants' stories. For example, in Rick's ecological reflections that "bio-abundance is actually an alternative to predator control. If there is heaps of food and no competition then animals can coexist." A similar thread is echoed in the impetus behind planting public fruit trees to create an abundance of food for people in a community. These ideas of deliberately creating an abundance of food directly contradict the scarcity-based economics of the dominant food system and 'supermarket culture' as described by Jon.

Instead of competing in a race or a game in which there are necessarily winners and losers, these local food providers envision and strive towards a system in which enough resources can be sustainably produced to meet everyone's needs. There is a strong underlying sense of social justice that goes beyond food, and delivers impetus to value and care for all people. This aligns with ontologies of connectedness, as from a perspective where everyone is connected, to negatively affect anyone is to negatively affect everyone. Similarly, within this ecological framework, the strong value of environmental justice, resonating with Leopold's (1949) land ethic, conceives every part of the environment including soil, air and microbes, as also intrinsically valuable. Navigating these, as human beings, means being mindful of our propensity for destruction. This destructiveness forms a central underlying paradox for participants, as does the inevitable interaction with the alienating globalising corporate capitalist system.

Faith's reflection on the situation at Wilderland contextualises these tensions within an interconnected spectrum of many challenges. She explains this spectrum as a having two ends of polarity: chaos and order. Some community participants seek to pull the community towards order and others seek more chaos with further potential for challenging learning. Faith's observation was that this tension continues to be underlying in the community. Most of the time the two polarities can coexist but sometimes generate conflicts that must be resolved.

The potential for tensions to coexist highlights that paradoxes do not always have to be resolved, and indeed, the overall reflections of Wilderland from my fieldwork showed that ideological or scarcity based tensions that seemed to relate to specific people tended to endure even when those people left the community, having been passed on to new people or re-emerging from particular situations.

The complexity of and interconnectedness of paradox is also reflected in resistance to 'corporate food' and 'supermarket culture' shared by many participants across locations. However, this resistance sits, sometimes uncomfortably, alongside tensions associated with various kinds of privilege. This is a challenging paradox to reconcile when participants' living experiences are intensified by both a strong sense of agency and a variety of complex difficulties. Faith thinks it should be acknowledged that self-sufficiency when it comes to food, even on a community scale, requires significant hard work. It is understandable, from her perspective, that people opt for off-the-shelf supermarket food that is accessible and cheap: "I wonder if we will ever have a system where good food is not just available to people who are privileged in some way. We've pretty-much, as a culture, lost those skills." From this perspective it is clear why the food sovereignty framework places such value in learning and teaching food-related skills (Rose 2013).

Positioning tensions

The broadly shared perspective among these local food providers is that large corporations are responsible for social and environmental injustices, and that this is problematic for both global and local well-being. This observation serves as a core understanding parallel to that of the framework of food sovereignty. As described in Chapter Five, the shared narrative of resistance against global corporate capitalism follows a line of reasoning along these lines:

1. There are major problems with corporate capitalism.
2. Something must be done to counteract these.
3. Asking the question: what do we have the power to do?
4. Focussing on the every-day and the local: what are we eating and where does it come from?
5. Doing whatever we can to resist the system and create solutions.

A central reflection from my fieldwork is that the definition and connotations of 'capitalism' are especially relevant here. Graeber (2011) describes 'capitalism' as a term invented by socialists as a critique of an exploitative model of power relations. Along with Graeber, I have noticed that contemporary capitalism has appropriated this term and transformed the meaning into something positive. This creates confusion, especially for those still using the word as a critique. Using the same word, but with very different meanings creates a disruption of communication. I noticed this when talking to people outside the 'bubble' where 'capitalism' is considered a positive thing, associated with the agency to trade goods and own property, but disassociated from the exploitative elements which produce social and environmental harms. The 'only' other alternative commonly posed in the form of an obvious straw-man argument, is a 'communist dictatorship' such as Stalinist Russia. Conversely, proponents of food sovereignty and other people critiquing capitalism are not usually advocating for a 'communist dictatorship' and are not necessarily opposed to owning property or to the trading of goods. Indeed, they are often engaged directly in (farmers') markets. This linguistic dissonance is more than a marginal technical issue – it is a very real barrier to facilitating wider conversation about significant social problems.

Negotiating paradoxes can be seen as an unavoidable part of living an ethically-guided life. For these local food providers, corporate tensions extend into day-to-day experiences alongside concerns over local and national government power to potentially strangle local food. The feeling of powerlessness in the face of national and global politics such as that described by Cally in Chapter Five, prompts questioning and action. At a basic and day-to-day level, this is enacted through food-related practices. In this sense, small deliberate actions can ease personal tensions in the face of powerlessness. The focus shifts from what participants cannot do, to what they can do. Similarly, Justin's reflection that in the hospitality industry resistance to big corporations can be particularly difficult prompts him to focus on finding options that he finds more ethically acceptable.

The shift from large-scale tensions to local solutions is a common theme. Attention often returns to injustices on a global scale, and then reverberates back again to the local. Robz's quote below illustrates this dynamic:

Everyone knows that we have enough food in the world but sometimes governments are using it to suppress people. It just feels so hopeless. There are all the issues in America with Monsanto with seed ownership. I remember reading years and years ago about them trying to take ownership of the native peoples' corn and it made me so angry – but I can't do anything about that. I can just do things in my own world.

People's lives are interconnected with corporations and government in ways that cannot be avoided. To some extent, the role of government as a regulator is acknowledged and encouraged, as Cally describes:

I think regulations are important to a degree because if you had no regulations, imagine what those big business people would be doing. It's very hard – where do you draw that line? – Yes these people have to be regulated but you don't. I certainly wouldn't want Fonterra going regulation-free, thank you very much.

As mentioned in Chapter Five, these day-to-day contradictions seem to be faced with reflexivity and pragmatism by participants. These characteristics are also resonant of the tensions experienced, resistance mounted, and inevitable entanglement faced by the wider food sovereignty movement and framework.

Although the food activism of focus here is informed and sometimes fuelled by resistance to corporate capitalism, the identities of participants did not seem to be primarily constructed in terms of this resistance. There was not an overriding drive for opposition to the mainstream. While it is considered important to stand up against things conceived as harmful and exploitative, there is more focus on what can be gained from positive action, in creating better models and in taking control back from corporations by producing and sharing food, amongst other things.

The proactive culture of positive resistance in Whaingaroa resonates with the wider New Zealand food activism. Alongside food sovereignty, as described by Rose (2013), these can be seen to be based in

ontologies of connectedness in comparison to the ontologies of alienation he associates with globalising capitalism. Similarly, the focus on
creative solutions in resistance to the perceived continuous threat of
disempowerment by corporations and the state resonates with Graeber's (2009) analysis of activist ontologies based on imagination, as
opposed to the corporate state's ontology of violence. As mentioned
in Chapter Five, this proactive resistance is deliberately engaged in
order to build connections and relationships between people, and to
experiment in building healthier and more resilient social, economic
and environmental eco-systems on a local level.

Connecting values

Ontologies of connectedness are particularly relevant to the values
described as the focus of chapter six. Rose's (2011) description of food
sovereignty as a particularly diverse and also particularly inclusive
movement and framework resonates with the perspectives here. In
analysing the data gathered during my fieldwork I noticed a
resounding openness to critical reflections coexisting alongside strong
values. Indigenous, particularly Māori, values in their myriad diverse
manifestations, are acknowledged, even if not well-understood, by all
the participants. Generally, they are seen as based in more holistic,
integrated value sytems, which have developed alongside ecological
systems. The openness to diverse understandings is also demon-
strated in the way local food providers here value each other and
avoid competition 'like an ecosystem', as reflected by Rick, in which a
balance of entities can coexist as long as sufficient resources are
available.

To some extent, this culture of inclusion is potentiated as a response
to an invisible but ever-present 'other': the dominant power structures of corporate capitalism. Strong values around 'organic food' can
be seen to coexist here alongside critical analysis of 'organic' labels,
especially with regards to highly processed, resource intensive, and
industrially produced organics. Likewise, the process of obtaining

organic certification is seen as a costly and time consuming process which is particularly difficult for small-scale producers. Participants are critical of the disconnection and alienation they experience in relating to industrial organic food. While they sometimes seek to avoid using synthetic pesticides or consuming food which has been exposed to them, they would rather support local producers with whom they can establish trust-based relationships, even if they cannot completely realise their ideals. There is an understanding here that the notion of 'organic' is more about what isn't in the food. It presents the absence of pesticide residues. It does not particularly account for nutrient density or sustainable land use. It is a place-holder for trust in a food-system of multiple disconnections, a sentiment that is shared by Ackerman-Leist (2012, 13). Tension regarding organic certification is mitigated in that it is less necessary for small scale producers who have greater connectivity with the people who consume their food and, therefore, do not require their function as "sanctioned brokers of trust" described by Ackerman-Leist (2012, 13).

The difficulties with organic certification experienced by Mike and Mady on their small dairy farm are generated more from the global food supply chain than from their local customers, with whom they share a high trust relationship. This resonates with the idea that local food is about relationships, as The Bro describes, and relates to the concept of whakapapa, connectedness across time and space. The ontological connectedness threaded through these various narratives emerges again and again, in a similar way to that which Rose (2013) ascribes to food sovereignty. This concept lends itself to an ecological perspective of human beings living in interconnection with ecosystems and nature, rather than as separate to them. The paradigms of permaculture and agroecology are based in this kind of understanding, and Ackerman-Leist's (2012) perspective of farming being about energy flows reflects movement within an ecological perspective. Echoing the food sovereignty focus on decommodification of food, there is a strong emphasis placed on reconnecting with 'real food'.

The ethics presented by the food providers in Whaingaroa, and those from the wider New Zealand vignettes, reflect similar values to those common in green consumerism. They simultaneously share varying critical reflections on green consumerism, particularly a scepticism about whether the ability of the market to fix the problems caused by the market, as well as distinct wariness of the high price of 'ethical' food and its lack of accessibility for those on low incomes. They navigate these tensions in their daily lives. Within this shared ethical paradigm participants hold varied perspectives on what is considered to be more important: animal or human rights, personal or environmental health. Different values, and their contextual relationship between one another, can be used to navigate contradictions. For example, The Bro's value of manākitanga [reciprocal respect] and respecting the hospitality of hosts is more important than his other personal food values in a context where someone offers him food.

Overall, these differences are reflected upon both individually and through conversations, perhaps opening up the space for transformation in the way that Seo and Creed (2002) describe, or perhaps in ways that reaffirm ethical identities similar to the process reflected on by Foote (2009). The food ethics presented here generally arise out of genuine concerns over exploitation and the desire to avoid social and environmental harm as much as possible. This awareness of wider ecological relationships is a core part of the ontologies of connectedness of food sovereignty (Rose 2013).

Connecting solutions and aspirations

To understand the focus on solutions in the practices of local food producers in Whaingaroa, it is helpful to have an understanding of permaculture which resonates with the complex system model articulated by Capra and Luisi (2014). This ecosystem-based and holistic way of perceiving relationality aligns strongly with Rose's (2013) positioning of food sovereignty's ontologies of connectedness. This complex systems theory opens space for designing organisations, models and systems at a local level that differ, fundamentally, from those based on the dominant corporate capitalist system. Complex systems view is radically inclusive. In line with Leopold's (1949) land ethic, it recognises intrinsic value in every element of an ecosystem. On a social level it includes being aware of cycles and flows within the community, an awareness that filters through to the organising and planning of meetings and the timing of activities.

One key difference in this ecological-based perspective is the awareness of waste as part of the food system. This is evidenced in Xtreme Waste's deliberate focus on solutions leading to a seventy-six percent diversion of landfill waste in the area, while restoring the surrounding water systems, previously contaminated by toxic leachate. Aside from these ecological successes, Xtreme Waste also has provided numerous social benefits, economic and educational benefits, and has been successful in activism involving a large corporation. Like Xtreme Waste, most of the other food sovereignty related activities in Whaingaroa happened despite resistance from the local council. The 'just did it anyway' approach is seen as the only way forward, through the sometimes stifling power structures, despite the risks involved with this kind of resistance.

The values of participants and their awareness of problems with globalising corporate capitalism and associated social and environmental exploitation, as described in chapters five and six, are directly connected to their 'focusing on solutions'. This proactive, deliberate focussing is a distinguishing characteristic shared by most participants. The response to perceived global problems with small-scale solutions is a strong characteristic of permaculture and wider community based activities associated with food sovereignty. Redirecting frustrations into fruitful local pursuits can be seen as a purposefully constructive coping strategy, helping people to cope with the often painful emotional burden of awareness of destructive injustice.

The successful experiments of Xtreme Waste and Whaingaroa Harbourcare both support the notion of Whaingaroa as a 'bubble' of experimentation towards sustainability, as Robz describes: 'I guess Whaingaroa's quite a bubble in a way... I see it as almost a child's playground. It's a place where you can do stuff.'

The potential to experiment in different systems that offer the possibility of alternatives to more destructive dominant structures was a key theme of interest to all the participants involved. Participants both channel their agency experimentation, and receive a sense of agency and satisfaction in return. These kinds of experiments can be sparked by incidents like the dump closing, which led to the formation of Xtreme Waste; by the man who couldn't catch a fish, which led to the establishment of Whaingaroa Harbourcare and the restoration of the harbour; or by questions like 'What would you want school to look like?', which led the home schooling parents of Te Mauri Tau to choose to affect the mainstream through their Enviroschools curriculum. These various marginal experiments have achieved wide-reaching change and had some influence on wider practices. This can also be related to the permaculture principle of 'valuing the margins' (interesting things happen at the intersections) which features in Figure 2 of the methodology section of Chapter One.

Although it can be argued that people always fall short of reaching aspirational ideals, overall the local food providers are in the habit of 'practicing what they preach' in terms of lifestyles and food consumption. This can be viewed as a kind of everyday 'direct action' (Graeber 2011). This also relates to the permaculture principle of 'small slow solutions' and can be seen to be a part of the enacting of personal food sovereignty (Dowling 2011, 17). Most participants attempt to grow the bulk of their fruit and vegetables, or to source produce locally rather than purchasing from supermarkets.

There is a commonly held understanding within the community that contemporary corporate capitalism, along with a history of colonisation and industrialisation, has created social disconnection and alienation, and that there is much work to be done in 'community-building'. Healthy communities are considered to be those with strong connection and shared celebrations. Among participants in Whaingaroa, there is a strongly expressed support for these small-scale local solutions, along with a sense of celebration and pride. When I asked The Bro what he would like to see happening in Whaingaroa, he responded: "It's already happening, just more of the same." Similarly, Jenny expressed pride in her small bread business, as well as the desire to see more small-scale local food initiatives. Tensions that build up in a community can also be resolved through celebrations, activism, and creating abundance.

Wilderland was founded on similarly resonant aspirations. As Faith's vignette describes, it is a place for sustainability-focussed holistic and interactive education and transformative learning. This sometimes idealised focus is not without challenges. Faith points to frustrations with the continuous change of participants and the lack of retention of knowledge:

Sometimes things are just not very realistic. People come with a purist outlook and want everything to be completely sustainable without really realising how much work is involved in producing the nuts, grains and legumes for an average of twenty people onsite all through the year. They don't really appreciate that it's not a model of perfection, in fact it's the very imperfection of Wilderland that makes it such a good opportunity for learning.

Accepting imperfection is part of the ongoing learning process. Educating for such big-picture wisdom, as Faith describes, involves a combination of attempts at explaining limitations, balanced with allowing participants to experiment. As community decisions at Wilderland are made by eighty percent consensus during meetings, the process of raising, explaining their impracticality, and sometimes convincing the group that there is valuable potential in attempting or re-attempting various projects can take up a lot of time. For example, in the time I have been visiting the community there have been several attempts at keeping chickens for eggs with varying levels of success.

Connecting economies

As long as analysts presume that individuals cannot change such situations themselves, they do not ask what internal or external variables can enhance or impede the efforts of communities of individuals to deal creatively and constructively with perverse problems such as the tragedy of the commons (Ostrom 1990, 21).

One of the powerful concepts involved in Permaculture is the principle of 'valuing the margins'. During the permaculture course I participated in in my fieldwork, Liz explained that "The margins is where the energy is." She said that this was true in her experience as a trained ecologist. Permaculture gardening systems often involved planting the margins of land with large trees to provide food and protect against wind and erosion, and letting the marginal parts of land 'to lay' and develop rich biodiversity. Liz also explained that this concept can be applied socially, in taking note of the myriad forms of unrecognised, yet important, labour that is being carried out in every community. From an ecological-economic perspective, Rick explained, "unemployment is a resource rather than a burden". This was an element of the kaupapa [philosophical foundation] on which Xtreme Waste was based. In Chapter Eight, the conversations around value, involve a lot of language typically associated with capitalism such as 'resources', 'richness', 'wealth', and 'social capital'. Discourses of alternative economics and value walk a fine line between the words associated with neoliberal capitalism and their holistic ethical value systems. To some extent these conversations involve reclaiming or repurposing language. To have conversations around value, the lexicon surrounding wealth must be re-contextualised. Difficult conversations are an important part of developing alternative economic thinking. In negotiating this paradox, participants tend to sway between rejection of money and corporate greed and perceiving money flow as useful, akin to Korten's (2010) analogy of the circulatory system of societal organism.

One of the most surprising things about the process of this research was how fascinating I have found economics, a topic that previously held very little interest for me. Korten's (2010) characteristics of healthy living systems and Ostrom's (1990) work on good community management of 'the commons' is particularly relevant to the local food providers. In understanding the intricacies of economics in a community like Whaingaroa it is helpful to first understand that the economics is deeply interconnected with culture. Terms such as 'moral economy', as described by MacRae (2016), have been employed for several decades in relation to peasant communities. They illustrate this interconnectedness and are relevant here in interpreting the experiences of participants. The concept of a moral economy pose something of a paradox, particularly to 'free market' economic ideology of neoliberalism. Proponents of free-market capitalist neoliberalism, as described in Chapter Six, struggle with ethical food concepts like 'fairtrade', portraying them as a socialist distortion of an otherwise pure free-market. These local food providers might see this distortion as an optimistic manifestation in an otherwise painfully exploitative system.

The values described in Chapter Five shape the moral economies in the context of the communities and organisations featured here. The moral and values-based economic dimensions can also be connected with the value of decommodification expressed in relation to food sovereignty as described by Rose (2013). This is expressed as resistance to the reductionist perspective through which food, as well as other things are constructed as mere 'resources' and 'commodities', to be bought and used by 'consumers'. From a food-sovereignty perspective, these things are seen as much more complex, interconnected, and inherently valuable.

One of the most remarkable economic reflections on the local food providers of Whaingaroa, as well as other participants, is that many of them live on relatively low incomes and yet, for the most part, enjoy particularly rich lives in terms of agency. Much of this phenomenon can be explained by people having different priorities, based on values, community and sharing, rather than on accumulation of other kinds of wealth. This raises the questions around privilege and class. Despite many participants living well on low incomes, the richness in their lives is supplemented by fresh, good quality food, by education, by community and other things that are difficult, if not impossible, to measure using conventional economic tools. This book's findings suggests the potential of a different kind of class of 'rich-poor' people, notable for their lack of financial means and the freedom to live lives that they choose to live. The concepts of gifting and sharing are particularly important in this values based, moral economy, as is access to land or other resources, often without ownership which can be mediated by wwoofing and land-sharing. This concept applies strongly to participants at Wilderland, and to a lesser degree among the urban participants, and those in Whaingaroa who have higher incomes.

It is key to acknowledge that myriad social and cultural factors are interconnected with economics, despite the difficulty in measuring them. Even outside of the food sovereignty bubble, at every level of society there are relationships in which sharing occur. Alongside financial transactions, there are unquantifiable but prevalent practices of gifting, swapping and trading, especially of surpluses. Another interconnected factor is the role of the government in giving subsidies to some participants. Jenny received a grant to start her business. Kaiwaka and Lynne formerly received subsidies from the Ministry of Social Development to employ workers who were considered difficult to employ. While some people would question the validity or sustainability of these subsidies, in the experiences of these participants they created far greater social, and local economic value. The workers at Kaiwhenua, like those at Xtreme waste, were able to gain valuable skills and experience. Jenny was able to come off a welfare benefit which otherwise would have been a far greater long-term cost. There are many other benefits in these kinds of subsidies that are difficult to measure and relate to enhancing the wellbeing of the community, which, in turn makes it a nicer place for tourists to visit.

Emerging ideas around alternative economics and collaborative economics have been subject to the critique, such as that presented by Walker (2015), that they further neoliberal agendas. Care must be taken in critiquing in order to raise awareness of ethical issues so that these might be addressed, rather than condemning these newly emerging different models for not addressing all the major systemic problems. The systemic problems we face do not have simple solutions. However, curiosity, experimentation, and shifting social attitudes may lead to less consumption and exploitation. If we can employ critique as an important tool, alongside experimentation with different economic models, then we will have the opportunity to improve these models (and the critique), rather than merely condemning and dismissing them which does not lead to any greater goal.

The concepts of abundance and scarcity are particularly relevant to the economic perspectives presented here. Tensions tend to emerge around scarce resources and high prices, particularly high food prices. Mike's reflection that people become less wasteful, and try to be more resilient by producing more of their own food in times of economic and resource scarcity is echoed by Knox (2013), as mentioned in Chapter Eight. Knox (2013) notes that the peaks of foraging in New Zealand have coincided with times of economic scarcity, notably during the world wars, the Great Depression, and the oil crisis of the 1970s. There is a sense of irony here: that it takes a crisis for people to act, and that while there are plenty of resources available people will continue to be wasteful, despite apparently having the capacity for foresight, and despite increasingly dire environmental warnings.

Alongside the emphasis within the community on voluntary simplicity and moral economic practices, there is also a strong emphasis on 'good business sense' and its practical application. For these small-scale food producers, 'good business sense' is about producing and selling enough food to stay afloat. It is about maintaining and building relationships within the community. It often means reaching compromises between values and cost-effectiveness. People whose livelihoods depend on putting this into practice, often do so through finding ways of adding value and diversifying their food production.

Justin expresses these values, and the tensions which much be navigated in his attitude of 'finding a balance' and treating food differently, demonstrating a greater level of connectedness to food. This perspective reflects food sovereignty's focus on decommodification and its ontologies of connectedness. Rather than a chicken being viewed as 'just a commodity', more value is placed on the quality of life of the animal. This value is followed through the process of its preparation and consumption, as well as its disposal, each of which is given more attention in relation to ethical and environmental factors.

Reflections on connectedness

The stories of local food providers that have been the focus of this book suggests that small-scale local food initiatives are often connected, if only in that they are responses by community groups to the tensions of struggle and scarcity created by the globalising corporate system. They present a logical response of focusing on small-scale solutions to large-scale problems, based on the minimal agency that people do have in a world where resources and power are becoming increasingly concentrated in the hands of the few. Similarities can also be seen in the strong ethical values held by key participants, as well as in the tensions they negotiate in their daily lives. They present a deliberate focus on solutions, and on what is possible and achievable by small groups of people with minimal resources, and they present a protest against the alienation inflicted by dominant power structures in the global corporate food system. I argue that these food-based initiatives are connected, not only with food sovereignty, but also with movements towards localised economies and alternative economics and with what has been called the 'Global Justice Movement' (Graeber 2009). This connectedness springs from shared values and the common theme of proactive resistance to corporate and government exploitation, along with a commitment to searching for and experimenting with potential solutions.

POSTSCRIPT: CONTINUED STORIES

People's lives are far more varied, shifting and complex than can be represented in text, and these continue to change long after interviews about their lives are conducted. I chose not to keep adding material after 2014, the main year of ethnographic fieldwork and in-depth interviews, in order to contain the collection of materials and make completion of this research a possibility. However, I have since kept in touch with participants, and here I touch on some of the many changes that have occurred in their lives.

Whilst Jono, who appeared in Chapter Two, is still living in Auckland, his rental property with the big garden has been sold and is likely to be developed into more intensive housing. At the time of writing he is looking for another house to rent where he can continue to garden. Kora has been living internationally and travelling the world for most of the time since 2014. She has been in Australia, the Philippines, Scotland, England, South Africa, Namibia, Botswana, Zimbabwe, Zambia, Tanzania and is currently living in Canada. Over this time, she has been involved in various kinds of volunteer work and activism that relates to the values she expressed in her interview.

Josh remained at Wilderland for most of the time since our interview. At the time of writing he has recently returned to city life to save money towards further education in permaculture design. He told me he feels much lighter, having left many of the frustrations of immersive community life behind for the time being, and is looking forward to his next steps. He is currently renting accommodation at a more urban community in Auckland, but intends to 'hit the road again' soon.

Faith, who was in the process of leaving Wilderland at the time of the interview, went on to live in South East Asia and then in rural France with her partner. They have now returned to live near where Faith grew up in Australia, and have recently had a baby. Since purchasing property suitable for permaculture, Faith is looking forward to a return to gardening.

Wilderland continues to hold space for the hundreds of volunteers who pass through every year. Its power structure and decision-making process have continued to change to meet the needs of participants. The income of the community has risen enough so that spending on communal resources is not as tight as in times past. However, financial sustainably is still an issue for people living there and as such Wilderland continues to deal with a high turnover of participants.

Liz and Rick continue to grow food and make delicious pesto at Taunga Kereru. They have had several long-term interns over the last few years, and still feature regularly at the local Creative Markets. Alongside this, they continue to be involved in Xtreme Waste, which has been re-named Xtreme Zero Waste to reflect their goal of reducing refuse to zero through reuse, recycling, upcycling and encouraging more sustainable packaging. Kaiwaka continues to garden at Kaiwhenua with Lynne. They have completed renovations on their big shed which can now be used to host courses on organic gardening.

Mike and Mady's farm lost its organic certification following another drought when they decided to use local feed to keep their animals healthy rather than buy in organic feed from further away at a greater cost. This was a blow for Mike, although he had previously been unsure whether the paperwork was worth the small profit margin organic milk received above the usual price for milk. More recently, the milk co-operative Fonterra has announced plans to pay the market rate for organic milk, a much higher amount than they previously paid. This may influence Mike to return to organic certification, and other dairy farmers to pursue organic conversion. Cally continues to garden and keep bees. Her recent increased focus on improving her nutrition has shown remarkable results in her health.

Jon decided to expand WOK into a much bigger shop in town. It still has a strong focus on local produce and he deliberately prices locally grown and food at a lower rate to encourage people to buy it. This change has made WOK much more accessible to the public and now, instead of only being open two days a week, it is open every day. This has also created more local jobs.

Jenny continues to make and sell her bread in the morning on the main street, and in other shops around Whaingaroa. She has extended her range of bread and now sells seasoned rolls and chockie buns (buns made with chocolate chips). She has also shared the space of her tiny shop with another local baker, who can use it in the later hours of the day.

Wayne continues to be involved in the Solscape gardens and the community garden at the Whaingaroa Police Station. He has been involved in setting up workshops in Whaingaroa that reflect his values. The Bro continues to enact his values through food. Recently he has travelled both overseas and back to his ancestral Tuhoe land. Justin continues to source local food for the Shack. Madi and her partner now also have a baby. They continue to live and garden at Te Mauri Tau. Robz is still foraging and living in the structures he built on a friend's land with his son Matai. They continue to travel the country regularly, especially during the warmer seasons.

Figure 26: Completed kete, created by my sister Piata, 2015.

RESEARCH THEORY AND
METHODOLOGY

Raranga kete

This research involved bringing together many different strands of understanding. As such, a fitting metaphor for the process of this research is one of raranga-kete [weaving a basket]. This kete has many different coloured strands – different threads of narratives: personal, political, ecological, ontological, theoretical; of values, tensions, visions and practices, of my story and of other people's stories. Kete have mythology. In the story often told during my bicultural upbringing, ngā kete o te wānanga, the baskets of knowledge, were obtained for human-kind by the great forest god Tāne:

To acquire the baskets of knowledge, Tāne had to ascend to the twelfth heaven, to Te Toi-o-ngā-rangi, and there be ushered into the presence of the Supreme God, of Io-matua-kore himself, to make his request. The request was granted and hence the knowledge we now have in our possession and at our disposal. Tāne had to reconnoitre and negotiate eleven other heavens before ascending to the twelfth and there receive the knowledge he sought. The three baskets of knowledge are usually called te kete tuauri [basket of sacred knowledge], te kete tuatea [basket of ancestral knowledge] and te kete aronui [basket of life's knowledge]... These are the kits of knowledge that Tāne fetched from Io the parent (Kete o te wānanga 2006, 1).

In Kete we can hold knowledge, we can hold seeds, we can hold stories and whakapapa, we can hold food. A kete has a structure, a framework, to be viable it must have a strong spine, but designs can vary; kete are adaptable. Weaving a kete is a creative process... a process of transformation. A kete can be held. It can be useful. Kete can also be taonga [precious or treasured], or the weaving can result in a rourou, a food basket, an everyday, ordinary, practical object. Kete are multi-dimensional, rather than linear, and deeply embedded in context, as is the research presented in this book.

The process of carrying out this research, from the earliest stages, has been a lot like the process of raranga [weaving], from the spark of an idea, to the gathering of materials, the learning and exploration and the sorting, the organising and the process of making connections along the way. This research is where strands of ontology, methodology, narratives, and theory are plaited, then woven, then folded together to make connections in a way that I hope makes sense, and can be useful.

Figure 1: Raranga in process, woven by my sister Piata, 2015.

Central to my chosen research methodology is the belief that all knowing is embedded in relationship. Ways of knowing, intellectually, emotionally, spiritually and intuitively while interwoven are differently valued, noticed and applied in my day to day life (Casey-Cox 2013, 39).

Research objectives

The traditional way to write a section about research objectives would be to set out in detail the aims of the project. This would be done by setting out a predetermined purpose, describing the plan for my work, and the analytical conventions through which I would provide an assertion arrived at from the integration of my literature reviews and field work. The problem with setting out my report in that traditional approach is that it would be misleading in this case. Certainly, in the initial stages of preparing a proposal for the consideration by the Post-Graduate Studies Committee, I did just that – even though I felt significant discomfort in doing so. Looking back, I can see that I approached 'Objectives' with a combination of curiosity and resistance. The term implies a particular set of aims or goals, a traditional notion of a hypothesis to be tested. The term also has linguistic connotations in the positivist sense of 'the objective world'. This made me ideologically uncomfortable at the time and even more so as I became immersed in my fieldwork. My orientation is towards a view of the world as always in creation, including through the processes of research.

Despite this early tentative and sometimes ambiguous attempt to avoid a positivist orientation to my work, I continued to be encouraged by some commentators on my work to 'be more objective' in separating my pre-conceived political views from the research design and process. This was hard to hear at the time. Interestingly and somewhat paradoxically, the transformative process of engaging in in-depth interviews generated a kind of broader perspective in itself. I more closely considered my own strong views, reflected (along with other, contrary views) in the words of the participants. I could also see what sometimes appeared to be leaps of logic and other inconsistencies in our narratives more clearly. I came to view my research as a process of exploration: of gathering and re-telling of stories, of weaving strands, working with, and through, these narratives in order to try to explore tensions, intensions; contradictions and paradox[1], and the insights that can be gained from their scrutiny. Therefore, it might be more accurate to state the research objectives as 'discovery' or 'getting through this PhD' or 'finding reflections of things I already thought and also changing my perspective in the process' or something similarly vague and open. For this reason, I will write my 'research objectives' as a story of conceptualising and reconceptualising my research journey.

I did not start with 'Objectives'. I started with a spark of inspiration. In 2011, at the very beginning of my Doctoral journey, I was excited about the 'free food' type initiatives I saw popping up in my neighbourhood and that I heard about from all around New Zealand and other parts of the world. I saw connections here with resistance to the global corporate food system and I saw the potential for research in exploring this – research that would focus on solutions rather than merely adding to the already volumes of recordings of the myriad of problems with the exploitation by that dominant system. In the process of first proposing this research I was asked to formulate research questions. This is what I came up with:

1. What values do different free food initiatives share (and what values differ)?
2. How can these micro level grass roots initiatives create wider social change?
3. How can they be supported or set up?
4. What motivates the initiatives at the micro level?

My understanding, at the time was based on these premises:

- The global corporate food industry creates a state of scarcity in order to maximise profits which means that food (especially good food) is less accessible to people of low socio-economic means.
- Free food movements create abundance through growing food or redistributing food that would otherwise be wasted (positive social change? Activism?)

In a later proposal I formulated the following similarly positioned questions:

1. What is the relationship between global capitalism and food?
2. Does the global corporate food industry create food scarcity in order to maximise profits?
3. In what ways have people responded to the global distribution of food (commodity chain and food scarcity)?
4. What is the relationship between the democratisation of food and food scarcity?

5. What groups and initiatives are involved in the democratisation of food?
6. What political and ethical values do different food democratising initiatives share (and what values differ)?
7. How can these micro-level grass roots initiatives create wider social change?
8. How can they be supported or set up?
9. What motivates the initiatives at the micro-level?
10. How can the discourses of these initiatives contribute to the critique of global capitalism?

After scouring the literature for the development of my full proposal I found very little on food democratisation and 'free-food' initiatives. However, in this process I came across a large and growing body of food sovereignty literature that seemed to align both with my own strong values around social and environmental justice, and with the values of the people involved in local free-food initiatives. This observation significantly changed the framing of my research. By the time I came to finishing my full proposal in 2012, I was still (uncomfortably) using a lexicon of 'objectives'. My focus was now more clearly positioned around food sovereignty in a New Zealand context, specifically around the small township of Whaingaroa:

The overall objective of my research is to question the relevance of the 'food sovereignty' term in New Zealand and to explore if and how the food sovereignty movement is being enacted in Whaingaroa and in wider New Zealand. My research addresses the following three questions:

1. What are the culturally and situationally specific ways that food sovereignty is enacted in Whaingaroa and other parts of New Zealand?
2. What motivates people to get involved, and remain involved, in food sovereignty-related activities?
3. What are the possible linkages between these local groups

and other New Zealand and global initiatives with a similar focus on food sovereignty?

These shifts show the influences both the literature I read and my supervisors' encouragement and perspectives have had on my understandings. Now, in 2016, I am not sure if any of these questions – or the objectives to answer them – are quite the right ones, but they go a long way to explaining where the research came from at those points in time, and how it has shifted. Over and above the changes in perspective and focus, my *aspirations* for this research have come to focus on the telling of the stories gathered through fieldwork and in-depth interviews. That has become my central process, along with deepening my understandings of the mahi [work], and my presentation of the insights I have gained from this work.

Theorising ontologies: ecology, connectedness, complexity and creativity

A good description, certainly, requires appeal to theory, but in ethnography, theory is properly deployed in the service of description rather than the other way around (Graeber 2009, 509).

Theory, of course, is nothing more than a fancy name for a story that presumes to explain how things work (Korten 2010, 23).

The pursuit for substantial, adequate and fitting theory, in this case, has been ongoing, trying, and at times quite confusing. The quotes above have helped to remind me that ethnographic researchers tend to use theory in the opposite direction from many other methods employed by researchers who may start with theory, to which they then apply 'data'. Data is the information they have chosen to take account of as significant. Their 'data' is then applied according to the protocols of their chosen methodology in order to test the veracity of the theory akin to positivist methods. These quotes also suggest that theory does not need to be complicated; it is a framework and tool for conscious meaning-making. Choosing appropriate frameworks and tools to go along with the stories gathered here has been a process of continuous questioning. With this kind of process, one begins to see recurrent themes that persistently emerge despite the questioning. This section provides a brief explanation of some of these recurrent themes based on the most compatible and useful theoretical material I have been able to find.

Organisational theorists, Fritjof Capra and Piere Luigi Luisi's (2014) notion of the 'systems view of life' is particularly relevant in explaining the theoretical, and indeed ontological underpinnings of my research approach. The systems view is an ecological approach to understanding connectedness and complex situations as Capra and Luisi (2014). They reject mechanistic ways of understanding the world that have become common under the dominant Western scientific approach, arguing that this positivist kind of ontology is unable to grasp complexity enough to address the numerous multi-faceted crises humanity is facing.

In her research exploring community gardening, Anna Casey-Cox (2014) builds on these ecological ideas in order to appreciate connectedness:

Within ecosystems there is a delicate balance of organisation. The epiphyte, for example, displays a deep dependency on another life form that, contrary to modern day notions of dependency, is non-destructive and life giving. Many plants live in symbiotic, interdependent relationship. While thriving ecosystems display the wonder of interdependent life forms, damaged ecosystems highlight the destruction of virulent competition and colonisation. (Casey-Cox 2014, 110)

Sociologist William Catton (1982) similarly criticised the prolific anthropocentrism of the social sciences and argued that an ecological-based framework must be adopted in order to address the demands of the multi-dimensional crises brought about by over-consumption. This encourages the perspective that human beings are always embedded in wider eco-systems and are indeed part of these systems from an ecological perspective. It constructs human beings as part of, rather than oppositional to, nature. This kind of theoretical perspective is compatible with many indigenous perspectives, including Māori conceptions of environmental ethics (Gunn 2007). This ecocentric perspective is also articulated in Aldo Leopold's pioneering Land Ethic:

The land ethic simply enlarges the boundaries of the community to include soils, waters, plants, and animals, or collectively: the land… In short, a land ethic changes the role of Homo Sapiens from conqueror of the land-community to plain member and citizen of it (Leopold 1949, 239).

This ecosystem framework resonates well with my experiences of Māori Cosmology, of the valuing of the anthropomorphic Ranginui [sky father] and Papatuanuku [earth mother]. These key deities are parents to many of the other gods in the pantheon who protect and care for domains such as Tāne Mahuta, god of forests and Tangaroa, god of the ocean. Through this perspective intrinsic value is also placed in anthropomorphised mountains, and in the taniwha [fabulous water monsters] that protect each bend in a river. Leopold's land ethic also relates well to the complex systems approach articulated by Capra and Luisi (2014), and these, in turn resonate with what Rose (2013), in his research on food sovereignty in Australia, calls: an ontology of connectedness.

The term 'ontology' invokes questions about the nature of 'the world', how the universe works and what forces can be said to exist within it. Both Rose (2013) and Graeber (2009) present ontological dichotomies. Graeber (2009) positions the anarchist activists which are the focus of his ethnographic study as operating from an ontology of imagination and creativity as in contrast to the dominant system's ontology of violence. He argues that the state and market are interdependent, and that the coercive force of the state is everywhere. Most of all, this force adheres in anything large, heavy, and economically valuable that cannot easily be hidden away. Nations are seen as purely imaginary constructs which become "real" when they threaten to send in the army (2009, 283). Graeber describes the ontology of the market and state as one that uses language to assert power as if their interplay were an expression of a natural or scientific law. He discusses how this conception of 'forces', such as 'market forces' or the 'police force' may stem from the Western language being based on nouns: static objects relying on largely invisible forces to demonstrate movement and change. He claims that while the state and the market operate on ontologies of violence, the activists he has worked with operate on an entirely different ontology: one of imagination. The former is continually engaged in destruction and maintaining lopsided power dynamics while the latter is continuously in the process of creation in order to challenge those power dynamics (2009, 511, 512). These represent basic underlying understandings upon which 'the activists' and those adhering to the dominant perspectives sometimes called 'the system' operate on which differ fundamentally.

The concept of alienation is also relevant in this theoretical framework:

Just as alienation forms part of the capitalist rationality in an ontological sense, it is connectedness which lies at the core of the food sovereignty rationality, which is aimed at healing the ecological and social rifts. In its practical manifestations to date, I regard food sovereignty as constituted by three foundational 'pillars', namely: redistributive agrarian reform, agro-ecological methods of production, and (re)localised and democratised food systems. Each in its own way contributes to the healing of the ecological and social rifts; and integrated as a whole they express the ontology of connectedness (Rose 2013, 11-12).

This ontology of connectedness is a recurring theme here. Rose (2013) argues that food sovereignty envisions and works towards replacing the capitalist food system, with its ontology of alienation and disconnection, with a more connected and democratised mode.

In place of the anonymous 'cash-nexus' which constitutes the sole bond between primary producer and end-consumer in the capitalist food system, food sovereignty is premised on the recovery of social connectivity via more intimate and direct personal relationships between producers (farmers) and the end consumers achieved through localised food systems. In such direct and personal exchanges, it can also be argued that something is being altered in the minds of the participants as regards their understanding of food itself. A monetary exchange is still taking place, but the value of food – its sensuous, cultural nature, and its true ecological and social cost – is being recovered, and more properly reflected in the price. The primary consideration is no longer simply about profit; in the process food becomes de-commodified; and this represents a deep and effective engagement with a central element of the common sense of the globalising capitalist food system (Rose 2013, 28).

Globalising capitalism's ontology of alienation can be seen to work through violent disconnection to amass and maintain power. This can be seen in the food system disconnections described by Hendrickson and Hefferman:

Space has been disconnected from place in the dominant food system... a problem that is being explicitly rejected by those involved in the local food system movements across the globe. This compression of space and the speed-up of time are key components of accumulation in the modern era.... Understanding the entwined forces of agency and structure are important (Hendrickson and Hefferman 2002, 349).

The notion of an ontology – or ontologies to signify diversity of perspective – of connectedness may serve to highlight the central difference between the ideological perspectives generally employed by food sovereignty practitioners, and the globalising corporate food system (Rose 2013). Ontological connectedness can be developed further with Ackerman-Leist's (2012) reflection that 'local food', a core theme of food sovereignty, is about relationships. In the context of this research, the concept of an 'ontology of connectedness' is particularly useful for its capacity to include, rather than exclude. This capacity makes room for indigenous values, ecological understandings, and even for the contradictions and tensions between ideals and capacity that people face on a daily basis, particularly in negotiating ethical relationships with food. These ideas are explored in more depth in Chapter Six.

Another contemporary theorist whose work is relevant to both the ecosystem framework and 'ontology of connectedness' is the Indian ecologist Vandana Shiva (2012). Shiva emphasises the importance of local knowledge systems which are disappearing and being colonised by dominant Western knowledge and the globalising system. She argues that although Western knowledge has been constructed as universal, it is actually just a globalised version of a local parochial system based in particular cultures, gender and class (2012, 9). Therefore, the common dichotomy between the universal and the local is misplaced when applied to Western and indigenous traditions because what is perceived as 'universal' was actually a local system "which has spread world-wide through intellectual colonisation" (Shiva 2012, 10).

Shiva argues that just as intensive corporate farming practices create unsustainable biological monocultures which erode both biodiversity and cultural diversity, the dominant scientific paradigm "breeds a monoculture of the mind" (2012, 12). It makes local alternative knowledge systems disappear by destroying the possible conditions required for alternatives to exist. It does this through its 'superior' exclusivity and through a violent process of reductionism which destroys diverse local meanings. Shiva states that in local knowledge systems there is no artificially imposed separation between 'resources': "the forest and the field are in ecological continuum". Local agriculture is modelled on forest ecology and both supply food (2012, 14). In contrast the supposedly 'scientific' system segregates forestry from agriculture. Forestry is reduced to resources like timber and is no longer connected to food. "Knowledge giving systems which have emerged from the food giving capacities of the forest are therefore eclipsed and finally destroyed, both through neglect and aggression" (2012, 14). Shiva uses the examples of 'scientific management' based on narrow commercial interests and enforced through legislation in India to illustrate her arguments on the destruction of diverse knowledge systems (2012, 18).

Shiva (2005) has also spoken out against corporate globalisation which destroys grassroots democracy through "new enclosures of the commons" which are based on violence. She is particularly critical of the patenting of genetics and the concept of 'ownership' of life and the rhetoric of 'ownership society' which she describes as 'anti-life'. From this perspective, living things have no intrinsic value and no integrity. She argues that the commons are the "highest expressions of economic democracy" (2005, 3). She also describes the movement against corporate globalisation as one toward 'Earth Democracy' the fate of which concerns the wellbeing of all living beings on earth. She describes an intentional shift:

...from vicious cycles of violence in which suicidal cultures, suicidal economies and the politics of suicide feed on each other to virtuous cycles of creative nonviolence in which living cultures nourish living democracies and living economies (sharing resources equitably to create meaningful liveli-hoods)" (2005, 5).

Along similar lines of critiquing corporate control and supporting more holistic understandings, critical economic theorist, David Korten (2010), adopts an organic analogy for economics: "The money system is to the modern economic system what the circulatory system is to the body. Where blood flows freely the body's cells flourish. Where blood flow is restricted, they become anaemic and may die" (170-171). Korten's organising principles of healthy living systems are as follows:

Organising principles of healthy living systems

1. *Self-organise into dynamic, inclusive self-reliant communities of place*
2. *Balance individual and community needs and interests*
3. *Practice frugality and reciprocity*
4. *Reward cooperation*
5. *Optimise the sustainable capture and use of energy and matter by adapting to the specific details of the microenvironment*

6. *Form and manage permeable boundaries*
7. *Cultivate diversity and share knowledge*

(Korten 2010, 147).

These can be seen to be reflected in the groups and stories featured here, presented in the following chapters. Korten (2010) argues that the economy's proper function should be to support healthy societal and environmental function, rather than exponential economic growth motivated by profit. Using another organic analogy Korten (2010) likens this growth that does not support wellbeing to cancerous tumours in the body. He sees the greatest barrier to healthy economic transformation as a flawed cultural story that misinforms our understandings of humanity and thus limits our possibilities. He argues that: "Just as fabricated stories are an instrument of social control, so authentic[2] stories are an instrument of liberation" (252). This might be a difficult dichotomy to define or sustain from an academic perspective, just as all dichotomies are only useful in their potential to draw awareness through contrast and comparison. Authentic stories, as conceptualised by Korten (2010), are characterised by their service towards social and environmental justice, and by their potential to liberate people from the chains of dominant discourse and the destructive economic system which is supports. This notion resonates with the perspectives of the community of which this research is the focus and therefore, is worth considering, along with Korten's version of an optimistic authentic story:

The new economy story that we humans are capable of creating vibrant, peaceful cooperative world bursting with life resonates deep within most people. Once that connection is made: the trance is broken... (Korten 2010 253)

We are privileged to live at the most exciting moment of creative opportunity in the whole of the human experience. Now is the hour. We have the power to turn this world around for the sake of ourselves and our children for generations to come. We are the ones we've been waiting for (Korten 2010, 283).

These quotes can be seen as examples of Korten's 'storying', his deliberate telling of a powerful story of hope and possibility, rather than
one of despair and powerlessness, in the face of multiple global
crises. It can be seen as a response to those, such as Graeber (2009)
and Shiva (2005), who posit the current system as violent. A similar
deliberate focus on peaceful and healthier economic solutions, in the
community of Whaingaroa, is explored in Chapter Seven. Korten
(2010) and several other alternative economic theorists will be drawn
upon, particularly in Chapter Eight.

As well as the theorists mentioned in this chapter, and in-line with the
emergent, reflexive design of this research, theoretical concepts
arising from participant observation, interviews and discussions
during the fieldwork are employed in my analysis. These concepts
include the notions of "supermarket culture" and "the green bubble".
Where possible, I have found other theories to explore the experiences of participants, including Seo and Creed's (2002) theorising of
the potential power of paradox. These diverse theoretical orientations
are applied in order to explain the frequently-encountered contradictions faced by people who have strong ethical codes who are navigating the complexities of the contemporary food-scape. Seo and
Creed (2002) suggest that exploration of the power of the paradox
holds potential for further reflexive engagement, which can be
disruptive to the status quo and facilitate further changes in action.

It is an academic tradition to justify one's research though demonstrating that it provides a unique contribution to the literature. The
understandings presented above provide central theoretical strands
which form the supporting base structure of the metaphoric kete, the
basket I introduced in my researcher positioning statement. In this
study, theory is primarily utilised to guide and support the interpretation of ethnographic material. These connecting theoretical strands
provide the support-structure of the kete of this research, in a way
that is compatible with the ethnographic tradition of theory being
used to support the findings, rather than the other way around
(Graeber 2009). It can also be argued that any reflexive research in

which the theory arises from the information gathered is bound to be unique. For these reasons it seems reasonable to suggest this research offers a unique theoretical contribution. In examining other similar research, there are few studies with which to draw comparison. Rose's (2013) study which engages ontology of connectedness to describe food sovereignty activism in Australia and internationally is one of the closest I have found to my own research. However, he does not go into detail in explaining this theoretical approach or use it in conjunction with complex systems theory, indigenous based under-standings, or many of the other theoretical work referred to in the body of this research. Casey-Cox (2015) draws on some of the complex systems theory in her exploration of community gardening, but does not focus on ontologies of connectedness in particular. These, along with others will be explored in more detail in the following chapters.

Method(ology): how I carried out the research

When I first embarked on this research I had never heard of food sovereignty. I began with an interest in 'free food' or the democratisa-tion of nourishment. I wanted to look into the emerging popularity of contemporary food foraging, dumpster diving, community gardening and other 'free food' activities which could be seen as outside 'the Market' and as potential resistance to the industrialised corporate food system. My research changed in direction due to a lack of litera-ture on food democratisation, the apparent difficulty in defining anything as outside the corporate system and because I came across a large body of food sovereignty literature that seemed to encompass and expand my initial focus.

I was drawn to ethnography because of its intuitive, immersive, comparative qualities, as well as its evolution towards more critical and reflexive inquiry (Gille 2001). The method resonated with me, and made sense in relation to the still-forming intentions of this research project which have always centred around understanding local food systems, values and democratisation. My research has worked well, simultaneously, along-side these 'organic' processes. I have taken what can be described as a critical-reflexive approach to research similar to that of critical-reflexive appreciative inquiry, as described by Grant and Humphries (2006), where being 'critical' means applying deliberate sensitivity to multiple constructions of identities, to power and to opening up possibilities:

Application of a critical perspective with its attendant reputation for nega-
tivity to the paradigm of appreciative inquiry may appear paradoxical.
Indeed our initial reaction was that the two approaches were almost contra-
dictory. However, as our reading and reflection on the relevant theoretical
foundations and applications matured, we began to both identify similarities
and value apparent differences. We treated the apparent contradiction as a
paradox. A paradox might be seen as an interesting and thought provoking
contradiction… The energy generated from working with/through the
paradox may manifest alternative insights that one would not have reached
by ignoring the paradox, or even working with just one dimension of it. The
idea that seemingly contradictory or opposing concepts may spring from a
common source differentiates paradox from conflict) and in doing so may
provide life giving and/or emancipatory opportunities. For example,
although they appear to reside in opposing paradigms, both appreciative
inquiry and critical theory share a common research objective. Through their
commitment to change, researchers in both paradigms seek to encourage and
facilitate 'human flourishing' (Grant and Humphries 2006, 406).

Appreciative inquiry seems to be an academic way of adopting a reflexive and transformative praxis for research, one that may be similar to the way in which many activists, community groups and engaged citizens practise. In the process of this research I did not often feel the need to attempt to raise the awareness of the partici-pants – most of the time, I felt I was learning from them.

As is generally the case with ethnographic fieldwork, the central research method engaged here is participant observation in conjunc-tion with semi-structured interviews as described by (DeWalt and

DeWalt 2011). Secondary sources have also been used. Some internet-based research involved gathering information from what was already available in the public sphere. Participants were found through existing networks as well as through participation in publicly open activities involved in the research process. Finding willing participants was not a problem as people were generally interested in the topic of research and open to contributing.

Site as siteless, Site as Whakapapa.

As Gille (2001) comments, the concept of 'site' as traditionally used in ethnography has been thoroughly contested by critical scholars. Gille describes 'site' as a construct of imagined boundaries which, through separation, can be cast as the exotic 'other' and examined, largely by white men. Sissons (1999) also challenges 'sited ethnography' as largely imagined, and proposes an alternative in his notion of 'siteless ethnography'. A more contemporary approach to 'site', particularly in a globalising world where concrete material boundaries are more and more difficult to imagine, is to conceptualise 'site' based on connectedness. David Boarder Giles (2013) similarly conceptualised interconnected globalised community sitedness in his ethnography of *Food Not Bombs*. The informal and interconnected nature of the communities that are the focus of my research mandated a similarly flexible approach to the research 'site'. Along with Sissons (1999) and Gille (2001), the critical reflexive approach adopted in this ethnography prioritises the interconnectedness of people over space and time, an approach resonant with the concept of whakapapa [interconnectedness, relatedness, ancestry], rather than attempting to justify ethnography through a limited physical location. The connectedness in this instance is related to values, to visions, to local food networks and to local alternative economic systems. Alongside Gupta and Ferguson (1997), I see value in the political purpose of ethnography, not in terms of sharing knowledge with people who lack it, but as something for which the purpose is to forge links between different understandings and perspectives, tracing possible alliances and common purposes, less as a 'field' for the collection of 'data' and more as a site for possibility.

My approach could also be described as a combination of classic 'sited' ethnography, in respect to my focus on the community of food producers in Whaingaroa, and 'siteless' as described by Sissons (1999). The site(s) of this research are as much located in the values, tensions and practices of the key participants in this primary community as well as others in New Zealand. This 'site' is also constructed in relationship with the values, tensions and practices associated with the global food sovereignty literature. Along with Gille (2001), I acknowledge that "space and society as well as place and community are mutually constituted" (329). As there was no obvious 'food sovereignty community' in New Zealand, in which I could locate my research site, the process of this research was one of making connections from the very beginning of conceptualising this study. From my original inspiration around food democratisation which developed into a focus on food sovereignty, I was able to work backwards: to find a variety of people involved in related activities, activism and community with what seemed to be similar focusses and values to those which had emerged from my reading of food sovereignty literature, and other related publications. I do not attempt to map food democratisation or food sovereignty in New Zealand as any map I make would be insufficient in complexity, flexibility, and inclusion. However, the 'site' itself can be seen in the similarities of values and tensions, practiced and encountered in the daily lives of participants, both in Whaingaroa, and wider New Zealand examples. The participants' stories with examples of the values they represent, have been chosen for both variety and commonality. The variety demonstrates the diversity of activities that seem to be related to food sovereignty. The similarity comes from participants' resonating values, compatible perspectives and shared tensions with those associated with food sovereignty.

There appears to be some resonance between the literature of the food sovereignty movement and other contemporary social movements, the most public of which is the Occupy Movement (Razsa and Kurnik 2012; Hickel and Khan 2012). These share resemblances in both their strong critique of social inequalities, neoliberalism, and corporate capitalism, and in their demand for conscious transformation toward democratisation and social justice. Along these lines, there exists a growing body of activist ethnography which is relevant to this study in a general way. For example, Graeber's (2009) insider ethnography warns the reader that it has no particular argument other than that the movement it describes is worth thinking about, that it makes a number of theoretical arguments, and that theory is invoked in order to assist description. I also make the connection between activist insider research (Graeber 2009; Razsa and Kurnik 2012) and my own, as an 'insider' member of the wider Whaingaroa community and, furthermore, a member, through friends and networks, of the broader New Zealand food sovereignty community. In making comparisons with activist ethnography I point out that although some of the participants in my research identify as activists, others do not. However, whether someone is consciously involved in organising food activism or just happens to enjoy community gardening, because of human and environmental interconnectedness, they might still be considered to be participating in the larger food sovereignty movement (Holt-Gimenez and Patel 2009).

David Foote (2009) explores the interconnectedness of vegan, anarchist, and punk subcultures in Hamilton, New Zealand. Foote's research is geographically relevant, being situated less than an hour's drive from Whaingaroa. His focus on 'siteless' interconnected subcultures within a community and the interpretive ethnographic methodology he employs in order to achieve the flexibility required to adequately document such a community is similarly relevant for the purposes of this research. Foote's research methods included participant observation and interviews. In his case, he did not go in search of a community to study, but found himself, through a new flatmate, living in an environment shared with the community that he decided to study. Similarly, I have been embedded in the community of

Whaingaroa, although not as a local food producer. Because of this, Foote's (2009) research also resembles mine in the liminal[3] relationship of the researcher to the community as neither outsider nor insider, but moving in between. For this reason, I identify my research as a liminal insider ethnography.

Ethnography as process:

The primary research method employed in my fieldwork was participant observation. The initial phase of my research was carried out over the first six months and involved getting to know various groups of people, attending meetings and gardening with people. After this I began conducting informal and semi-structured interviews in order to gather more in-depth information, understanding, and to document people's stories. I also gathered information from the internet, largely from websites and blogs, as a kind of netnography research (Kozinets 2009). This was carried out in order to further assist in locating the food sovereignty movement within New Zealand. I began by talking to people I knew, and by attending meetings, festivals and courses that seemed relevant to the initial topic of food democratisation. This canvassing was fairly broad, extending as far south as Dunedin in the South Island, New Zealand, and as far north as Kaitaia, at the top of the North Island, New Zealand. Through these conversations I learned about various food democratisation initiatives on various scales and with different collective organisation methods. These included community gardens, seed banks, free food shops, dumpster diving, land-sharing, food co-ops, and other forms of food hubs, courses, workshops and internships, sustainability-focussed intentional communities and eco-villages, revivals of traditional Māori gardening, groups focussed on planting fruit trees on public land, groups focussed on harvesting fruit that would otherwise go to waste, and wild foraging initiatives, among others. I also learned about initiatives based in various different countries, from the car-park community gardens in the largely deserted urban slums of Detroit to the allotment gardens of Hawaii.

As a resident of Whaingaroa, I inquired within my existing contacts and networks to recruit participants. I also became more actively involved with the groups and activities associated with food sovereignty in order to carry out participant observation. This included joining in activities that were open to the public such as gardening working-bees and public meetings. I also inquired within my existing network of contacts, in order to be able to represent the activities and initiatives that are not represented locally, for example, urban gardening which is carried out in cities. This research project involved one year of intensive ethnographic fieldwork in the Whaingaroa community with additional information collection being undertaken as necessary throughout the writing up period. My research can be considered a liminal insider ethnography, as I already lived in the area when the research began and my interest and my participation pre-dated this study. My relationship with the community is described in more detail in Chapter Three.

Following a qualitative methodological approach, interviews were deliberately flexible in their focus as to allow them to be co-directed by the participants. The interviews employed open-ended questions. Interview participants were drawn largely from the Whaingaroa community but also included members of the wider New Zealand food sovereignty community, particularly in instances where their particular activities were not found in Whaingaroa; for instance, urban gardening or Freegans activities that require a different environment. Factors such as whether or not potential participants feel comfortable being interviewed could mean that the people represented here are those more likely to be open to sharing their stories and views. I set out to find a variety of people with connections to local food so as to be as representative as possible. I endeavoured to include a variety of ages, ethnic backgrounds, and income levels, as well as a gender balance where possible. I also aimed to source participants to represent a variety of different kinds of local food related activities and groups.

I acknowledge that in selecting participants and facilitating interviews, as well as in analysing the information gathered in this study
and writing it up my voice, as the researcher, has been influential. As
an interested human being, a participant as well as an observer, my
own views and biases have undoubtedly effected the direction and
outcomes of the research. I attempted to balance this as much as
possible by fostering conscious and deliberate reflexivity in order for
my voice to better represent just one among the many others.

In addition to carrying out their regular activities during my participant observation (which ranged from public meetings to garden
working-bees), key research participants were interviewed for
periods of between one and three hours. If permission to do so was
granted by participants, interviews were recorded. After I selectively
transcribed recorded interviews, participants had the option of
viewing their interview transcription, in line with their preference.
They also had the option to check over their transcription and to
make corrections or additions. All participants chose to have their
interviews recorded and several chose to review their transcripts.
Only minor changes relating to accuracy were requested by participants. I incorporated these changes into the transcripts before I began
my analysis.

The structure of these interviews was based on themes in line with
the initial objectives of the research. As intended in my full proposal, I
conducted eleven interviews within the local Whaingaroa community
with twelve key participants featured in Chapter Four. I also
conducted six interviews outside the Whaingaroa community, particularly in instances where activities included under the broader
research topic are not carried out in Whaingaroa itself. Two of these
were with people involved in urban food activities, these interviews
feature in Chapter Two. The remainder of the interviews were carried
out in a community and sustainability education centre in the Coromandel[4]. Only four of these six are documented in Chapter Two as
the other two did not contain information that added to what had
already been gathered. This indicates a level of saturation of informa-

tion. Interviews were selectively transcribed[5] and organised into themes that had emerged in the process of the initial participant observation, as shown in the picture at the beginning of this section. The kinds of analysis and theory applied has been informed by the stories gathered in this process. Because of the wide range of participants involved in different groups and activities the questions asked in each interview were necessarily flexible to account for this diversity.

Figure 2: Mapping various strands on paper, organising ideas, 2014.

Permaculture as method

During the process of this fieldwork I participated in a Permaculture Design Certificate (PDC) course in Whaingaroa in 2014. This was particularly useful for deepening my understanding of the area. I learnt many things which I had not been aware of in several years of living there. There were also issues described which many long-standing Whaingaroa residents did not know about such as details of the regeneration successes of Whaingaroa Harbourcare [described in Chapter Three], or about the local man who accidentally started farming eels sustainably, for example. Permaculture is a system of sustainable design pioneered by Bill Mollison and David Holmgren in the mid-1970s (PiNZ 2009). Many people apply the concept of permaculture to vegetable gardening. However, as we were informed during this course, permaculture design principles can be applied, metaphorically or literally, to anything.

Here is my interpretation of the principles of permaculture:

- Observe and interact: listen, watch, pay attention
- Catch and store energy: harvest while abundance and preserve
- Obtain a yield: collect enough of what holds value
- Self-regulate: be reflexive, accept feedback
- Use and value renewables: reduce dependency on scarce resources
- Design from pattern to detail: observe ecosystem patterns and apply to design
- Integrate: look at how things work together
- Use small slow solutions: local, manageable scale and pace
- Value diversity: richness in complexity
- Value the marginal: the edges is where the energy builds
- Creatively respond to change: look for the opportunities

The main assignment of the PDC was a permaculture-based project. Many people chose to develop sustainable food producing systems for properties they were familiar with. I chose to apply the principles to my research, as seemed appropriate. This process was very useful in my conceptions and organising of information. It has become part of my research method and has informed my choice of theory as well.

My description of permaculture as methodology is not exhaustive or comprehensive. My purpose in including this here is in order to identify another strand in the kete that will be woven into later chapters, particularly Chapter Six, on values, and Chapter Seven, on 'focusing on solutions'. As such, I have included diagrams I made for the PDC project, to demonstrate the reflexivity of the process of doing the PDC as part of my PhD and of focussing on my PhD as part of the PDC. Just as permaculture is about complex systems and understanding connectedness, food sovereignty also values connectedness. For the presentation at the end of the course I prepared a diagram, in an attempt to show intersections of movements that are also related to food sovereignty in New Zealand, particularly in Whaingaroa:

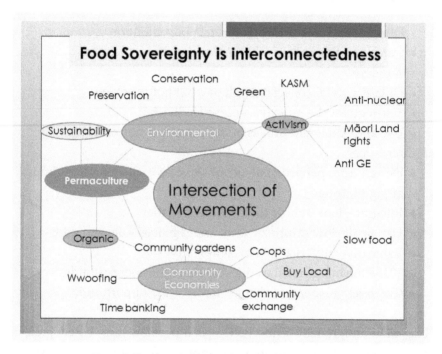

Figure 3: Food sovereignty as interconnectedness, 2014.

I then looked at each of the permaculture principles, usually depicted in diagrams such as the one following, in light of my research. The text in purple is my guess at what research concepts could relate to the twelve principles which are described in the black text:

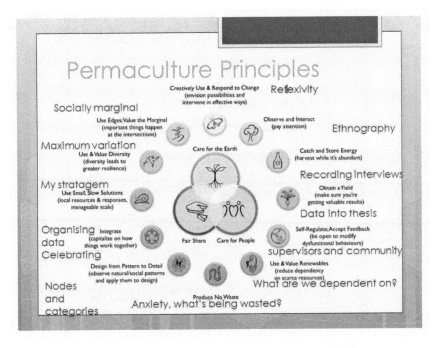

Figure 4: Permaculture principles related to research, 2014.

Another diagram employed regularly in permaculture is the design flower. Again I took each area represented by a petal and examined its research resemblance. Sometimes these comparisons were obvious, others seemed more like grasping at straws, however, this was very useful in terms of conceptualising my research, in terms of a complex system, which it has always resembled, an organic pattern rather than a linear process.

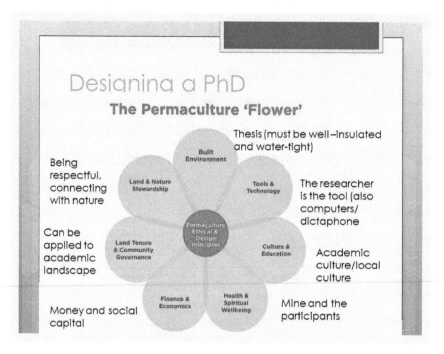

Figure 5: Designing a Permaculture PhD, 2014.

None of the diagrams represented here are intended as complete representations. They are all indications and illustrations of various points, and most are intended to demonstrate the kind of connectedness and liminality described in the theory section. The theory and method described here are just some of many strands that were attempted, explored and followed at various points. Many of these strands did not have sufficient load-bearing capacity, relevance, flexibility or length to be included here. The strands here demonstrate a unique approach to both theory and method. It has been designed to account for the complex systems of community, values, contradictions, practices and economy which are described and explored in the body of this research. For me, as a researcher, accounting for such complexity has been a challenging mental exercise. What I have written here is intended as scaffolding for understanding the rest of this work.

Ethical statement

This research project has been approved by the Human Research Ethics Committee of the University of Waikato Faculty of Arts and Social Sciences.

As I shifted between perspectives of framing myself as a researcher doing participant observation and an enquirer in communication with a community, the ethical nuances also shifted. Throughout this process I informed people of my research in the interests of maintaining transparency about and upholding my own integrity. I followed the guidance of the Human Research Ethics Committee and provided all participants with a copy of a general information sheet and answered any questions participants had in relation to their participation in or contributions to the research project. The process of going through the ethics committee application was useful at that early stage of my research because it encouraged me to think in more detail about different aspects and possibilities that might or might not eventuate.

In every instance I attained informed consent verbally and through a written information sheet and consent form. Participants were not paid although I attempted to bring food to some of the interviews, as was culturally appropriate. Participants were informed of the right to withdraw all or part of their contribution, however none have requested this. I did encounter a strange tension between the checkbox exercise dictated by the ethics committee and the perceptions of participants, with whom in many cases I had already established a good level of trust. The requirement for them to fill out ethics forms sometimes came across as a formality, rather than something that they particularly valued. Despite this, it was a useful exercise in clarifying the details such as whether they wanted to be provided with a transcript of their interview or whether to use a pseudonym. These were the only options where some participants diverged in their choices. Most chose to use their own names. Indeed, many considered it important to be connected with their stories.

Experiences and conversations from the initial participant observation informed the themes and direction of the research. No major
ethical problems emerged in the course of my Doctoral research. For
each of the interviews I first provided information and consent sheets
as well as the interview questions in advance where possible, so that
the participants were broadly aware of what I intended to ask them
and had time to think about their responses beforehand. The in-depth
interviews were recorded with the informed consent of each participant. I have carefully analysed the information from these interviews,
consulting with participants to ensure their stories were fairly represented within the research. A draft interview schedule was provided
to participants, with some suggested questions that I might ask, along
with the general information sheet and the interview participant
information sheet as part of the informed consent process. I also
discussed important points on the information sheet with participants
to ensure that people were giving their informed consent, including
the rights of the participants to anonymity through pseudonym, and
their rights to withdraw all or part of their contribution and to ask
further questions. Participants were made aware, both verbally and
through participant information sheets, that they could refuse to
answer questions or withdraw some or all of their information from
my research within one month of participating in the interview;
however, none chose to.

The netnography (Kozinets 2009) research employed for this study
involved retrieving information from blogs, social media sites and
websites that were already largely in the public domain. I employed
similar research methods to those employed in my Master's degree
looking at alternative narratives of health and nutrition (Ritchie 2011),
including the use of my own research blog (Ritchie 2012). In doing so
I clearly stated that my blog was for my PhD research into food sovereignty in New Zealand and that comments on my blog may be used
in my research unless the person who makes them requests otherwise. In blog posts I took care not to post comment about my participant observation or interviews unless it was with the consent of

participants. As in my Master's research, I wrote a specific post on ethics which linked back to the ethics committee so that anyone with queries about the ethics of my research could contact them if they so desired. I took care to treat information gathered from blogs and websites with the same sensitivity as other information that I gathered. In any interactions on the internet I was deliberately as transparent about my research as I was through in-person participant observation, in line with the guidelines of the Human Research Ethics Committee of the University of Waikato Faculty of Arts and Social Sciences[6] as well as the ethical guidelines of the Association of Social Anthropologists of Aotearoa New Zealand[7].

At the beginning of this research process I did not anticipate encountering difficulties in finding willing participants because, from my previous experience of talking to people informally on this topic, people involved in potential food sovereignty related activities tended to be willing to discuss their activities and ideas because they wanted to share their views widely in order to create more influence in the world. I approached participants either face-to-face, over the phone, or by email depending on appropriate tikanga [protocol]. I did not encounter any difficulties in this regard. I have taken particular care to protect participants by omitting any information which participants expressed they would be uncomfortable about sharing. These were either identified by participants or by my inquiring as to whether they would like those details on record. I communicated clearly that I would use only information that key participants would be comfortable with me using in my research.

In relation to the ethics of working across domains that encompass te ao Māori [the Māori world] the following statement is from my ethics proposal:

The Treaty of Waitangi[8]/Cultural Sensitivity

In this research I am likely to explore some territories governed by Te Ao Māori that are interconnected with the wider Whaingaroa community I am intending to study. In these situations I intend to use my own knowledge of

Māori tikanga garnered from a bicultural childhood and consult experts if I feel out of my depth.

These 'territories' could be seen in terms of physical land-based 'sites' and also as other culture-based things. This makes sense in a Māori context where values, words and practices can be regarded as tapu [sacred] and tāonga [treasures]. My understandings of tikanga Māori and of te reo [Māori language] were more useful than I originally anticipated, especially when some participants described their Māori cultural values and used words and concepts from te reo in our discussions and interviews.

GLOSSARY OF MĀORI WORDS

Aotearoa: North Island – now used as the Māori name for New Zealand.

Atua: God, deity.

Haumia Tikitiki: God of cultivated food.

Iwi: Tribal group, extended kinship group, tribe.

Kaitiakitanga: Guardianship, stewardship, caretaking role.

Kai: Food

Kaupapa: Foundation, topic, policy, purpose, theme, issue, initiative.

Kaupapa Māori: Māori approach, Māori institution, Māori principles.

Kete: Woven basket, kit.

Kōhanga reo: Māori language early childhood learning centre.

Kura kaupapa: Primary school operating under Māori custom and language.

Mahi: Work, job, practice, occupation, activity, exercise, operation, function.

Mana: Integrity, prestige.

Manākitanga: Hospitality, kindness, generosity, support, respect

Māra Māori: Traditional Māori gardens.

Marae: Traditional meeting place, Māori settlement.

Mātauranga: Knowledge, wisdom, understanding, skill.

Pākehā: Non-indigenous, often used to refer to European settlers.

Papatuanuku: Earth mother goddess.

Rangatiratanga: Chieftainship, sovereignty, self-determination.

Ranginui: Sky father god.

Raranga: Weaving, to weave, plait (mats, baskets, etc.).

Rongo Mā Tane: God of wild or uncultivated foods.

Rourou: Food basket.

Tāne (Mahuta): God of the forests and birds.

Tangaroa: God of the ocean and sea-life.

Taniwha: Fabulous water monsters, protectors of each bend in a river.

Taonga: Precious gift, treasure.

Tapu: Sacred, prohibited, restricted, set apart, forbidden.

Te ao Māori: The Māori world.

Te reo: Māori language.

Tikanga: Custom, rule, code, meaning, plan, practice, convention, protocol.

Wairua: Spirit, soul, attitude, quintessence, feel, mood, feeling, nature, essence.

Whakapapa: Genealogy, ancestry, lineage, descent, connectedness over space and time.

Whanaungatanga: Relatedness, relationship, kinship, sense of family connection.

REFERENCES

Ackerman-Leist, P (2012). *Rebuilding the Foodshed*. Chelsea Vermont: Green.

Aerni, P. (2011). *Food Sovereignty and its Discontents*. African Technology Development Forum, 8(2). 23–40.

Alkon, A. & Mares, T. (2012). Food Sovereignty in US Food Movements: Radical Visions and Neoliberal Constraints. *Agriculture and Human Values*, 29(3), 347–359.

Arnould, E. J., Plastina, J. & Ball, D. (2009). Does Fair Trade Deliver on Its Core Value Proposition? Effects on Income, Educational Attainment, and Health in Three Countries. *Journal of Public Policy & Marketing*, 28(2), 186–201.

Bello, W. & Baviera, M. (2010). Capitalist Agriculture, the Food Price Crisis & Peasant Resistance. In Wittman, H. K., Desmarais, A. A., & Wiebe, N. (Eds.). *Food Sovereignty: Reconnecting Food, Nature and Community*, 62–75. Oxford: Food First Books.

Bernstein, H. (2009). Agrarian Questions from Transition to Globalization. In A. Akram-Lodhi (Ed.), *Peasants and Globalization: Political*

Economy, Agrarian Transformation and Development Vol. 2, 255–284. New York: Routledge.

Borras, S. M. & Franco, J. C. (2010). Food Sovereignty and Redistributive Land Policies. In Wittman, H. K., Desmarais, A. A., & Wiebe, N. (Eds.). *Food Sovereignty: Reconnecting Food, Nature and Community*, 106–118. Oxford: Food First Books.

Botsman, R. & Rogers, R. (2010). *What's Mine Is Yours Intl: The Rise of Collaborative Consumption.* New York: Harper Collins.

Capra, F. & Luisi, L. P. (2014). *The Systems View of Life.* Cambridge: Cambridge University Press.

Came, H. (2012). Institutional Racism and the Dynamics of Privilege in Public Health (Doctor of Philosophy). University of Waikato, Hamilton, New Zealand.

Casey-Cox, A. M. (2014). The Transformative Possibilities of 'Noticing' in Community Gardening and my Life (Doctor of Philosophy). University of Waikato, Hamilton, New Zealand.

Catton, W. R. (1982). *Overshoot: The ecological basis of revolutionary change.* Chicago: University of Illinois Press.

Corner, S. B. (2008). An Ethnographic Exploration of Gender Experiences of a New Zealand Surf Culture (Master of Social Sciences). The University of Waikato, Hamilton, New Zealand.

Curry, P. (2011). *Ecological Ethics.* Malden: Polity.

Dann, C. (2012). *Food @ home.* Christchurch: Canterbury University Press.

DeWalt, K. M. & DeWalt, B. R. (2011). *Participant observation: a guide for fieldworkers* (2nd ed). Plymouth: AltaMira Press.

Donati, K. (2005). The Pleasure of Diversity in Slow Food's Ethics of Taste. *Food, Culture and Society: An International Journal of Multidisciplinary Research*, 8(2), 227–242.

Dowling, K. (2011). *Chicken Poop for the Soul: In Search of Food Sovereignty*. Prince George: Caitlin Press.

Elgin, D. (1981). *Voluntary Simplicity*. New York: Harper Collins.

Fairbairn, M. (2010). Framing Resistance: International Food Regimes and the Roots of Food Sovereignty. In Wittman, H. K., Desmarais, A. A., & Wiebe, N. (Eds.). *Food Sovereignty: Reconnecting Food, Nature and Community*, 15–32. Oxford: Food First Books.

Flachs, A. (2010). Food for Thought: The Social Impact of Community Gardens in the Greater Cleveland Area. *Electronic Green Journal*, 1(30). Retrieved from http://escholarship.org.

Food Act (1981). Food Act 1981. Retrieved September 2016 from: http://www.legislation.govt.nz.

Food Act (2014). Food Act 2014. Retrieved September 2016 from: http://www.legislation.govt.nz.

Foodbill.org. (2012). Food Bill Issues List. Retrieved August 21, 2012, from http://www.foodbill.org.nz/wiki/Food_Bill_Issues_List.

Foote, D. M. (2009). Anarchists, Punks and Vegans: oh my!: Ethnography of an Anti-Capitalist Community of Dissent. (Master of Social Sciences). University of Waikato, Hamilton, New Zealand.

Freire, P. (1992). *Pedagogy of Hope*. London: Continuum International Publishing Group.

Galli, A. M., & Clift, B. C. (2012). Food Justice. *The Wiley-Blackwell Encyclopaedia of Globalization*. Blackwell Publishing Ltd. Retrieved from http://onlinelibrary.wiley.com.

Germov, J., & Williams, L. (2008). *A Sociology of Food and Nutrition: the Social Appetite*. New York: Oxford University Press.

Gibson-Graham, J. K. (2006). *Postcapitalist politics*. Minneapolis: University of Minnesota Press.

Giles, D. B. (2013). "A Mass Conspiracy to Feed People": Globalizing Cities, World-Class Waste, and the Biopolitics of Food Not Bombs. (Doctor of Philosophy). University of Washington, Seattle, United States.

Gille, Z. (2001). Critical ethnography in the time of globalisation: towards a new conception of site. *Cultural Studies – Critical Methodologies*, 1 (3), 319–334.

Gordon Nembhard, J. (2008). Theorizing and practicing democratic community economics: engaged scholarship, economic justice, and the academy, in Charles R. Hale (Ed.) *Engaging contradictions: theory, politics, and methods of activist scholarship*. Berkley: University of California Press, 265–298.

Graeber, D. (2001). *Toward an Anthropological Theory of Value: The False Coin of Our Own Dreams*. Palgrave: New York.

Graeber, D. (2002). The New Anarchists. *The New Left Review* (13), 61–73.

Graeber, D. (2009). *Direct action: an ethnography*. Oakland: AK Press.

Graeber, D. (2011). *Debt: the first 5000 years*. Melville House: New York.

Grant, S. & Humphries, M.T. (2006). Critical evaluation of appreciative inquiry: Bridging an apparent paradox. *Action Research*, 4(4) 401–418.

Gunn, A. S. (2007). Environmental ethics in a New Zealand context. New Zealand *Journal of Forestry*, 51(4), 7–12.

Gupta, A. & Ferguson, J. (1997). *Anthropological Locations*. UC Press: Oakland.

Guthman, J. (2008). Bringing Good Food to Others: Investigating the Subjects of Alternative Food Practice. *Cultural Geographies*, 15(4), 431–447.

Guthman, J. (2003). Fast food/organic food: Reflexive tastes and the making of "yuppie chow." *Social & Cultural Geography*, 4(1), 45–58.

Handy, J. & Fehr, C. (2010). Drawing Forth the Force that Slumbered in Peasants' Arms. In Wittman, H. K., Desmarais, A. A., & Wiebe, N. (Eds.). *Food Sovereignty: Reconnecting Food, Nature and Community*, 45–61. Oxford: Food First Books.

Hendrickson, M. K. & Hefferman, W. D. (2002). Opening spaces through relocalization: locating potential resistance in the weaknessed of the global food system. *Sociologia Ruralis*, 42 (4), 347–396.

Hickel, J. & Khan, A. (2012). The Culture of Capitalism and the Crisis of Critique. *Anthropological Quarterly*, 85(1), 203–227.

Holt-Gimenez, E. & Patel, R. (2009). *Food Rebellions! Crisis and the Hunger for Justice*. Oxford: Pambazuka Books.

Hutchings, J., Tipene, P., Carney, P., Greensill, A., Skelton, P. & Baker, M. (2013). Hua parakore: an indigenous food sovereignty initiative and hallmark of excellence for food and product production. *Mai*, 131–145.

International Planning Committee for Food Sovereignty. (2007). *Definition and Principles of Food Sovereignty*. Retrieved, October 15, 2012, from http://www.foodsovereignty.org.

Kete o te wānanga. (2006). Māori Dictionary. August 18, Retrieved 2015 from http://www.Māoridictionary.co.nz.

Kelsey, J. (1995). *Economic Fundamentalism – The New Zealand Experiment: A World Model for Structural Adjustment?*. London: Pluto Press.

Klein, N. (2015). *This changes everything (documentary)*. Klein Lewis Productions. Abramorama: New York.

Knox, J. (2013). *A Forager's Treasury: A New Zealand Guide to Finding and Using Wild Plants*. Auckland: Allen and Unwin.

Korten, D. (2010). *Agenda for a new economy.* San Francisco: Berret-Koehler.

Kozinets, R. V. (2009). *Netnography: Doing Ethnographic Research Online.* Sage Publications.

Larner, W. (2000). Neo-liberalism: Policy, ideology, governmentality. Studies in *Political Economy,* 63(0).

Laudan, R. (2001). A Plea for Culinary Modernism: Why We Should Love New, Fast, Processed Food. *Gastronomica,* 1(1), 36–44.

Le Grand, Y. (2010). Activism through Commensality: Food and Politics in the Temporary Vegan Zone (Masters). Universidade de Lisboa, Lisbon, Portugal. Retrieved from http://repositorio.ul.pt.

Leopold, A. (1949). *A Sand County Almanac.* Oxford: Oxford University Press.

MacRae, G. S. (2016). Forgotten moralities of agrarian economy in Bali: Production and Exchange, business and friendship. *Focaal,* 2016(17), 89–104.

Masioli, I. & Nicholson, P. (2010). Seeing Like a Peasant. In Wittman, H. K., Desmarais, A. A., & Wiebe, N. (Eds.). *Food Sovereignty: Reconnecting Food, Nature and Community,* 33–44. Oxford: Food First Books.

Mason, J. & Singer, P. (2006). *The Ethics of What We Eat.* Melbourne: Text Publishing.

McCormack, F. (2011). Levels of Indigineity: The Māori and Neoliberalism. *Journal of the Royal Anthropological Institute,* 17, 281–300.

McMichael, P. (2010). Food Sovereignty in Movement. In Wittman, H. K., Desmarais, A. A., & Wiebe, N. (Eds.). *Food Sovereignty: Reconnecting Food, Nature and Community,* 168-183. Oxford: Food First Books.

McNeil, K. I. B. (2011). *Talking with Their Mouths Half Full: Food Insecurity in the Hamilton Community.* (Doctor of Philosophy). University of Waikato, Hamilton, New Zealand.

Ministry for Culture and Heritage (updated 25-Nov-2015). 'Eva Rickard', Retrieved from: http://www.nzhistory.net.nz/people/eva-rickard.

National Family Farm Coalition. (2012). *NFFC.* Retrieved August 24, 2012, from http://www.nffc.net.

Ostrom, E. (1990). *Governing the Commons: The Evolution of Institutions for Collective Action.* Cambridge: Cambridge University Press.

Partridge, B. (2011). Food Waste, Freeganism and Sustainable Consumption: A Qualitative Investigation into Eating from the Bin (Master of Arts). King's College, London. Retrieved from http://www.kcl.ac.uk.

Patel, R. (2009). Food Sovereignty. *Journal of Peasant Studies,* 36(3), 663–706.

PiNZ. (2009). About Permaculture. Retrieved August 24, 2015, from http://www.permaculture.org.nz.

Pollan, M. (2006). *The Omnivore's Dilemma: A Natural History of Four Meals.* New York: Penguin.

Radio New Zealand National. (2014). Bill threatens food standards MPs hear. Retrieved, September 14, 2016, from: http://www.radionz.co.nz.

Raglan Chronicle. July 2014. Quirky furnishings real Raglan style. Raglan Chronicle (404), 2.

Razsa, M. & Kurnik, A. (2012). The Occupy Movement in Žižek's Hometown: Direct Democracy and a Politics of Becoming. *American Ethnologist,* 39(2), 238–258.

Ritchie, I. P. (2011). The Nourishing Revolution: Exploring the Praxis of the Weston A. Price Foundation (Master of Social Sciences). University of Waikato, Hamilton.

Ritchie, I. P. (2012). The Nourishing Revolution. www.nourishingrevolution.blogspot.co.nz.

Roche, M. (2012). Food Regimes Revisited: A New Zealand Perspective. *Urbaniizziv*, 23(s 2), s62–s75.doi:10.5379/urbani-izziv-en-2012-23-supplement-2-005.

Rose, N. (2013). Optimism of the will: Food sovereignty as transformative counter-hegemony in the 21st century, (Doctor of Philosophy (PhD)). RMIT University, Melbourne, Australia.

Rosin, C. (2014). Engaging the Productivist Ideology through Utopian Politics. *Dialogues in Human Geography*, 4 (2). 221-224.

Rosset, P., Patel, R., & Courville, M. (2006). *Promised Land: Competing Visions of Agrarian Reform*. New York: Food First Books.

Scanlan, S. J. (2009). New Direction and Discovery on the Hunger Front: Toward a Sociology of Food Security/Insecurity. *Humanity & Society*, 33(4), 292–316.

Seo, M.G., & Creed, W.E.D. (2002). Institutional Contradictions, Praxis, and Institutional Change: A Dialectical Perspective. *Academy of Management Review*, 27(2), 222-247.

Shiva, V. (2005). *Earth democracy: justice, sustainability and peace*. Brooklyn: South End Press.

Shiva, V. (2012). *Monocultures of the mind: perspectives on biodiversity and biotechnology*. New Delhi: Natraj.

Singh, H. (2014). Where are NZ's most deprived areas? *New Zealand Herald*. Retrieved June 2016 from: http://www.nzherald.co.nz.

Sissons, J. (1999). Siteless ethnography: possibilities and limits. *Social Analysis*, 43(2), 88-95.

Slocum, R. (2007). Whiteness, space and alternative food practice. *Geoforum*, 38(3), 520-533.

Smith, J.M. (2003). *Hard to Swallow: The dangers of GE food: an international expose*. Nelson: Craig Potton Publishing.

Statistics New Zealand. (2006). Quick stats about Whaingaroa – Statistics New Zealand. Retrieved September 24, 2012, from http://www.stats.govt.nz.

Stuart, T. (2009). *Waste: Uncovering the Global Food Scandal*. London: Penguin.

Te Ara. (2011). Whaingaroa and the West Coast. Te Ara Encyclopaedia of New Zealand. Retrieved September 24, 2012, from http://www.teara.govt.nz.

Vaarst, M., & González-García, E. (2012). The Concept of Food Sovereignty in Relation to European Food Systems. International Farming Systems Association Conference, Aarhus, Denmark. Retrieved from http://ifsa.boku.ac.at.

Vazquez, J. M. (2011). The Role of Indigenous Knowledge and Innovation in Creating Food Sovereignty in the Oneida Nation of Wisconsin (Master of Arts). Iowa State University, Ames, Iowa. Retrieved from http://gradworks.umi.com/14/99/1499492.html.

Vennell, .W.C & Williams, S. (1976). *Raglan County Hills and Sea: a Centennial History 1876-1976*. Auckland: Wilson & Horton.

Vernon, R.T. (1981). *Around Raglan*. Hamilton: University of Waikato.

Walker, R. (2004). *Ka Whawhai Tonu Matou. Struggle without end* (revised ed.). Auckland: Penguin.

Walker, E.T. (2015). Beyond the rhetoric of the "sharing economy". Retrieved from: https://contexts.org.

Waring, M. (1988). *If Women Counted: A New Feminist Economics*. San Francisco: Harper & Row.

Wittman, H. (2009). Reworking the Metabolic Rift: Vía Campesina, Agrarian Citizenship, and Food Sovereignty. *Journal of Peasant Studies*, 36(4), 805–826.

Wittman, H. K., Desmarais, A. A., & Wiebe, N. (Eds.). (2010). *Food Sovereignty: Reconnecting Food, Nature and Community*. Oxford: Food First Books.

NOTES

1. Local solutions and the power of authentic stories

1. To make interpretation easier I use square brackets next to most instances of Māori words with approximate translations for them in the context in which they are used. A glossary of Māori words is also included in the appendices.
2. Similarity is acknowledged that grass-roots movements around food production movements also have a much longer history.
3. This co-option of terminology is also discussed by Graeber (2011).
4. Māori refers to the indigenous people of New Zealand. In this context Kaupapa means basis or foundation.
5. My great grandfather Ernest Beaglehole earned a PhD, as did his daughter Jane (my grandmother), and her husband James. My mother, Jenny, completed her PhD around the time I started my undergraduate university studies.
6. The decile school system in New Zealand ranks schools from lowest income areas (1) to highest (10). See: http://www.education.govt.nz/school/running-a-school/resourcing/operational-funding/school-decile-ratings/
7. From the documentary 'This Changes Everything'.
8. I have chosen to use the Māori name for the area, 'Whaingaroa', in place of the English name 'Raglan'. In most cases I use English name for New Zealand, rather than Aotearoa, to provide more clarity for international readers.

2. Food sovereignty and Aotearoa

1. See: http://www.enviroschools.org.nz/
2. Wwoofing began as an acronym for Willing Workers on Organic Farms. It refers to the practice of exchanging labour for food and board. In New Zealand it is commonly practiced by international visitors who find farms to work on through various wwoofing directories.
3. Commercially exploiting naturally occurring biochemical or genetic material.
4. As mentioned in Chapter Two, GM (Genetic Modification) is used interchangeably with GE (Genetic Engineering) for the purposes of this research. Participants did not see a particular distinction appear to distinguish between these terms.
5. See: https://nz.freecycle.org/
6. See: http://www.kaibosh.org.nz/
7. See: http://foodnotbombs.net/

3. Whaingaroa

1. From: Raglan Kopua Holidaypark brochure, 2014.
2. From: Waikato District visitor guide, 2013/2014.
3. See: http://kasm.org.nz/
4. As seen in election results such as:
   http://www.electionresults.govt.nz/electionresults_2014/e9/html/e9_-part8_party_65.html
5. Goods and Services Tax, a 15% tax added to goods and services in New Zealand, see: www.ird.govt.nz/gst/
6. One issue with text-based communication is the ambiguity. It is hard to imagine what such a conversation might look like if it played out in person.

4. Local food producers in Whaingaroa

1. United States Food and Drug Administration, see: http://www.fda.gov/

5. Cultivating resistance

1. As mentioned in chapter one, the Treaty of Waitangi is New Zealand's founding document – intended as a partnership between Māori and the British Crown. For more information see Walker (2004)
2. For example: The Corporation (2003), by Joel Bakan and Mark Achbar, or Food Inc (2010), by Robert Kenner.
3. As mentioned in Chapter Two, GM (Genetic Modification) is used interchangeably with GE (Genetic Engineering) for the purposes of this research. Participants did not see a particular distinction between these terms.
4. A sedative given to pregnant women in the late 1950s resulting in foetuses with malformed limbs.

7. Values and ontologies of connection

1. Although not all indigenous people express such values.
2. God of cultivated food.
3. God of wild or uncultivated foods.
4. An organisation that helps businesses to become more sustainable. See: http://consciousconsumers.org.nz/
5. Many of the participants do not consider cities to be sustainable in the future, given diminishing resources. This sentiment is shared by Korten (2010).
6. See www.plasticfreejuly.org
7. The notion of 'real', much like Korten's (2010) notion of 'authentic' can be problematic to those rejecting a modernist framing of 'objective reality'. Here both words speak to a deeper connectedness, and a lack of 'fakeness'. This can also be related to decommodification as the meaning and complex value of 'real food'

and 'authentic stories' are beyond the alienated capitalist framing of 'commodity'.

8. Focusing on solutions: community economies and ecology

1. 'Whaea' is a common way of addressing women in Māori.
2. Although this might seem like an unrealistic and romantic notion, given New Zealand's geographic isolation, I recently learned that the Wellington Chocolate Factory is in the process of purchasing a yacht for precisely this purpose.
3. Pollan (2006), See: http://michaelpollan.com/books/the-omnivores-dilemma/
4. See: http://www.transitiontowns.org.nz/

9. Living Economies

1. This refers to the neo-liberal de-regulation of New Zealand politics in the 1980's described in Chapter Two.
2. The website http://www.landshare.net/ is an example of land sharing focussed networking through the internet.
3. For more information see: http://www.wfto.com/

Research Theory and Methodology

1. For the purposes of this research, 'contradiction' is apparent when two ideas appear to in conflict, in a kind of opposition where it is difficult to see how they could possibly co-exist. On further exploration, a contradiction is often revealed to be a paradox: a dialectic relationship between two or more competing yet coexisting influences creating tension. Seo and Creed (2002) suggest the conscious and reflective negotiation of paradox presents opportunity for raising awareness, resolving tensions or stimulating further action.
2. I see 'authentic', in this sense, as something standing its own integrity, resonating and connecting with context, in line with ontologies of connectedness.
3. Liminal in the sense of feeling 'in between': of relating and connecting, but not quite belonging, rather than in any particular theoretical use of the word.
4. Located on the east coast of the North Island of New Zealand, about four hour's drive from Whaingaroa.
5. Although changes occurred after the interviews took place I decided to keep the focus of the thesis to the year of 2014 in which the fieldwork was conducted. Many changes in the lives of participants have occurred since this time. I touch on these in the epilogue 'Post script: continued stories' at the end of chapter nine.
6. See: http://www.waikato.ac.nz/research-enterprise/ethics/human-ethics-research-committee

7. See: http://www.asaanz.org/code-of-ethics/
8. The Treaty of Waitangi is New Zealand's founding document – intended as a partnership between Māori and the British Crown. For more information see Walker (2004)